COLLECTE

D0120949

Edith Sitwell

COLLECTED POEMS

M

*This book is copyright in all countries which
are signatories to the Berne Convention*

All rights reserved. No part of this publication
may be reproduced or transmitted, in any form or by
any means, without permission.

First published 1957 by Macmillan & Co Limited
Reprinted 1979 by
Macmillan London Limited
4 Little Essex Street London WC2R 3LF
and Basingstoke

First published 1982 by
PAPERMAC
a division of Macmillan Publishers Limited
London and Basingstoke

Associated companies in Auckland, Dallas,
Delhi, Dublin, Hong Kong, Johannesburg,
Lagos, Manzini, Melbourne, Nairobi,
New York, Singapore, Tokyo, Washington
and Zaria

ISBN 0 333 33391 8

Printed in Hong Kong

To

BRYHER

OSBERT SITWELL

and

SACHEVERELL SITWELL

PREFATORY NOTE

THE following poems appeared in *Street Songs*, dedicated to Osbert Sitwell : ' An Old Woman (I),' ' Still Falls the Rain,' ' Lullaby,' ' Serenade : Any Man to Any Woman,' ' Street Song,' ' Poor Young Simpleton,' ' Once my heart was a summer rose,' ' Tattered Serenade : Beggar to Shadow,' ' Tears,' ' The Flowering Forest,' ' How Many Heavens,' ' We are the darkness in the heat of the day,' ' The Youth with the Red-Gold Hair,' ' You, the Young Rainbow,' ' Most Lovely Shade,' ' The Swans.'

The following poems appeared in *Green Song and Other Poems*, dedicated to Bryher : ' Invocation,' ' An Old Woman (II),' ' Song for Two Voices,' ' O yet forgive,' ' Green Flows the River of Lethe — O,' ' A Mother to her Dead Child,' ' Heart and Mind,' ' Green Song,' ' Anne Boleyn's Song,' ' A Young Girl,' ' Holiday,' ' Girl and Butterfly,' ' The Queen Bee sighed,' ' O bitter love, O Death,' ' Lo, this is she that was the world's desire,' ' One Day in Spring.'

The dedication of these two books is continued in this, as the dedication of the individual poems is also continued.

E. S.

ACKNOWLEDGMENTS

My thanks are due to the Editors of *The Times Literary Supplement*, *The Listener*, *The London Magazine*, *Life and Letters*, *To-Day*, *New Writing and Daylight*, the ' Penguin ' *New Writing*, *Orpheus*, *Orion*, *Horizon*, *Poetry London*, *View*, *Adam*, *The Atlantic Monthly*, and *Poetry Chicago*, for permission to reprint poems first published by them.

My thanks are also due to Sir Basil Blackwell for his kind permission to reprint my *Early Poems*; to Messrs. Gerald Duckworth for their kindness in allowing me to reprint my 'Bucolic Comedies,' 'Façade,' 'Marine,' 'Elegy on Dead Fashion,' 'Gold Coast Customs,' and other poems taken from *Façade and Other Poems*, *1910–1935*; to Messrs. Faber & Faber for being so good as to allow me to reprint ' Lullaby ' and ' Serenade ' from *Poems Old and New*; and to Messrs. John Lehmann for allowing me to reprint ' The Shadow of Cain.'

CONTENTS

FAÇADE

LATER POEMS
(from 1940 onwards)

SOME NOTES ON MY OWN POETRY

In every age we find poets discussing the problems of poetry, defending their verses and giving reasons for innovations in various Prefaces and Defences of Poetry. Among the earliest English examples is the *Apologie for Poetry* written by Sir Philip Sidney about the year 1580. Ben Jonson treated of the problems of poetry in his *Discoveries*, and Thomas Campion wrote his *Observations on the Art of English Poesie* in 1602. It therefore may not seem out of place or the result of an undue vanity if I gather together these notes — mainly technical — about the developments in my own verse.

At the time I began to write, a change in the direction, imagery, and rhythms in poetry had become necessary, owing to the rhythmical flaccidity, the verbal deadness, the dead and expected patterns, of some of the poetry immediately preceding us.

Rhythm is one of the principal translators between dream and reality. Rhythm might be described as, to the world of sound, what light is to the world of sight. It shapes and gives new meaning. Rhythm was described by Schopenhauer as melody deprived of its pitch.

The great architect, Monsieur Le Corbusier, said that, as the result of the Machine Age, ' new organs awake in us, another diapason, a new vision.' He said of persons listening to the sound of certain machinery that ' the noise was so round that one believed a change in the acoustic functions was taking place.' It was therefore necessary to find rhythmical expressions for the heightened speed of our time.

In spite of the fact that the rhythms in which I practised, in *Façade*, were heightened, concentrated, and frequently more violent than those of the poets who had preceded us immediately, it was supposed by many that I had discarded rhythm.

There was a great deal of opposition to the revivification of rhythmic patterns. But even the greatest of all rhythmic patterns, those not made by the hand of Man, have been misapprehended. The otherwise great mind of Bishop Burnet, who died in 1715, was so seriously disturbed by the unsymmetrical arrangement of the stars that he rebuked the Creator for His lack of technique. ' What a beautiful hemisphere they would have made,' he exclaimed, 'if they had been placed in rank and order; if they had all been disposed in regular figures . . . all finished and made up into one fair piece, or great composition, according to the rules of art and symmetry.'

We must not complain, therefore, if the patterns in the humble works of Man are not perceived immediately by the unobservant.

Therefore, to rebukes and protests, I returned the answer 'God comfort thy capacity,' and went on my way.

The poems in *Façade* are *abstract* poems — that is, they are patterns in sound. They are, too, in many cases, virtuoso exercises in technique of an extreme difficulty, in the same sense as that in which certain studies by Liszt are studies in transcendental technique in music.

My experiments in *Façade* consist of inquiries into the effect on rhythm and on speed of the use of rhymes, assonances, and dissonances, placed at the beginning and in the middle of lines, as well as at the end, and in most elaborate patterns. I experimented, too, with the effect upon speed of the use of equivalent syllables — a system that produces great variation.

The rhythm and speed of a skilful unrhymed poem differ from the rhythm and speed of a rhymed poem containing the same number of feet, and both the rhymed and the unrhymed poems differ slightly in these respects from a poem ending with assonances or dissonances but containing the same number of feet. Again, assonances and dissonances put at different places within the lines and intermingled with equally skilfully placed internal rhymes have an immense effect upon rhythm and speed; and their effect on rhythm, and sometimes, but not always, on speed, is different from that of lines containing elaborately schemed internal rhymes without assonances or dissonances. And how slight, how subtle, are the changes of speed or of depth in English poetry due to differences in texture, and due to the fact that the English, in their cunning over the matter of poetry, have adopted the idea of equivalence. For is it really to be supposed that two words, each of one syllable, equal in speed one word of two syllables? The two-syllabled words, if unweighted by heavy consonants, move far more quickly. The system of equivalent syllables, therefore, produces great variation — as, for instance, in 'Fox Trot,' a poem to be discussed later.

I experimented, also, in texture, in the subtle variations of thickness and thinness brought about in assonances by the changing of one consonant or labial, from word to word — as, for instance, in the softening from ' apiaries ' to ' aviaries ' in these lines from ' Waltz ' :

> The stars in their apiaries,
> Sylphs in their aviaries.

Many years ago, Villiers de l'Isle Adam wrote of his own work, *Tribulat Bonhomet*, that it was ' an enormous and sombre clowning, the colour of the century.' ' Words and thoughts,' said Arthur Symons of this work, ' never brought together since Babel, clash into a protesting combination.' This might also be said of certain poems in *Façade*.

At other moments, as Jean Cocteau said of another work of more or less the same kind, the ballet ' Parade,' in which he, Picasso, and Satie collaborated, the work is ' the poetry of childhood overtaken by a technician.'

He added, ' For the majority, a work of art cannot be beautiful without a plot, involving mysticism or love. Beauty, gaiety, sadness without romance are suspect.' It is certain that an empty work which appears to be serious, because it is dull and heavy and has no vitality, will be acclaimed as a masterpiece, while a work of this kind will be at first derided, and its author insulted.

The poems appeared strange, sometimes because of the heightened imagery and sometimes because, to quote a phrase of the scientist Henri Poincaré, ' the accident of a rhyme can call forth a system.' To this I would add — sometimes a planetary system.

Some of these poems are about materialism and the world crumbling into dust ; some have as protagonists shadows, or ghosts, moving, not in my country world, but in a highly mechanised universe ; others have beings moving

> To the small sound of Time's drum in the heart

— figures gesticulating against the darkness, from the warmth and light of their little candle-show.

Some of the poems have a violent exhilaration, others have a veiled melancholy, a sadness masked by gaiety.

Their apparent gaiety caused them to be suspect. They were useless. They were butterflies. They were spivs. And yet I cannot but remember that when the great seventeenth-century naturalist John Ray was asked, ' What is the use of butterflies ? ', he replied, ' To adorn the world and delight the eyes of men, to brighten the countryside, serving like so many golden spangles to decorate the fields.' And he added, of these butterflies made by the hand of God, ' Who can contemplate their exquisite beauty and not acknowledge and adore the traces of divine Art upon them ? ' At least these butterflies made by the hand of Man may have the traces of human art upon their wings.

And are they, indeed, spivs ? The gaiety of some masks darkness — the see-saw world in which giant and dwarf take it in turns to rush into the glaring light, the sight of the crowds, then, with a terrifying swiftness, go down to the yawning dark. An example is ' Said King Pompey ' — a poem about the triumphant dust.

It is built on a scheme of R's, which in this case produces a faint fluttering sound, like dust fluttering from the ground, or the beat of a dying heart.

> Said King Pompey, the emperor's ape,
> Shuddering black in his temporal cape
> Of dust, ' The dust is everything —
> The heart to love and the voice to sing,
> Indianapolis
> And the Acropolis,
> Also the hairy sky that we
> Take for a coverlet comfortably.'
> Said the Bishop,
> Eating his ketchup :
> ' There still remains Eternity
> Swelling the diocese,
> That elephantiasis,
> The flunkeyed and trumpeting sea.'

In the first two lines, the sound rises. ' Pompey,' in sound, is a dark distorted shadow of ' Emperor ' and of its crouching echo, ' temporal ' — a shadow upside down, one might say, for in ' Emperor ' the sound dies down in hollow darkness, whereas in ' Pompey ' it begins in thick muffling animal darkness and then rises, dying away into a little thin whining air. The crazy reversed sound of ' Indianapolis,' ' Acropolis ' — ' Acropolis ' being a hollow darkened echo of ' Indianapolis,' broken down and toppling over into the abyss — this effect is deliberate.

The poem deliberately guttered down into nothingness, mean-inglessness. But lately, since the circumstances of the world have changed from the moronic cackling of the 1920's over ruin, over their bright-coloured hell, to a naked menace, where the only bright colour is that of blood, I have now changed the end to this :

Said the Bishop, ' The world is flat. . . .'
But the see-saw Crowd sent the Emperor down
To the howling dust — and up went the Clown
With his face that is filched from the new young Dead. . . .
And the Tyrant's ghost and the Low-Man-Flea
Are emperor-brothers, cast shades that are red
From the tide of blood — (Red Sea, Dead Sea),
And Attila's voice or the hum of a gnat
Can usher in Eternity.

Why ' hairy sky ' ? I was speaking of streaks of dark cloud in a hot summer sky, and I meant, too, that now everything, even the heaven, seems to be of an animal, a material, nature.

At that time I was much occupied in examining the meaning of material phenomena and attempting to see what they revealed to us of the spiritual world.

Seeing the immense design of the world, one image of wonder mirrored by another image of wonder — the pattern of fern and of feather by the frost on the window-pane, the six rays of the snowflake mirrored in the rock-crystal's six-rayed eternity — seeing the pattern on the scaly legs of birds mirrored in the pattern of knot-grass, I asked myself, were those shapes moulded by blindness ? Are not these the ' correspondences,' to quote a phrase of Swedenborg, ' whereby we may speak with angels ' ?

It was said that the images in these poems were strange. This was partly the result of condensement — partly because, where the language of one sense was insufficient to cover the meaning, the sensation, I used the language of another, and by this means attempted to pierce down to the essence of the thing seen, by discovering in it attributes which at first sight appear alien but which are acutely related — by producing its quint-essential colour (sharper, brighter than that seen by an eye grown stale) and by stripping it of all unessential details.

The ' Waltz ' in *Façade* is an example at once of the technical exercises and of this heightened imagery.

Here, the rhythm is produced by the use of rhymes at the beginning of certain lines, and, occasionally, in the middle as well as at the end, and by the use of carefully arranged assonances and half-assonances. The rhyme-assonance scheme — Walk, Shore, Talking — with their various degrees of darkness, gives a kind of ground rhythm.

The phrase ' wan grassy sea ' means that the sea was the

colour of faded summer grass and seemed, from a distance to be like a grassy plain.

By ' swan-bosomed tree ' I mean a tree covered thickly with snow. ' Each foam-bell of ermine ' means thick foam.

I was thinking of flower-bells, not bells that ring.

Towards the end of the ' Waltz ' come these lines :

> Our élégantes favouring bonnets of blond,
> The stars in their apiaries,
> Sylphs in their aviaries,
> Seeing them, spangle these, and the sylphs fond
> From their aviaries fanned
> With each long fluid hand
> The manteaux espagnols,
> Mimic the waterfalls
> Over the long and the light summer land.

Here the movement is got partly by the use of assonances — in one case softening — ' apiaries,' ' aviaries ' — in one case rising — ' fond,' ' fanned.'

' Aviaries ' is a reversed, trembling assonance to ' favouring ' ; — the ' p 's in ' spangle ' and in ' espagnols ' form, with the ' p ' in ' apiaries,' a ground rhythm. The alliterative 'b's of ' bonnets ' and ' blond,' the ' m 's of ' manteaux ' and ' mimic ' also form a ground rhythm.

It is admissible that certain arrangements of words ending in ' ck ' (' black,' ' quack,' ' duck,' ' clack,' etc.) cast little, almost imperceptible shadows. In ' The Bat,' a poem about the waiting, watching world of the Shade, I have contrasted these shadows, so small yet so menacing, with those flat and shadeless words that end with ' t ' and with ' d,' experimenting, too, as do all poets, with the different vibrations gained from the alternate use of poignant, dark, and flat ' a ' sounds.

In this poem, some of the ' a 's and the ' u 's have neither depth nor body, are flat and death-rotten ; yet at times the words in which they occur cast a small menacing shadow because of the ' ck ' endings, though frequently these shadows are followed almost immediately by flatter, deader, more shadeless words ending in ' t ' or in ' d.'

> Where decoy-duck dust
> Began to clack,
> Watched Heliogabalusene the Bat
> In his furred cloak hang head down from the flat
> Wall . . .

The only body in the first three lines of this passage (if we except the round second syllable of ' decoy ') is in the consonants (casting those little threatening shadows) of ' duck ' and ' clack.' In the lines

> Shades on heroic
> Lonely grass,
> Where the moonlight's echoes die and pass.
> Near the rustic boorish,
> Fustian Moorish
> Castle wall of the ultimate Shade,

the long ' o 's of ' heroic ' and ' lonely,' cast at opposite ends of two succeeding lines (' lonely ' being slightly longer than ' heroic '), the still deeper ' oo ' of ' moonlight,' the hollow sound of ' echoes ' — these throw long, and opposed, shadows, and in the case of ' heroic ' and ' echoes ' they seem broken columns of shade. The ' oo 's in ' boorish ' and ' Moorish ' are still darker, and the shadows seem at once blown forward by the ' r 's, as by a gust of wind, and broken by these. ' Rustic,' ' Fustian,' and ' ultimate ' are broken echoes of one another ; but ' rustic ' is harder than the other echoes, because of the ' c,' and it is less wavering and indeterminate. The varying length and depth of the ' a ' sounds in

> Castle wall of the ultimate Shade,
> With his cloak castellated as that wall, afraid,
> The mountebank doctor,
> The old stage quack,

give a sense of fear, of something that alternately tries to shrink away into the darkness and to rear itself up in self-protection. The long second ' a ' in ' castellated ' (coming after the huddled beginning of the word) and its exact counterpart, the second ' a ' of ' afraid,' coming after the short crouching first ' a ' and the shuddering ' fr ' — these, falling in their particular places in the line, give a feeling that the half-unreal figure of the old stage quack (the Bat's half-human counterpart) — a figure that is so flat and empty that its only reality seems to lie in the slightly thicker muffling-cloak-sound of ' mountebank,' and whose shadow, being part and parcel of the Shade, is not a shadow cast by a man but like small menacing shadows that prophesy of the ultimate darkness — this figure seems raising itself up to its full height, as if fearing attack.

In the line

> The old stage quack

the word 'stage,' with its crumbling 'ge,' is a reversed, dry, and crumbling echo or shadow of the 'sh' of 'shade,' and in that word we have already the beginning of the deathlike rottenness that will be completed by the dull 'a' and the shades cast by the 'ck' in 'quack.'

The poem called 'The Drum,' which belongs neither to the world of *Façade* nor to that of *Bucolic Comedies* but to a nightworld that lies between, is founded on a story told by that very odd clergyman, the Reverend Joseph Glanvil, chaplain to King Charles II, in his records of witches and witchcraft. It contains, at the beginning, certain of the same experiments as are to be found in 'The Bat,' but in 'The Drum' the rhythm and the variations in it are much more complicated.

In the first few lines of 'The Drum' I attempted to convey the sense of menace, of deepening darkness, by the use of the dissonances, so subtle they might almost be assonances, of 'tall,' 'senatorial,' 'manorial' — the 'o' of 'senatorial' being deeper than the dissonantal 'a' in 'tall.' 'Black,' 'duck,' 'clatter,' and 'quack,' with their hard consonants and dead vowels, are dry as dust, and the deadness of dust is conveyed thus, and, as well, by the dulled dissonance of the 'a's, of the 'u' in 'duck' followed by its crumbling assonance 'dust.' (By 'decoy-duck dust' I mean very thick dry dust. A duck's quacking is, to me, one of the driest of sounds, and it has a peculiar deadness.)

The sharp and menacing rhythm of the first four lines is given by the fact that 'black' in the second line is at the opposite side from 'duck' and 'clack' in the third and fourth, and this throws reversed shadows. In the lines

> Clatter and quack
> To a shadow black, —

'clatter,' coming, as it does, immediately after 'clack,' has an odd sound, like that of a challenge thrown down in an empty place by one who, having offered it, then shrinks away in fear. It is a fact that the second syllable of 'clatter,' instead of casting a shadow, shrinks away into itself and dies. Its flatness is of a different quality from the flatness of the word 'shadow,' which is less dead, but still more bodiless — more bodiless because the 'd' is less thick than the two 't's — less dead because the last syllable has the length and depth of the dark vowel sound.

In the lines

> Said the musty Justice Mompesson,
> 'What is that dark stark beating drum . . . ? '

the thick assonance of 'musty Justice,' the rhymes 'dark stark,' placed so closely together, produce a menacing echo. These latter do not leap into the air, as do the rhymes placed immediately together in 'Fox Trot,' for the reason that in 'Fox Trot' they have light and bodiless endings, while in 'The Drum' they are weighed down by the shadow-casting 'k's.

We find, occasionally, subtle variations of thickness and thinness (and consequently variations of darkness) brought about in assonances and rhymes by the changing of a consonant or labial, from word to word, as in the first two lines of the poem, where the grave darkness of 'senatorial' changes to the thicker, more impenetrable 'manorial' (which, for all its thickness, is hollow), and in the seventh line — here it is the case of a distorted dissonance — where the fat sloth of 'musty Justice' changes to the thick, black, muffled bulk and darkness of 'Mompesson.' Again, in the twentieth and twenty-first lines,

> In the pomp of the Mompesson house is one
> Candle that lolls like the midnight sun,

the round body and concentration of 'pomp' is changed to the softness and shapelessness of 'lolls,' while in

> Out go the candles one by one,
> Hearing the rolling of a drum!

we have the change from the disembodied sound of 'one,' with its faint echo, to the thickness of 'drum,' wherein darkness takes on a body. In the lines

> Black as Hecate howls a star
> Wolfishly, and whined
> The wind from very far

the small-vowelled quick three-syllabled word 'Hecate' makes the line rock up and down. In the next line, the word 'wolfishly' *pretends* to balance 'Hecate' but in reality does nothing of the kind, because of the longish 'o,' and because the 'c' and 't' in 'Hecate' are thin and dry, and the 'lf' and 'sh' of 'wolfishly' are thick and soft, and therefore 'wolfishly' is a longer, slower word. The soft 'w' and the dim vowels, the 'i' dimming from whined ' down to ' wind,' are meant to give the impression of a faint breeze.

In the next verse,

> In the pomp of the Mompesson house is one
> Candle that lolls like the midnight sun,
> Or the coral comb of a cock ; . . . it rocks. . . .
> Only the goatish snow's locks
> Watch the candles lit by fright
> One by one through the black night

leaving aside the effects produced by the variations in thickness to which I have referred already, the rhythm, the drum-beating, the inevitable march onward of the menace — these are produced by the very elaborate schemes of rhymes, assonances, and dissonances —' lolls,' ' coral,' ' cock,' ' rocks,' ' locks ' — dissonances so faint they might almost be assonances, but each having its own particular thickness and depth, varying with an extraordinary subtlety. Then there are the more discordant dissonances to these, ' one,' ' sun,' and their dissonance ' candle,' and its shadow ' black,' and all these make the line heave up and down, like something struggling to escape.

In the line

> Or the coral comb of a cock ; . . . it rocks . . .

the sharp ' c 's seem pin-points of light, which leap into a sudden flare with the word ' comb.' Later on, when we come to the lines

> Through the kitchen there runs a hare —
> Whinnying, whines like grass, the air

the rhythm is given by the assonances ' kitchen ' and ' whinnying,' rising to the high ' i ' of ' whines,' and by the balance of the two-syllabled, three-syllabled, and one-syllabled words. The image was brought to my mind by the fact that thin grass trembling in the wind seems to me to resemble in its movement a high whining or whinnying sound, while the dampness and coldness of the air on certain winter days resembles the dampness and coldness of grass.

If we take the lines

> Black angels in a heavenly place,
> Her shady locks and her dangerous grace

we shall see that the rhythm is given by the high assonantal ' a 's and the balance (which is completely different from that of the

xxiv

couplet quoted previously) of the two-syllabled, one-syllabled, and three-syllabled words.

A completely different balance, again, is given by the assonances and the arrangement of one-syllabled, two-syllabled, and three-syllabled words in

> ' I thought I saw the wicked old witch in
> The richest gallipot in the kitchen ! '

in which the sound alternately intertwines and marches forward. In

> A lolloping galloping candle confesses

' lolloping ' is a queer reversed dissonance of ' gallipot,' and ' galloping ' is an almost equally crazy assonance ; they are intended to convey the impression of candle flames, blown now backwards, now sideways, and the ' l 's in these, together with the ' s ' sounds in ' confesses ' and in the lines following :

> ' Outside in the passage are wildernesses
> Of darkness rustling like witches' dresses '

give the softness of the flame that is speaking. Then, much later, we come to the line

> The mocking money in the pockets

where the faint variations in the castanet-thin, elfish sound seem like pin-points of candlelight, blown by the cold air.

As, earlier in the poem, we found variations in degrees of thickness, so in

> Whinnying, neighed the maned blue wind

we find variations in the degrees of thinness, and this, too, has significance.

In the poem ' The Wind's Bastinado,' the strange ghostly rhythm is formed largely by the fact that the lines end (with a deliberate tunelessness) with words whose first syllable is a dissonance, whose last syllable rhymes — dissonances which, therefore, shrink as with cold, or are blown backwards and forwards as by a cold wind, changing their direction aimlessly from time to time or gathering the rhythm together into a ghostly march tune.

The lines in which dissonances occur blow aimlessly backwards and forwards ; but in the lines

> Beneath the galloon
> Of the midnight sky

the rhythm is gathered together, shows a faint, not quite formulated, purpose.

Throughout the poem the rhythm changes again and again, owing largely to the constant shifting of the accent from one syllable of the words ending the lines to another — from the dissonance beginning the end word to the rhyming last syllable and back again.

In the lines quoted below :

> ' This melon,
> Sir Mammon,
> Comes out of Babylon :
> Buy for a patacoon —
> Sir, you must buy ! '

the change from the word ' melon ' to ' Mammon ' (the latter word is like thick dust that has gathered itself into some embodiment), the change from the dreaminess of ' Babylon,' which is in part a matter of association, to the sharp sound, like that of a hard coin falling on dry ground, of ' patacoon ' — this is deliberate.

In the nine lines beginning with

> Said Il Magnifico

a final shaping and embodiment of the dust comes to pass. But this shaping and voicing of the dust is followed immediately by the dreaminess, in which there is no emphasis save that of the little cold air produced by the faint wavering pauses in the lines

> ' It is my friend King Pharaoh's head
> That nodding blew out of the Pyramid . . .'

and their echoes (which are echoes only rhythmically, not verbally) :

> For it is winter and cold winds sigh . . .

and

> Of bunchèd leaves let her singing die.

An impression of cold is obtained in the lines

> The tree's small corinths
> Were hard as jacinths,
> For it is winter and cold winds sigh . . .
> No nightingale
> In her farthingale
> Of bunchèd leaves let her singing die

by the fading dissonance of ' jacinths ' after ' corinths ' and the identical ending of ' nightingale,' ' farthingale,' which sounds like something shrinking from the cold.

' Fox Trot ' is an experiment in the effect, on rhythm and on speed, of certain arrangements of assonances and dissonances, and of a certain arrangement of intertwining one-syllabled, two-syllabled, and three-syllabled words.

The ground rhythm of the beginning of this poem is partly the result of the drone sounds in the first lines, the dissonances, so subtle they might almost be assonances, of 'Faulk,' 'tall,' 'stork,' 'before,' 'walk' — each having a different depth of darkness. 'Tall' and the second syllable of 'before,' for instance, while the sounds differ (though with an almost incredible faintness) both in darkness and in length, dip much deeper in both cases than 'Faulk' or 'stork,' while the sound of 'stork' is slightly darker than 'Faulk.' All these drone sounds seem pleasant country shadows, varying slightly in depth, in warmth, in length. In the fifth and seventh lines, the words 'honeyed' and 'reynard' are a little rounder than 'pheasant-feathered,' and each casts a little dipping, reversed shadow, because the light, fleeting character of the second syllable of 'honeyed' suddenly grows dark in its dissonance, the second syllable of 'reynard,' while the first syllable of 'honeyed' is a faintly darker dissonance of the 'rey' of 'reynard.' The shadows, therefore, fall in opposite directions.

The fact that in the line

The reynard-coloured sun

the words ending in 'd' are placed so close together, makes, in this particular case, a slight leap into the air, while, some lines farther on, the three-syllabled words of

Periwigged as William and Mary, weep . . .

twirl round on themselves : and the assonances, placed in such juxtaposition, of

Among the pheasant-feathered corn the unicorn has torn, forlorn the

gives a particular smoothness ; the line might consist of one word only were it not for the change from sunniness to darkness.

The 'ea' sounds, on which much of the poem is based, vary in lightness ; at moments the effect is of light pleasant stretches of cornfields, as in

Among the pheasant-feathered corn the unicorn has torn, forlorn the

over which the flying shadows of the darker-vowelled 'corn,' 'unicorn,' 'torn,' 'forlorn,' dip and are gone.

In the line

'Sally, Mary, Mattie, what's the matter, why cry ? '

the changing of the assonances, from the limpness of 'Sally' to the hardness of 'Mattie,' the reversal of sound in the second syllables, from 'Mattie' to 'matter'—these have a very faint effect upon the rhythm, while the exact rhymes 'Why cry,' placed together, give a high leap into the air. Throughout the poem the assonances and dissonances are placed in a closely concerted and interwoven design, some being accented, and some so un-accented as to be almost muted; they are largely responsible for the rhythm, and often counterpoint it slightly, as in

> Oh, the nursery-*maid* Meg
> With a leg like a peg
> *Chased* the feathered dreams like hens, and when *they laid* an egg

where the high 'a' sounds counterpoint the 'Meg,' 'leg,' 'peg,' 'egg' sound of the ground rhythm.

These 'a' (or 'ai') sounds are echoed, farther on, more insistently, and with a deeper emphasis, by

> . . . In the
> Corn, towers *strain*,
> Feathered tall as a *crane*,
> And whistling down the feathered *rain*, old Noah goes again —

where these assonances, while they are slightly counterpointed, are yet nearly as important as the ground rhythm given by 'corn' and 'tall.'

It will be seen how slack is the rhythm, in comparison with the rest, of such lines as have only an end rhyme and no apparent assonances or dissonances, as in the second line of

> An old dull mome
> With a head like a pome.

Though 'head' is immediately linked up again in the next line with 'egg,' yet, because it had no previous related sound, there is no effect on rhythm.

A faint and fleeting country shadow is cast again, later in the poem, by the changing of the 'aph' of 'Japhet' to the dimmer 'v' of 'gave' in the lines

> Of Japhet, Shem, and Ham; she gave it
> Underneath the trees.

'Dark Song' is a poem about the beginning of things and their relationship — the fire that purrs like an animal and has a beast's thick coat (the crumbling, furry black coal), and a girl whose blood has the dark pulse and instinct of the earth.

The long, harsh, animal-purring ' r 's and the occasional double vowels, as in ' bear ' and ' fire,' though these last are divided by a muted ' r,' are intended to convey the uncombatable animal instinct. The poem is built on a scheme of harsh ' r 's, alternating with dulled ' r 's, and the latter, with the thickness of the ' br ' and the ' mb ' in

> The brown bear rambles in his chain

are meant to give the thickness of the bear's dull fur. The dissonances of the first line :

> The fire was furry as a bear

the one and a half syllables of ' fire,' stretching forward and upward and then breaking, contrasted with the dark, thick, numb insistence of the first syllable in ' furry ' — the fact that the dissonances ending the first six lines are *dropping* dissonances — this conveys the feeling of the animal's thick paws that have not the power of lifting. The sinking or dulled dissonances which end some of the lines in the place of rhymes, ' bear,' ' purr ' — ' chain,' ' men ' — the way in which, in the midst of this darkness, there is an occasional high insistent vowel sound — these effects are deliberate and are meant to convey a darkened groping.

In most of the *Bucolic Comedies* there are no technical experiments, and usually the rhythm is a drone-sound like that of a hive or the wind in the trees. Some of the poems, again, have a goat-footed, rustic sound, deliberately uncouth — a hard, quick, uncouth rhythm — so that it seems as if we are not listening to the peasants' boots falling on a soft soil but to the far earlier sound of satyr hooves falling on a ground that is hard with winter, or harsh and sharp with spring, or mad and harsh with summer — or, to quote Rimbaud, to ' the eclogues in sabots, grunting in the orchards.'

At moments, the shortness and roundness of the lines produce the effect of small uncouth buds breaking from the earth — daisy-buds, for instance ; or they spurt like a hard, shrill jet of water, as in the shorter lines of ' Gardener Janus Catches a Naiad ' :

> Feathered masks,
> Pots of peas,
> Janus asks
> Naught of these.

> Creaking water
> Brightly stripèd,
> Now, I've caught her —
> Shrieking biped. . . .

In one of the *Bucolic Comedies*, ' Early Spring,' the effect of windless cold, of that time of waiting and watching, when the first buds are spurting from the dark boughs, and when the winter is about to change into spring — these sensations are produced by the absolute stillness of the lines, the faintness of the pauses when they occur (and they are very rare, excepting at the ends of lines).

There are, indeed, only two long pauses to be found *within* the lines — one after ' whimper,' because the second syllable dies away like a little cold air ; the other after ' milk,' because this is a word of one syllable and a fraction, and, this extra fraction being extremely faint, the effect is not that of a flutter or a movement, but of a tiny pause.

Any other definite movement in this poem is caused by words ending in ' d ' being placed in juxtaposition — slowing, in this instance, the lines

> Our faces, furre*d* with col*d* like re*d*
> Furre*d* bu*d*s of satyr springs, long *dead*!
>
> The col*d* win*d* creaking in my bloo*d*
> Seems part of it, as grain of woo*d*;

and by the unmuted ' r 's in the above lines and in some others, which give the faintest possible movement, like that of a bough stirring in the air.

Such other pauses as occur, so faint as to be almost imperceptible, give the lines a strange chilliness, all the stranger because the ' o ' and ' ou ' sounds throughout the poem (when they are not sharp with spring, as in ' cloud,' ' shroud,' ' bough,' ' slough ') are warm, and are meant to give the impression of growing things waiting beneath the hard soil in the darkness till the winter shall be gone. From time to time a poignant cold air creeps into these lines, with the sharp freezing ' e ' sounds, while the subtle faint change from the cold wind to the swaddled warmth of the growing things waiting beneath the hard soil — these are conveyed by the varying lengths and depths of these ' o ' and ' ou ' sounds, sometimes dulling and shrinking with cold into a ' u ' that is only a shrunken echo of these.

The feeling of cold air comes, too, with an occasional dissonance, as in the ' dull,' ' crystal,' ' bells ' sounds of the first two couplets. The subtle variations which lie between the dissonances and assonances, as well as the faint pauses, do, indeed, give a slight movement. ' Blunt,' for instance, is faintly higher, longer, more numb with cold than is ' dull '; ' bells ' is slightly longer than ' red '; ' buds ' is sharper yet rounder and less dark than ' furred.' And these, as well, gather together the rhythm while conveying the sense of this time of waiting.

In many of these poems the subject is the growth of consciousness. Sometimes it is like that of a person who has always been blind and who, suddenly endowed with sight, must *learn* to see ; or it is the cry of that waiting, watching world, where everything we see is a symbol of something beyond, to the consciousness that is yet buried in this earth-sleep ; and it is this last that we find in ' Aubade.'

The reason I said ' The morning light creaks ' is this : after rain, the early light seems as if it does not run quite smoothly. Also, it has a quality of great hardness and seems to present a physical obstacle to the shadows — and this gives one the impression of a creaking sound because it is at once hard and uncertain.

> Each dull blunt wooden stalactite
> Of rain creaks, hardened by the light,
>
> Sounding like an overtone
> From some lonely world unknown.

At dawn, long raindrops hanging from boughs seem transformed by the light, have the dull, blunt, tasteless quality of wood : as they move in the wind they seem to creak. Though the sound is unheard in reality, it has the quality of an overtone from some unknown and mysterious world.

The poem is about a country girl, a servant on a farm, plain, neglected, and unhappy, with a bucolic stupidity, coming down in the dawn to light the fire. And the lines

> But the creaking empty light
> Will never harden into sight,
>
> Will never penetrate your brain
> With overtones like the blunt rain

mean that to her the light is an empty thing which conveys nothing. It cannot bring her sight, because she is not capable of seeing.

The light would show (if it could harden)
Eternities of kitchen garden,

Cockscomb flowers that none will pluck,
And wooden flowers that 'gin to cluck.

If she were capable of seeing anything, still she would only see
the whole of eternity as the world of kitchen gardens to which
she is accustomed, with flowers red and lank as cockscombs
(uncared for, as she is uncared for), and hard-looking flowers
that dip and bend beneath the rain with a movement like that of
hens when they cluck.

Where the cold dawn light lies whining.

To me, the shivering movement of a certain cold dawn light
upon the floor suggests a kind of high animal whining or whimper-
ing, a half-frightened and subservient urge to something outside
our consciousness.

The world I see is a country world, a universe of growing
things, where magic and growth are one, and wherein, as in
George Peele's lines :

God in the whizzing of a pleasant wind
Shall march upon the tops of mulberry trees ;

a world of rough, fruitful suns, and the age of the innocence of
man — of the forests

Where the wolf Nature from maternal breast
Fed us with strong brown milk . . .

the age

When Time's vast sculptures from rough dust began,
And natural law and moral were but one, —
Derived from the rich wisdom of the sun.

Sometimes we find poems whose movement is like the growth
of a slower plant life, as in verse twenty-two of ' Romance ' :

When the green century of summer rains
Lay on the leaves, then like the rose I wept.
For I had dwelt in sorrow as the rose
In the deep heaven of her leaves lies close.
Then you, my gardener, with green fingers stroked my leaves
Till all the gold drops turned to honey. Grieves

This empire of green shade when honeyed rains
And amber blood flush all the sharp green veins
Of the rich rose?
                    So doth my rose-shaped heart
Feel the first flush of summer; love's first smart
Seemed no more sorrowful than the deep tears
The rose wept in that green and honeyed clime.

Here the ethereal quality of the plant world, the slow growth of the plant, the colour and scent of the rose are conveyed by the different wave-lengths of the vowels.

At other moments, as a contrast to this world, we find one of heavy, brutish, greedy darkness:

    . . . the countrysides where people know
That Destiny is wingless and bemired,
With feathers dirty as a hen's, too tired
To fly — where old pig-snouted Darkness grovels
For life's mired rags among the broken hovels —

or a countryside where everything we see is a symbol of something beyond the world, but where the people live the life of growing things rooted deeply in the mould, understanding only the world of the unawakened senses but not the significance of their language — seeing the stars as no more remote than the flowers in their potting-sheds, and the vast and unknown splendours as something homely; so that death and the stars are no more strange:

    It seemed a low-hung country of the blind, —
A sensual touch upon the heart and mind,
Like crazy creaking chalets hanging low
From the dark hairiness of bestial skies
The clouds seem, like a potting-shed where grow
The flower-like planets for the gay flower-show.

Sometimes the poems speak of an unawakened consciousness fumbling toward a higher state, and sometimes of a purely animal consciousness — the beginning of all earthly things.

Thus, a flower, in 'Springing Jack,' is a

    Clear angel-face on hairy stalk
(Soul grown from flesh, an ape's young talk).

The images of my early poems were regarded as unreal and intended to shock. But were they more shocking than this lovely image of Gerard Manley Hopkins, written in 1868 but not published until 1938 ? —

Antares sparkled like a bright crab-apple tingling in the wind.

When, in 1924, fourteen years before the publication of that sentence, I wrote of

> . . . boughs of cherries
> That seem the lovely lucent coral bough
> (From streams of starry milk those branches grow)
> That Cassiopeia feeds with her faint light
> Like Ethiopia ever jewelled bright

my image was regarded as very odd.

Images in other poems in *Bucolic Comedies* were regarded as still stranger. But they now form part of the currency of the language —' purring fire,' ' creaking light,' to take only two examples.

For all their condensement, I have tried to make my images exact — though heightened.

When I say :

> . . . with a sweet and velvet lip
> The snapdragons within the fire
> Of their red summer never tire

I try to give to the imagination a red and glowing fire.

Writing of spring, I say :

> In Midas' garden the simple flowers
> Laugh, and the tulips are bright as the showers,

> For spring is here ; the auriculas,
> And the Emily-coloured primulas

> Bob in their pinafores on the grass
> As they watch the gardener's daughter pass.

Emily is a countrified old-fashioned name, and pink primulas remind one of the bright pink cheeks of country girls. Obviously I could not mean yellow primulas, since nobody is of that bright yellow colour.

By ' Bob in their pinafores ' I meant to give the impression of frilled flowers bending in the wind.

In ' Père Amelot,' which is a poem about an unawakened being whose death, sharp and sudden, and inflicted for no purpose, leaves him nodding in his nightcap as he had done throughout his life, the image 'hen-cackling grass' refers to quaking grass, and it was suggested by the fact that the colour and dusty aspect of the pods are like the colour and dustiness of a hen, are dry and have markings like those on a hen's legs, and, as well, by the fact that the shaking movement resembles, for me at least, the quick dry sound and dipping movement of a cackling hen.

In the poem 'Madam Mouse Trots' I have these lines :

> Hoarse as a dog's bark
> The heavy leaves are furled. . . .

Certain leaves have a rough and furry texture and jut violently from their branches — the young leaves of a chestnut tree, for instance. In the same poem, when I say

> Furred is the light

I was thinking of misty moonlight.

In this edition I have included both the first and second versions of 'Metamorphosis,' for I have returned now to my original feeling about the first version and am as much at home with it as with the second version. At the time when I had, to my present feeling, mistakenly discarded it (the poem was written in 1929), I incorporated the first two lines of verse twenty-one, the verses thirty-eight, thirty-nine, forty, forty-one, forty-two, and forty-three, and verses ninety-seven and ninety-eight in a much later poem, 'Lo, this is she that was the world's desire,' and verses twenty-seven, twenty-eight, twenty-nine, thirty, and verses thirty-three and thirty-four, in 'One Day in Spring.'

My actual experiments led eventually to the poem 'Gold Coast Customs.' It is a poem about the state that led up to the second World War. It is a definite prophecy of what would arise from such a state — what *has* arisen. (It was written in 1929.)

> . . . Do we smell and see
>
> The sick thick smoke from London burning . . .?

In this poem the bottom of the world has fallen out.

The organisation of the poem, speaking of this world that has broken down, but where a feverish, intertwining, seething movement, a vain seeking for excitement, still existed, presented considerable difficulty. I tried to give a concentrated essence of that world through a movement which at times interweaves like worms intertwining, which at times has a jaunty wire-jerked sound, or rears itself up like a tidal wave rushing forward, or swells like a black sea-swell by means of violently stretching vowels, then, as in the lines

> Hidden behind
> The Worm's mask, grown
> White as a bone
> Where eyeholes rot wide
> And are painted for sight,

sinks into a deliberate pulselessness. In this world of the 'Rich man Judas, Brother Cain,' and of that world's confession, Lady Bamburgher, man is part ravenous beast of prey, part worm, part ape, or is but the worm turned vertebrate. It is a world where the light is no longer a reality but a high ventriloquist sound (so high none knows whence it comes) — the octave of the black clotted night — no longer the true and guiltless Light :

> Christ that takest away the sin
> Of the world, and the rich man's bone-dead grin

We see everything reduced to the primal mud — the 'Rich man Judas, Brother Cain,' and the epitome of his civilisation, Lady Bamburgher, are at one with the slum-ignorance and the blackness and superstition of the African swamp. The beating of their fevered hearts and pulses is no more than the beating of the drums that heralded the Customs, as they were called in Ashantee, a hundred and fifty years ago, when, at the death of any rich or important person, slaves and poor persons were killed so that the bones of the dead might be washed by human blood. So, the spiritual dead-in-life cry, in our time, for a sacrifice — that of the starved. And these, sacrificed, are watched by the appalling dumb agony of

> . . . the rat-eaten bones
> Of a fashionable god that lived not
> Ever, but still has bones to rot.

Down to the end of the sixth verse the poem is obviously nothing but abstract sound — abstract, but I would like to think significant. In the first verse, the rocking drum-beating movement is produced by the various flatnesses and depths of the ' a 's, the thicknesses and dullnesses of the ' u 's, and by the intertwining of words of different lengths (since these produce different speeds). In the first four lines :

> One fantee wave
> Is grave and tall
> As brave Ashantee's
> Thick mud wall

the first line begins with a jaunty wire-jerked movement. From the fawning, crouching sound of ' fantee ' it rises suddenly (stretching outward), with ' wave,' to one of the utmost heights of which a vowel-sound is capable — echoed by ' grave ' in the next line, which rocks up and down between that enormous height and the deepest darkness with the hollow sound of ' tall.' The first line is echoed, but upside down, in the third. By this means the lines toss up and down violently, from a world-height down into the deepest gulf imaginable, and this tossing up and down is repeated in the third verse :

> Like monkey-skin
> Is the sea — one sin
> Like a weasel is nailed to bleach on the rocks
> Where the eyeless mud screeched fawning, mocks

by means of the high screaming ' e 's alternating with dulled ' o 's, while the arrangement of soft ' s 's and of their slightly firmer counterpart, the ' ch 's, gives a feeling of gradually rotting flesh.
    In the following verse :

> At a Negro that wipes
> His knife . . . dug there,
> A bugbear bellowing
> Bone dared rear —
> A bugbear bone that bellows white
> As the ventriloquist sound of light,

we find the most giddy rocking sound that has yet been pro-duced in this poem — and this is the result of the rhymes ' dug there ' and ' bugbear ' being placed so close together, followed by the deafening blows of the alliterative ' b 's, with gaps between (numb like deafness), where a continued alliteration is expected and is not found. (Note: In ' Fox Trot,' two rhymes placed close together, ' Why cry,' ' I sigh,' produced a leap into the air ; but the result of ' dug there,' ' bugbear ' is entirely different, because ' there ' and ' bear ' are words of faintly more than one syllable, and because 'dug' and 'bug' are low sounds and 'there' and 'bear' are both higher and stretch forward instead of crouching.)

The long echoing hollowness of

> A bugbear bellowing
> Bone dared rear —
> A bugbear bone that bellows white

actually lengthens and slows the lines, the first two being stretched violently and to their uttermost capacity.

The verse about a slum, which begins with the line

> Here, tier on tier

gives a suggestion of flapping emptiness, because of the word 'tier' having a fraction of an extra syllable.

Certain images in the poem were taken from objects seen in the ethnographical section of the British Museum — the shrunken heads, for instance, and that image in which the sun

> . . . hangs like a skull
> With a yellow dull
> Face made of clay
> (Where tainted, painted, the plague-spots bray)
> To hide where the real face rotted away.

Here, though in quite a different sense, with a different sound, from that of a previous verse, we have again — resulting this time from the dull crumbling 'l's — the sense of flesh decaying. But in this verse we have a hopeless endeavour to rise, produced this time by using poignant vowels alternating with thick muddy ones ; but this endeavour, in lines seven, eight, and nine of the verse in question, becomes mere hallucination and fever. With the succeeding verse, when we come to the lines

> Of the shapeless worm-soft unshaping Sin —
> Unshaping till no more the beat of the blood
> Can raise up the body from endless mud

the position of the 'a's and 's's in the first line gives an impression of formlessness endeavouring (in the second and third lines) to regain shape (by means of the alliterative '.b's). To attain this aim, however, there should have been a third 'b' where the word 'no' stands — the omission was deliberate — and the formless matter sinks back once more, therefore, into the mud and slime, in the line

> Are painted upon each unshaped form —

where the position of the ' a 's produces this impression of form-
lessness, because they were put, deliberately, in the wrong place.
And the formlessness is not that of primeval matter, it is that of
matter which has chosen to be part of the slime and mud. The
lines purposely have an unpleasant softness — the softness of
corruption.

Throughout the poem, my method of producing the different
degrees of darkness has been that of using changing wave-lengths
of vowels, as in the description of Lady Bamburgher's unborn
god who

> . . . still has bones to rot :
> A bloodless and an unborn thing.

But this deadness changes suddenly to the piteous stirring,
the upheaval caused by the internal rhymes, the upward-heaving
vowels, sinking and heaving upward again, of

> That cannot wake, yet cannot sleep,
> That makes no sound, that cannot weep,
> That hears all, bears all, cannot move —
> It is buried so deep
> Like a shameful thing
> In that plague-spot heart, Death's last dust-heap.

Much earlier in the poem, in the lines

> Where flaps degraded
> The black and sated
> Slack macerated
> And antiquated
> Beckoning Negress
> Nun of the shade,

the degrees of the mud are given by the ' s 's, by the softening of
the sound of ' degraded ' to that of ' sated,' and by the change
from the squelching sound of the ' qu ' in ' antiquated ' to the
still softer sound of ' shade.'

In the succeeding lines :

> And the rickety houses
> Rock and rot,
> Lady Bamburgher airs
> That foul plague-spot
> Her romantic heart.
> From the cannibal mart,
> That smart Plague-cart,
> Lady Bamburgher rolls where the foul news-sheet
> And the shambles for souls are set in the street

'Rock' is a shrunken, darker echo of 'rickety,' 'rot' is a still deader, flatter echo of 'rock,' while the dissonances of 'plague-spot' and 'heart' are deliberate. The arrangement of 'l's placed near one another gives the effect of a stretch of mud, clinging to our feet and impeding our progress. Later in the same verse we return to the rocking movement, tossing up and down, which is effected by the internal rhymes and dissonances.

Much later in the poem, when we come to the verse

> In the sailor's tall
> Ventriloquist street
> The calico dummies
> Flap and meet :
> Calculate : ' Sally go
> Pick up a sailor.'
> Behind that façade
> The worm is a jailer,

the worm-twisting movement, the horrible softness, is produced in part by the half-rhymes — some broken or crumbled, some scarcely rhymes at all, but assonances : 'calico,' 'calculate,' 'Sally go' — in part by the soft 'l's and the dull, lifeless 'a's. And four verses farther on, in

> Once I saw it come
> Through the canvas slum,
> Rattle and beat what seemed a drum,
> Rattle and beat it with a bone.
> O Christ, that bone was dead, alone.
> Christ, who will speak to such ragged Dead
> As me, I am dead, alone and bare,
> They expose me still to the grinning air,
> I shall never gather my bones and my dust
> Together (so changed and scattered, lost . . .)
> So I can be decently burièd !
> What is that whimpering like a child
> That this mad ghost beats like a drum in the air ?
> The heart of Sal
> That once was a girl
> And now is a calico thing to loll
> Over the easy steps of the slum
> Waiting for something dead to come

the language has, in part, produced the effect, with the horrible thick deadness of the sound of ' slum ' and ' drum ' ; while the deliberate tuneless, soft deadness of the dissonances 'Sal,' 'girl,' 'loll' seem toppling downhill into some deep abyss.

Throughout the poem, I have tried to produce, not so much the record of a world as the wounded and suffering soul of that world, its living evocation, not its history, seen through the eyes of a protagonist whose personal tragedy is echoed in that vaster tragedy.

Yet the poem ends thus :

> Yet the time will come
> To the heart's dark slum
> When the rich man's gold and the rich man's wheat
> Will grow in the street, that the starved may eat, —
> And the sea of the rich will give up its dead —
> And the last blood and fire from my side will be shed.
> For the fires of God go marching on.

It was of that gold and that wheat, of that blood and fire, and of the fires of God that I was to write next.

After 'Gold Coast Customs' I wrote no poetry for several years, with the exception of a long poem called 'Romance,' and one poem in which I was finding my way.

Then, after a year of war, I began to write again — of the state of the world, of the terrible rain

> Dark as the world of man, black as our loss —
> Blind as the nineteen hundred and forty nails
> Upon the Cross —

falling alike upon guilty and guiltless, upon Dives and Lazarus. I wrote of the sufferings of Christ, the Starved Man hung upon the Cross, the God of the Poor Man, who bears in His Heart all wounds.

In one poem I wrote of the world reduced to the Ape as mother, teacher, protector.

But, too, with poor Christopher Smart, I blessed Jesus Christ with the Rose and his people, which is a nation of living sweetness.

My time of experiments was done.

Now, for the most part, I use lines of great length — these need considerable technical control — sometimes unrhymed, but with occasional rhymes, assonances, and half-assonances, used, outwardly and inwardly in the lines, to act as a ground rhythm.

'The profit of rhyme,' said Whitman, 'is that it drops seeds of a sweeter and more luxuriant rhyme ; and of uniformity that it conveys itself into its own roots in the ground out of sight. The rhyme and uniformity of perfect poems show the free growth of metrical laws, and bud from them as unerringly and loosely as lilacs or roses on a bush, and take shapes as compact as the shapes of chestnuts, and oranges, and melons, and pears, and shed the perfume impalpable to form.'

With such long lines, I wrote of harvest.

Before the time came for ' The Shadow of Cain ' to be written, various of my poems spoke of the change from the worship of the holy, living, life-giving gold of the wheat to the destructive gold of Dives — the change from the warmth of love that makes all men brothers to the state in which men only call their fellow men ' Brother ' in order to act the part of Cain.

In ' The Two Loves,' a poem written about eighteen months before ' The Shadow of Cain,' I wrote of the summer of the earth and of the heart, and of how the warmth of the heart faded and only a false brotherhood remained. But as yet the sun itself had not been harnessed to a war-machine and used against us. We could still remember the holy life-giving warmth. In ' The Shadow of Cain,' however, we moved still farther from the Sun that is Christ and the Sun of the heart.

This poem is about the fission of the world into warring particles, destroying and self-destructive. It is about the gradual migration of mankind, after that Second Fall of Man that took the form of the separation of brother and brother, of Cain and Abel, of nation and nation, of the rich and the poor — the spiritual migration of these into the desert of the Cold, towards the final disaster, the first symbol of which fell on Hiroshima.

The poem came into being thus.

On the 10th of September 1945, nearly five weeks after the fall of the first atom bomb, my brother Sir Osbert Sitwell and I were in the train going to Brighton, where we were to give a reading. He pointed out to me a paragraph in *The Times*, a description by an eye-witness of the immediate effect of the atomic bomb upon Hiroshima. That witness saw a totem pole of dust arise to the sun as a witness against the murder of mankind. . . . A totem pole, the symbol of creation, the symbol of generation.

From that moment the poem began, although it was not actually written until April of the next year. It passed through many stages.

I wrote of how, after the desert of the Cold, the wanderers

reached an open door, although all that was left to them were the primal Realities.

> There was great lightning
> In flashes coming to us over the floor :
> The Whiteness of the Bread —
> The Whiteness of the Dead —
> The Whiteness of the Claw —
> All this coming to us in flashes through the open door.

I *dreamed* those lines about two months before I began to write the poem as a whole. The open door, in my dream, was the door of birth, through which we would come to Bread, Struggle (the Claw), and Death. As I used the symbol of the door in the poem, it is still the door of birth ; but it is also the door through which we must find our own path. The three lightnings are still those three primal Realities. Reduced to these, in the very house of Birth and of Death, having found our way in the desert of the Cold, I saw the Spring returning. There was still the grandeur of the Sun ; and of Christ returning to us with the life-giving wheat of harvest.

' The Son of God is sowed in every furrow ' was a phrase used in a completely different sense by John Donne in a sermon. The furrows, to him, were the lines of the Bible.

Succeeding this line came the horror, the symbol of which was seen by that witness at Hiroshima :

> We did not heed the Cloud in the Heavens shaped like the hand
> Of Man . . .
>
>   . . . the Primal Matter
> Was broken, the womb from which all life began.
> Then to the murdered Sun a totem pole of dust arose in
>   memory of Man.

I cannot conceive how anyone could have so misread this poem as not to know that it was about the dropping of the Bomb. What is the splitting of the atom but the breaking of the Primal Matter ? However, it was misunderstood.

A great critic, Jack Lindsay, writing of the passage beginning with the lines

> They brought the Aeons of Blindness and the Night
> Of the World, crying to him, ' Lazarus, give us sight ! '

said that ' Lazarus is the poor man, the maker of bread who is also the living wheat, the murdered man round whom the forces of redemption most powerfully play. To him hurry " the civilisation of the Maimed," and, too, " Life's lepers." They cry for salvation in the midst of terrible pressures of retrogression.

' Then Dives was brought. . . . He lay like a leprous Sun

' There lie the two dead men who are Man (Lazarus and Dives), with their conflicting forces, their opposed symbols of gold — gold that is quick of light in the corn, alchemic moment of transmutation and the healing of all sores ; money, the defilement, and the fires of corruption.' And he says of the end of the poem : ' the golds fight and unite ; the opposed forces are broken down into a new unity ; the fission in Man, reaching down through all levels, is made the basis of a new wholeness. Because the horror is faced and understood at all levels, Christ arises out of the split sepulchre and womb. A Judgment Day of all that distorted and divided.'

Often a line can mean several things — all equally true. What Mr. Lindsay says of the use of Lazarus as a symbol is of the deepest truth. I used the symbol thus. I used the symbol, also, as that of Poverty, now moved into a new tomb of useless gold, in which, until the fires of love and spiritual rebirth reach him, he will lie as dead as in his tomb of mud. Lazarus, the symbol of the new *earthly* resurrection of Man, that cold idealists believe is to be brought about by the new experiments. Lazarus, the terrible ideal of useless Suffering. Lazarus, the hero of death and the mud, taking the place in men's minds of the Hero of Life Who was born in a stable.

Dives speaks of the healing qualities of Gold.

But near him a gold sound —
The voice of an unborn wheat-ear accusing Dives —
Said, ' Soon I shall be more rare, more precious than gold.'

The first two pages move partly on a physical, partly on a spiritual plane. Some people say they have found this difficult. So I will explain certain images.

The first line of the poem refers to the torn yellow heavens of the extreme cold, that seem like ancient and ragged banners. That is a physical image. But if I were to return to that which exists ' below the threshold of awareness, like a sun below the horizon ' (to quote Dr. Jung), I might remember that the hair of Judas, according to legend, was yellow, and that he has often been painted in a yellow dress. I might also have a vision of the silent advance of the yellow banners of terrible Asian hordes advancing across a vast desert.

But the poem occurs in no particular place, until it moves to Hiroshima. It would be dwarfed by a human space. Hiroshima is no longer that : it has taken a third place beside Heaven and Hell.

> But the Cold is the highest mathematical Idea . . . the Cold is
>   Zero —
> The Nothing from which arose
> All Being and all variation. . . . the Point that flows
>
> Till it becomes the line of Time . . . an endless positing
> Of Nothing, or the Ideal that tries to burgeon
> Into Reality . . .

Here the physical state and the spiritual are fused.

The Cold is the highest mathematical Idea, the Cold is Zero —

This refers to the feeling one has, in the most intense Cold, that all material things are abolished, all is reduced to Nothingness, to a desert, to Zero. There are no longer boundaries.

' Zero is the highest mathematical idea,' Lorenz Oken said.

In this present state of the world, Man is almost reduced to complete bareness — to the bareness of all but the Central Point . . . the bone, the small spark of the spirit. . . . All else is gone. But the theorists, the experimenters who believe that from such a reduction to Nothingness a new civilisation, the betterment of mankind, will come, actually see in this complete destitution, hope.

> . . . It is the sound too high for our hearing . . .

The intense cold has always seemed to me to have an affinity with an unheard sound — the sound too high for our hearing.

After that poem, haunted ever by the shadow that fell on Hiroshima, I yet ' blessed Jesus Christ with the Rose and his people,' as in ' The Canticle of the Rose.'

To what ideals would I reach in my poetry ? (How far I am from these no one could see more clearly than I.)

Technically, I would come to a vital language — each word possessing an infinite power of germination — I would attain to the ' hard and bounding line ' that Blake said was necessary to all art, as to all virtue. Spiritually, to give holiness to each common day. To ' speak for a moment with all men of their other lives.'[1] To produce a poetry that is the light of the Great Morning, wherein all beings whom we see passing in the common street are transformed into the epitome of all beauty, or of al joy, or of all sorrow.

> ' Who were those went by ? '
> ' Queen Hecuba and Helen.'

My poems are hymns of praise to the glory of Life.

To these truths I came, seeing, to quote Whitman, that ' all truths lie waiting in all things. . . . They unfold themselves more fragrant than . . . roses from living buds, whenever you fetch the spring sunshine moistened with summer rain. But it must be in yourself. It shall come from your soul. It shall be love.'

[1] Arthur Rimbaud, *Une Saison en enfer.*

EARLY POEMS

1. *Serenade*

THE tremulous gold of stars within your hair
Are yellow bees flown from the hive of night,
Finding the blossom of your eyes more fair
Than all the pale flowers folded from the light.
Then, Sweet, awake, and ope your dreaming eyes
Ere those bright bees have flown and darkness dies.

2. *Mandoline*

Down in Hell's gilded street
Snow dances fleet and sweet,
Bright as a parakeet,

Or Punchinello,
All glistening yellow,
As fruit-jewels mellow,

Glittering white and black
As the swan's glassy back
On the Styx' soundless track,

Sharp as bird's painted bill,
Pecking fruit, sweet and shrill,
On a dark window-sill.

See the glass house as smooth
As a wide puppet-booth. . . .
Snow strikes it like a sooth

Melon-shaped mandoline
With the sharp tang and sheen
Of flames that cry, ' Unclean ! '

Dinah with scarlet ruche,
Gay-plumaged Fanfreluche,
Watch shrill as Scaramouche

In the huge house of glass
Old shadows bent, alas !
On ebon sticks now pass —

Lean on a shadow boy,
Creep like a broken toy —
Wooden and painted joy.

4

Trains sweep the empty floors —
Pelongs and pallampores,
Bulchauls and sallampores,

Soundless as any breeze
(Amber and orangeries)
From isles in Indian seas.

Black spangled veils falling
(The cold is appalling),
They wave fans, hear calling

The adder-flames shrieking slow,
Stinging bright fruitlike snow,
Down in the street below ;

While an ape, with black spangled veil,
Plum'd head-dress, face dust-pale,
Scratch'd with a finger-nail

Sounds from a mandoline,
Tuneless and sharp as sin :
Shutters whose tang and sheen,

Shrieking all down the scale,
Seem like the flames that fail
Under that onyx nail,

Light as snow dancing fleet,
Bright as a parakeet,
Down in Hell's empty street.

3. Barber's Shop

TWANG the sharp mandoline !
Hail, falling in the lean
Street of Hell, sweeps it clean.

Under the puppet booth
Down in Hell, see the smooth
Snow bright as fruit and sooth.

Cherries and plums all freeze —
(Rubies upon the trees).
Rubied hail falls through these,

Pelting each young Snow Queen —
(A swan's breath, as whitely seen),
Flirting her fan in lean

Streets, passing to and fro,
White as the flamelike snow,
Fruit of lips all aglow

As isles of the cherry
Or ruby-sweet berry
All plump sweet and merry.

Mantillas hide the shame
Of each duenna dame,
(Fans made of plumes of flame)

Pelted with coral bells
Out of the orchard hells,
Hail with sweet fruitage smells.

Now on the platform seen,
Hoofs clatter with the clean
Sound of a mandoline. . .

Beelzebub in a chair
Sits on the platform there ;
Candles like cold eyes stare.

' Master has got the gout.'
Adder-flames flare and spout
From his lips — shadows rout.

Tiptoe the Barber crept,
On his furred black locks leapt.
Candles shrieked, flaring wept.

The Barber takes up the shears. . . .
' Fur for the shivering fears
Cold in Hell these long years

Where the hail in the lean
Street of Hell, sweeps it clean.'
Twang the sharp mandoline !

4. *Singerie*

SUMMER afternoon in Hell!
Down the empty street it fell,
Pantaloon and Scaramouche —
Tongues like flames and shadows louche —
Flickered down the street together
In the spangled weather.
Flames, bright singing birds that pass,
Whistled wares as shrill as grass
(Landscapes clear as glittering glass),
Whistled all together :
Papagei, O Papagei,
Buy our greenest fruits, oh buy,
Melons misty from the bloom
Of mellow moons on some hot night,
Melting in the August light ;
Apples like an emerald shower ;
Nectarines that falling boom
On the grass in greenest gloom ;
Peaches bright as parrot's feather
Glistening from the moon's bower ;
Chequered like fritillaries,
Fat and red are strawberries.
Parrot-voices shrill together —
Now they pelt each monkey-face
(Pantaloon with simian grace)
From the soft gloom till they smother
Both the plumèd head-dresses
With the green fruit-gems that glitter
(Twinkling sharp sounds like a zither).
Sharp each bird-tongue shrills and hisses,
Parrot-voices shrieking bane ;
Down comes every spangled shutter
With a sudden noise like rain.

5. *The Avenue*

In the huge and glassy room,
Pantaloon, with his tail feather
Spangled like the weather,
Panached, too, with many a plume,
Watched the monkey Fanfreluche,
Shivering in his gilded ruche,
Fawn upon the piano keys —
Flatter till they answer back,
Through the scale of centuries,
Difference between white and black.
Winds like hurricanes of light
Change the blackest vacuums
To a light-barred avenue —
Semitones of might and right;
Then, from matter, life comes.
Down that lengthy avenue,
Leading us we know not where,
Sudden views creep through the air;
Oh, the keys we stumble through!
Jungles splashed with violent light,
Promenades all hard and bright,
Long tails like the swish of seas,
Avenue of piano keys.
Meaning comes to bind the whole,
Fingers separate from thumbs,
Soon the shapeless tune comes :
Bestial efforts at man's soul.
What though notes are false and shrill —
Black streets tumbling down a hill?
Fundamentally
I am you, and you are me —
Octaves fall as emptily.

6. The King of China's Daughter

THE King of China's daughter,
She never would love me
Though I hung my cap and bells upon
Her nutmeg tree.
For oranges and lemons,
The stars in bright blue air
(I stole them long ago, my dear),
Were dangling there.
The Moon did give me silver pence,
The Sun did give me gold,
And both together softly blew
And made my porridge cold;
But the King of China's daughter
Pretended not to see
When I hung my cap and bells upon
Her nutmeg tree.

BUCOLIC COMEDIES

1. *Early Spring*

THE wooden chalets of the cloud
Hang down their dull blunt ropes to shroud

Red crystal bells upon each bough
(Fruit-buds that whimper).   No winds slough

Our faces, furred with cold like red
Furred buds of satyr springs, long dead !

The cold wind creaking in my blood
Seems part of it, as grain of wood ;

Among the coarse goat-locks of snow
Mamzelle still drags me, to and fro ;

Her feet make marks like centaur hoofs
In hairy snow ; her cold reproofs

Die, and her strange eyes look oblique
As the slant crystal buds that creak.

If she could think me distant, she
In the snow's goat-locks certainly

Would try to milk those teats, the buds,
Of their warm sticky milk — the cuds

Of strange long-past fruit-hairy springs —
The beginnings of first earthy things.

2. *Spring*

WHEN spring begins, the maids in flocks
Walk in soft fields, and their sheepskin locks

Fall shadowless, soft as music, round
Their jonquil eyelids, and reach the ground.

Where the small fruit-buds begin to harden
Into sweet tunes in the palace garden,

They peck at the fruit-buds' hairy herds
With their lips like the gentle bills of birds.

  . . . . .

But King Midas heard the swan-bosomed sky
Say ' All is surface, and so must die.'

And he said : ' It is spring ; I will have a feast
To woo eternity ; for my least

Palace is like a berg of ice ;
And the spring winds, for birds of paradise,

With the leaping goat-footed waterfalls cold,
Shall be served for me on a dish of gold

By a maiden fair as an almond-tree,
With hair like the waterfalls' goat-locks ; she

Has lips like that jangling harsh pink rain,
The flower-bells that spirt on the trees again.'

In Midas' garden the simple flowers
Laugh, and the tulips are bright as the showers,

For spring is here ; the auriculas,
And the Emily-coloured primulas

Bob in their pinafores on the grass
As they watch the gardener's daughter pass.

Then King Midas said, ' At last I feel
Eternity conquered beneath my heel

Like the glittering snake of Paradise —
And you are my Eve ! ' — but the maiden flies,

Like the leaping goat-footed waterfalls
Singing their cold, forlorn madrigals.

3. Aubade

JANE, Jane,
Tall as a crane,
The morning light creaks down again;

Comb your cockscomb-ragged hair,
Jane, Jane, come down the stair.

Each dull blunt wooden stalactite
Of rain creaks, hardened by the light,

Sounding like an overtone
From some lonely world unknown.

But the creaking empty light
Will never harden into sight,

Will never penetrate your brain
With overtones like the blunt rain.

The light would show (if it could harden)
Eternities of kitchen garden,

Cockscomb flowers that none will pluck,
And wooden flowers that 'gin to cluck.

In the kitchen you must light
Flames as staring, red and white,

As carrots or as turnips, shining
Where the cold dawn light lies whining.

Cockscomb hair on the cold wind
Hangs limp, turns the milk's weak mind. . . .
          Jane, Jane,
          Tall as a crane,
          The morning light creaks down again!

4. *Three Poor Witches*

FOR W. T. WALTON

WHIRRING, walking
On the tree-top,
Three poor witches
Mow and mop.
Three poor witches
Fly on switches
Of a broom,
From their cottage room.
Like goat's-beard rivers,
Black and lean,
Are Moll and Meg,
And Myrrhaline.
' Of those whirring witches, Meg '
(Bird-voiced fire screams)
' Has one leg ;
Moll has two, on tree-tops see,
Goat-foot Myrrhaline has three ! '
When she walks
Turned to a wreath
Is every hedge ;
She walks beneath
Flowered trees like water
Splashing down ;
Her rich and dark silk
Plumcake gown
Has folds so stiff
It stands alone
Within the fields
When she is gone.
And when she walks
Upon the ground
You'd never know
How she can bound
Upon the tree-tops, for she creeps
With a snail's slow silver pace ;

Her milky silky wrinkled face
Shows no sign of her disgrace.
But walking on each
Leafy tree-top, —
Those old witches,
See them hop !
Across the blue-leaved
Mulberry-tree
Of the rustling
Bunchèd sea,
To China, thick trees whence there floats
From wrens' and finches' feathered throats
Songs.   The North Pole is a tree
With thickest chestnut flowers. . . . We see
Them whizz and turn
Through Lisbon, churn
The butter-pats to coins gold,
Sheep's milk to muslin, thin and cold.
Then one on one leg,
One on two,
One on three legs
Home they flew
To their cottage ; there one sees
And hears no sound but wind in trees ;
One candle spills out thick gold coins
Where quilted dark with tree shade joins.

5. *Two Kitchen Songs*

I

THE harsh bray and hollow
Of the pot and the pan
Seems Midas defying
The great god Apollo !
The leaves' great golden crowns
Hang on the trees ;
The maids in their long gowns
Hunt me through these.
Grand'am, Grand'am,
From the pan I am
Flying . . . country gentlemen
Took flying Psyche for a hen
And aimed at her ; then turned a gun
On harmless chicken-me — for fun.
The beggars' dogs howl all together,
Their tails turn to a ragged feather ;
Pools, like mirrors hung in garrets,
Show each face as red as a parrot's,
Whistling hair that raises ire
In cocks and hens in the kitchen fire !
Every flame shrieks cockle-doo-doo
(With their cockscombs flaring high too) ;
The witch's rag-rug takes its flight
Beneath the willows' watery light :
The wells of water seem a-plume —
The old witch sweeps them with her broom —
All are chasing chicken-me. . . .
But Psyche — where, oh where, is she ?

II

GREY as a guinea-fowl is the rain
Squawking down from the boughs again.
     ' Anne, Anne,
      Go fill the pail,'

Said the old witch who sat on the rail.
' Though there is a hole in the bucket,
Anne, Anne,
It will fill my pocket ;
The water-drops when they cross my doors
Will turn to guineas and gold moidores. . . .'
The well-water hops across the floors ;
Whimpering, ' Anne ' it cries, implores,
And the guinea-fowl-plumaged rain,
Squawking down from the boughs again,
Cried, ' Anne, Anne, go fill the bucket,
There is a hole in the witch's pocket —
And the water-drops like gold moidores,
Obedient girl, will surely be yours.
So, Anne, Anne,
Go fill the pail
Of the old witch who sits on the rail ! '

6. King Cophetua and the Beggar Maid

THE five-pointed crude pink tinsel star
Laughed loudly at King Cophetua ;

Across the plain that is black as mind
And limitless, it laughed unkind

To see him whitened like a clown
With the moon's flour, come in a golden crown.

The moon shone softer than a peach
Upon the round leaves in its reach ;

The dark air sparkled like a sea —
The beggar maid leaned out through a tree

And sighed (that pink flower-spike full of honey),
' Oh, for Love ragged as Time, with no money ! '

Then through the black night the gardener's boy
As sunburnt as hay, came whispering, ' Troy

Long ago was as sweet as the honey-chimes
In the flower-bells jangling into rhymes,

And, oh, my heart's sweet as a honey-hive
Because of a wandering maid, and I live

But to tend the pale flower-bells of the skies
That shall drop down their dew on her sleeping eyes.'

7. *Gardener Janus Catches a Naiad*

BASKETS of ripe fruit in air
The bird-songs seem, suspended where

Between the hairy leaves trills dew,
All tasting of fresh green anew.

Ma'am, I've heard your laughter flare
Through your waspish-gilded hair :

Feathered masks,
Pots of peas,
Janus asks
Naught of these.
Creaking water
Brightly stripèd,
Now, I've caught her —
Shrieking biped.
Flute sounds jump
And turn together,
Changing clumps
Of glassy feather.
In among the
Pots of peas
Naiad changes —
Quick as these.

8. Green Geese

THE trees were hissing like green geese . . .
The words they tried to say were these :

' When the great Queen Claude was dead
They buried her deep in the potting-shed.'

The moon smelt sweet as nutmeg-root
On the ripe peach-trees' leaves and fruit,

And her sandal-wood body leans upright,
To the gardener's fright, through the summer night.

.   .   .   .   .

The bee-wing'd warm afternoon light roves
Gilding her hair (wooden nutmegs and cloves),

And the gardener plants his seedsman's samples
Where no wild unicorn herd tramples —

In clouds like potting-sheds he pots
The budding planets in leaves cool as grots,

For the great Queen Claude when the light's gilded gaud
Sings Miserere, Gloria, Laud.

But when he passes the potting-shed,
Fawning upon him comes the dead —

Each cupboard's wooden skeleton
Is a towel-horse when the clock strikes one,

And light is high — yet with ghosts it winces
All night 'mid wrinkled tarnished quinces,

When the dark air seems soft down
Of the wandering owl brown.

They know the clock-faced sun and moon
Must wrinkle like the quinces soon

(That once in dark blue grass dew-dabbled
Lay) . . . those ghosts like turkeys gabbled

To the scullion baking the Castle bread —
' The Spirit, too, must be fed, be fed ;

Without our flesh we cannot see —
Oh, give us back Stupidity ! ' . . .

But death had twisted their thin speech,
It could not fit the mind's small niche —

Upon the warm blue grass outside,
They realised that they had died.

Only the light from their wooden curls roves
Like the sweet smell of nutmegs and cloves

Buried deep in the potting-shed,
Sighed those green geese, ' Now the Queen is dead.'

9. The Higher Sensualism

QUEEN CIRCE, the farmer's wife at the Fair,
Met three sailor-men stumping there,

Who came from the parrot-plumed sea, Yo-Ho !
And each his own trumpet began to blow.

' We come,' said they, ' from the Indian seas,
All bright as a parrot's feathers, and these

Break on gold sands of the perfumed isles,
Where the fruit is soft as a siren's smiles,

And the sun is as black as a Nubian.
We singed the beard of the King of Spain . . .

Then we wandered once more on the South Sea strand,
Where the icebergs seem Heavenly Mansions fanned

By the softest wind from the groves of spice,
And the angels like birds of paradise

Flit there : and we caught this queer-plumaged boy
(An angel, he calls himself) for a toy.'

.   .   .   .   .

The Angel sighed, ' Please, ma'am, if you'll spare
Me a trumpet, the angels will come to the Fair ;

For even an angel must have his fling
And ride on the roundabout, in the swing ! '

She gave him a trumpet, but never a blare
Reached the angels from Midsummer Fair,

Though he played ' Will You Hear a Spanish Lady ? '
And ' Jack the Sailor,' ' Sweet Nelly,' ' Trees Shady ' —

For only the gay hosannas of flowers
Sound, loud as brass bands, in those heavenly bowers.

Queen Circe said, ' Young man, I will buy
Your plumaged coat for my pig to try —

Then with angels he'll go a-dancing hence
From sensuality into sense ! '

The Fair's tunes like cherries and apricots
Ripened ; the angels danced from their green grots ;

Their hair was curled like the fruit on the trees. . . .
Rigaudon, sarabande, danced they these.

And the pig points his toe and he curves his wings,
The music starts, and away he flings —

Dancing with angels all in a round,
Hornpipe and rigaudon on the Fair ground.

10. *Springing Jack*

GREEN wooden leaves clap light away
From the young flowers as white as day —

Clear angel-face on hairy stalk
(Soul grown from flesh, an ape's young talk).

The showman's face is cubed, clear as
The shapes reflected in a glass

Of water (Glog, glut, a ghost's speech
Fumbling for space from each to each).

The fusty showman fumbles, must
Fit in a particle of dust

The universe, for fear it gain
Its freedom from my box of brain.

Yet dust bears seeds that grow to grace
Behind my crude-striped wooden face,

As I, a puppet tinsel-pink,
Leap on my springs, learn how to think,

Then, like the trembling golden stalk
Of some long-petalled star, I walk

Through the dark heavens, until dew
Falls on my eyes and sense thrills through.

11. *Pavane*

ANNUNCIATA stands
On the flat lands
Under the pear-tree
(Jangling sweetly).   See,
The curé-black leaves
Are cawing like a rook. . . .
Annunciata grieves,
' No young man will look
At me with my harsh jangling hair
Pink as the one pear
(A flapping crude fish tinsel-pink
Flapping across the consciousness
Like laughter) and my tattered dress.'
Then from the brink
Of the deep well,
Sounding like a bell,
From the castles under water
The old men seek the beggar's daughter. . . .
Some were wrinkled grey
From suicide grown gay
And smiling, some were seen
With ivy limbs green
And gnarled like the water. . . .
' Dance a pavane, beggar's daughter.' . . .
They wooed her with book ;
And the water's tuneless bell
Wooed her as well —
A water-hidden sound achieves ;
And cawing like a rook
Were the curé-black leaves. . . .
One feather-breast of dew was grey
Upon round leaves — they fled away.
Only a moaning sound
From the castles that lie drowned
Beneath the fruit-boughs of the water
Reached the beggar's daughter.

12. *When the Sailor*

WHEN the sailor left the seas
They swayed like June's thick-leavèd trees ;

The winds seemed only nightingales
That sang so sweetly leafy tales

Of rustic vows among deep leaves —
Of Thisbe's love, how Priam grieves.

The sailor stumps his wooden leg
In shady lanes where he must beg,

Till skies shone like the fields he knew —
Golden with buttercups and dew ;

Then, slightly drunk, he sees an Inn
Beckon him to step within.

The parlour runs on feathered feet ;
Bird-like, ' Neptune, thee we greet,'

It cries ; the flames, an albatross,
Float on blue air like waves that toss,

Bird-like shriek, ' The sea floats still
Just above the window-sill ! '

' No, it is June's thick blue trees.'
Heeding not the sound of these,

Across the bar, through silver spray
Of the sweet and blossomed May,

Leaned the Circean landlady,
With her dark locks leafy shady

And eyes that seemed the dancing sound
Of waves upon enchanted ground.

' Did you batter down Troy's wall
(Silver hawthorn-trees grown tall),

Did you beg the Khan for mercy,
Did you meet the lady Circe ? '

' She is changing like the sea . . .
Shadow, like a lovely lady

With an elegant footfall,
Never seemed so lovely ; all

Her airs were beautiful as sleep,
Or dew too fair for flower to weep.'

13. Evening

PRINCE ABSALOM and Sir Rotherham Redde
Rode on a rocking-horse home to bed,

With dreams like cherries ripening big
Beneath the frondage of each wig.

In a flat field on the road to Sleep
They ride together, a-hunting sheep

That like the swan-bright fountains seem ;
Their tails hang down as meek as a dream.

Prince Absalom seems a long-fleeced bush,
The heat's tabernacle, in the hush

And the glamour of eve, when buds the dew
Into bright tales that never come true ;

And as he passes a cherry-tree,
Caught by his long hair, bound is he,

While all his gold fleece flows like water
Into the lap of Sir Rotherham's daughter.

Come, then, and sit upon the grass
With cherries to pelt you as bright as glass —

Vermilion bells that sound as clear
As the bright swans whose sighing you hear

When they float to their crystal death
Of water, scarcely plumed by the breath

Of air — so clear in the round leaves
They look, this crystal sound scarce grieves,

As they pelt down like tears fall'n bright
From music or some deep delight.

The gardener cut off his beard of bast
And tied up the fountain-tree, made it fast

And bound it together till who could see
Which is Prince Absalom, which is the tree?

Only his gold fleece flows like water
Into the lap of Sir Rotherham's daughter;

Sir Rotherham Redde gathers bags of gold
Instead of the cherries ruddy and cold.

14. *Winter*

TO VERONICA

DAGOBERT lay in front of the fire.
Each thin flame seemed a feathery spire

Of the grasses that like goslings quack
On the castle walls : ' Bring Gargotte back ' ;

But Gargotte the goose-girl, bright as hail,
Has faded into a fairy-tale.

The kings and queens on the nursery wall
Seem chain-armoured fish in the moat, and all

The frost-flowers upon the window-panes,
Grown fertilate from the fire's gold grains,

Ripen to gold-freckled strawberries,
Raspberries, glassy-pale gooseberries

(We never could touch them, early or late,
They would chill our hands like the touch of Fate).

But Anne was five years old and must know
Reality ; in the goose-soft snow

She was made to walk with her three tall aunts
Drooping beneath the snow's cold plants.

They dread the hour when with book and bell
Their mother, the old fell Countess of L——

Is disrobed of her wig and embalmed for the night's
Sweet mummified dark ; her invective affrights

The maids till you hear them scamper like mice
In the wainscoting — trembling, neat and nice.

Each clustered bouquet of the snows is
Like stephanotis and white roses ;

The muted airs sing Palestrina
In trees like monstrances, grown leaner

Than she is ; the unripe snow falls
Like little tunes on the virginals

Whose sound is bright, unripe and sour
As small fruits fall'n before their hour.

The Countess sits and plays fantan
Beneath the portrait of great Queen Anne

(Who sleeps beneath the strawberry bed) ;
And all her maids have scampered, fled.

The shuffled cards like the tail of a bird
Unfolding its shining plumes are heard. . . .

The maid in her powder-closet soon
Beneath the fire of the calm full moon,

Whose sparkles, rubies, sapphires, spill
For her upon the window-sill,

Will nod her head, grown sleepy, I wis,
As Alaciel, or Semiramis,

Pasiphae, or the lady Isis,
Embalmed in the precious airs like spices.

But her ladyship stamps with her stick . . .
    ' Grown cold
Are my small feet, from my chilly gold —

Unwarmed by buds of the lamb's wool . . . go
And gather for me the soft polar snow

To line with that silver chilly-sweet
The little slippers upon my feet —

With snow clear-petalled as lemon blossom —
Crystal-clear — perfumed as Venus' bosom.'

.   .   .   .   .

Can this be Eternity ? — snow peach-cold,
Sleeping and rising and growing old,

While she lies embalmed in the fire's gold sheen,
Like a cross wasp in a ripe nectarine,

And the golden seed of the fire droops dead
And ripens not in the heart or head !

15. *Spinning Song*

THE miller's daughter
Combs her hair,
Like flocks of doves
As soft as vair . . .

Oh, how those soft flocks flutter down
Over the empty grassy town.

Like a queen in a crown
Of gold light, she
Sits 'neath the shadows'
Flickering tree —

Till the old dame went the way she came,
Playing bob-cherry with a candle-flame.

Now Min the cat
With her white velvet gloves
Watches where sat
The mouse with her loves —

(Old and malicious Mrs. Grundy
Whose washing-day is from Monday to Monday).

' Not a crumb,' said Min,
' To a mouse I'll be giving,
For a mouse must spin
To earn her living.'

So poor Mrs. Mouse and her three cross Aunts
Nibble snow that rustles like gold wheat plants.

And the miller's daughter
Combs her locks,
Like running water
Those dove-soft flocks

And her mouth is sweet as a honey-flower cold
But her heart is heavy as bags of gold.

     The shadow-mice said,
     ' We will line with down
     From those doves, our bed
     And our slippers and gown,

For everything comes to the shadows at last
If the spinning-wheel Time move slow or fast.'

16. The White Owl

THE currants, moonwhite as Mother Bunch,
In their thick-bustled leaves were laughing like Punch;
And ruched as their country waterfalls
The cherried maids walk beneath the dark walls.
Where the moonlight was falling thick as curd
Through the cherry branches, half unheard,
Said old Mrs. Bunch, the crop-eared owl,
To her gossip : ' If once I began to howl,
I am sure that my sobs would drown the seas —
With my " oh's " and my " ah's " and my " oh dear me's ! "
Everything wrong from cradle to grave —
No money to spend, no money to save ! '
And the currant bush began to rustle
As poor Mrs. Bunch arranged her bustle.

17. Cacophony for Clarinet

THE dairy-maid's ghost
In a hooped petticoat
Swishing like water
Said to the buttercups
And to the sheep and goat
' I am Pan's daughter.'
Dark as Africa, Asia,
The vast trees weep,
And the Margravine, learned as Lady Aspasia,
Is nodding down in an afternoon sleep.
Now dense as her mind is the Margravine's shade
On the golden world of the buttercups laid,
And her small head is ribboned
With her yellow satin hair
Like satin ribbons that shine butter-yellow.
The faunal afternoon makes more mellow
The snore forlorn
That sounds like Pan's horn.
The dairy-maid's ghost through the diamonded pane
Of the window, stares at the cream in the dairy ;
Then through the meadows she slips again —
Soundless and shadeless as Morgane the Fairy.
The glazed chintz buttercups shining like summer
Seem the butter-hued print of a still-room-maid's gown
Where the kingly cock with a water-dark feather smock,
Golden feet and a five-pointed crown,
Rants and struts like a barn-door mummer.
Then I heard the Margravine say
To the ancient bewigged abbé,
' I think it so clever
Of people to discover
New planets — and how ever
Do they find out what their names are ? '
Then clear as a clarinet-note, her long hair
Called Pan over the fields — Pan, the forlorn wind
From the Asian or African darkness of trees
To play with her dense, with her tree-dark mind.

18. Two Songs

I

In Summer when the rose-bushes
Have names like all the sweetest hushes
In a bird's song, — Susan, Hannah,
Martha, Harriet, and Susannah,
My coral neck
And my little song
Are very extra
And very Susie ;
A little kiss like a gold bee stings
My childish life so sweet and rosy . . .
Like country clouds of clouted cream
The round and flaxen blond leaves seem,
And dew in trills
And dew in pearls
Falls from every gardener's posy ;
Marguerites, roses,
A flaxen lily,
Water-chilly
Buttercups where the dew reposes,
In fact each flower young and silly
The gardener ties in childish posies.

II

The clouds are bunchèd roses,
And the bunches seem
As thick as cream,
The country dozes, and I dream.
In a gown like a cauliflower,
My country cousin is —
So said Susie
And her sister Liz.
Blossoms hang on trees above,
Soft and thick as any dove,
They mock my love ;

Yet I pluck those feathers sweet
With my cold coral hands so like the
Small cold feet
Of a little sad bird,
On a budding branch heard.

19. *The Bear*

WATER-GREEN is the flowing pollard
In Drowsytown ; a smocked dullard
Sits upon the noodle-
Soft and milky grass, —
Clownish-white was that fopdoodle
As he watched the brown bear pass . . .
' Who speaks of Alexander
And General Hercules,
And who speaks of Lysander ?
For I am strong as these !
The housekeeper's old rug
Is shabby brown as me,
And if I wished to hug
Those heroes, they would flee, —
For always when I show affection
They take the contrary direction.
I passed the barrack square
In nodding Drowsytown, —
Where four-and-twenty soldiers stare
Through slits of windows at the Bear,'
(So he told the Clown.)
' Twelve were black as Night the Zambo,
(Black shades playing at dumb crambo !)
Twelve were gilded as the light,
Goggling Negro eyes of fright.
There they stood and each mentero,
Striped and pointed, leaned to Zero . . .
Grumbling footsteps of the Bear
Came near . . . they did fade in air,
The window shut and they were gone;
The Brown Bear lumbered on alone.'
So he told the smocked fopdoodle,
White and flapping as the air,
Sprawling on the grass for pillow —
(Milky soft as any noodle)
'Neath the water-green willow

There in Drowsytown
Where one crumpled cottage nods —
Nodding
        Nodding
                Down.

20. On the Vanity of Human Aspirations

'In the time of King James I, the aged Countess of Desmond met her death,
at the age of a hundred and forty years, through falling from an apple-tree.'
— *A chronicle of the time.*

In the cold wind, towers grind round,
Turning, turning, on the ground ;

In among the plains of corn
Each tower seems a unicorn.

Beneath a sad umbrageous tree
Anne, the goose-girl, could I see —

But the umbrageous tree behind
Ne'er cast a shadow on her mind —

A goose-round breast she had, goose-brains,
And a nose longer than a crane's ;

A clarinet sound, cold, forlorn,
Her harsh hair, straight as yellow corn,

And her eyes were round, inane
As the blue pebbles of the rain.

Young Anne, the goose-girl, said to me,
' There's been a sad catastrophe !

The aged Countess still could walk
At a hundred and forty years, could talk,

And every eve in the crystal cool
Would walk by the side of the clear fish-pool.

But today when the Countess took her walk
Beneath the apple-trees, from their stalk

44

The apples fell like the red-gold crown
Of those kings that the Countess had lived down,

And they fell into the crystal pool;
The grandmother fish enjoying the cool —

(Like the bright queens dyed on a playing-card
They seemed as they fanned themselves, flat and hard) —

Floated in long and chequered gowns
And darting, searched for the red-gold crowns

In the Castles drownèd long ago
Where the empty years pass weedy-slow,

And the water is flat as equality
That reigns over all in the heavenly

State we aspire to, where none can choose
Which is the goose-girl, which is the goose . . .

But the Countess climbed up the apple-tree,
Only to see what she could see —

Because to persons of her rank
The usual standpoint is that of the bank ! . . .'

The goose-girl smoothed down her feather-soft
Breast . . . 'When the Countess came aloft,

King James and his courtiers, dressed in smocks,
Rode by a-hunting the red-gold fox,

And King James, who was giving the view-halloo
Across the corn, too loudly blew,

And the next that happened was — what did I see
But the Countess fall'n from the family tree !

Yet King James could only see it was naughty
To aspire to the high at a hundred and forty,

" Though if " (as he said) " she aspired to climb
To Heaven — she certainly has, this time ! " '

. . . And Anne, the goose-girl, laughed, ' Tee-hee,
It was a sad catastrophe ! '

21. *The Man with the Green Patch*

Look through those periwigged green trees
At the tall house . . . impressions seize !

Trees periwigged and snuffy ; old
Is silence, with its tales all told,
And Time is shrunken, bare and cold,

And here the malefactor Death
Snuffs out the candle with our breath.

  . . . . .

The Admiral had soon returned
From active service ; ' home to die,'
Said he, a patch upon one eye.
The green shade of Death's own yew-tree,
So sightless, seemed that shade to me.

All day in the limp helpless breeze
Beneath the empty platform trees
He sits with Brobdingnagian asses,
Talking while the lame time passes —
And each voice seemed the hard trombone
Of harsh seas (blue and white dead bone).
He speaks of friendships long ago
With fairy aristocracies
Who dream in murmurous palaces
Haunted by gold eves — Chinese,
And apes superior to man,
Whose life outlives our mortal span,
And all the strange inhabitants
Of gardens under leaflike seas,
And the Admiral Yang among his plants,
Asking his god what no one grants
When the gold rain begins to fall.
But that green shade of Death's yew-tree,
His patch, will never let him see

The real world, terrible and old,
Where seraphs in the mart are sold
And fires from Bedlam's madness flare
Like blue palm-leaves in desert air ;
The prisons where the maimed men pined
Because their mothers bore them blind —
Starved men so thin they seem to be
The shadow of that awful Tree
Cast down on us from Calvary.

Beside the sea (blue-white harsh bone
Hard as a ship's deck) while the lone
Great sun with flames like leaves flares slow
In an empty sky like the great Mikado,
The Admiral is lulling these
Unreal owlish people there
Who, though asleep, still sit and stare,
Their dullard faces, planet-round,
Fringed all leafily with sound
Growth of their long heritage :
Beasthood, but grown tame with age.

The Admiral is such a bore,
Sleep murmurs, flows in the heart's core.
Gold as a planet system, rain
Falls in the gardens once again.
The cook as red as an aubergine
Sleeps in her kitchen, fallen between
Two clear-scrubbed wooden kitchen tables
Where creep the growing vegetables. . . .
Crowned are they, and rough and bold. . . .
The ass-hide grass grows over her ears,
And Midas Silence turns to gold
Each little sound she never hears.
The rain is gold as a planet system
Or the silent gardens of the Khan,
And all the world is changed to a green
Growing world to be touched and seen ;

And the folk in the caves of far Japan
Hear the triumphant growing sound
And say, ' Are the gold-melon flowers we see
The sunrise sound, young pleasure isles,
The soft wind from an incense tree,
Or the gold Mikado's shadowy smiles ? '

But the ancient Admiral was loath
To see or hear or dream of growth. . . .
For his existence was not life
But a tired stranger's conversations
(Modulated dull gradations)
With Life, that sleepy old housewife.

And all night long he lies and cowers. . . .
Pink moonlight turns to feathered flowers,
And sleep should be a coral cave
Haunted by a siren wave.

Yet moonlight lies as harsh as brine,
Noah's Flood, or a disused saltmine ;
Cold airs prick like grass or the sword
Of zanies . . . he falls overboard
Into that briny Noah's Flood,
The moonlight, drowning bestial blood.

His house is haunted by the shade
Of Death — no greenness in earth laid . . .
But a monstrous difference agape
Between the nations of the Dead,
A ghost that ne'er took human shape
But has a swinish pig-tailed head
Crowned with trembling ghostly flowers. . . .
It seems a candle guttered down
In a green deserted town.
It can alter at its will —
Batlike to the window-sill
It will cling, with squeaking shrill
Miming Triviality.

Or, shapeless now as a black sea,
Clattering a hellish hoof
With the other dragging after —
(Elephantine, muffled o'er) . . .
Oh, that tread breaks down the floor !
And we shall hear its numbing speech —
A roar that will break down the world,
A speech unknown of the race of Man.

The Admiral hears through his door
That shape flow down the corridor. . . .
He trembles when the ghost wind comes. . . .
Outside, among the tallest trees
The grey flowers hang
Like a snipe's plumes, clang
In the wrinkled and the withered breeze.

Come softly and we will look through
The windows from this avenue. . . .
For there my youth passed like a sleep,
Yet in my heart, still murmuring deep,
The small green airs from Eternity,
Murmuring softly, never die.

THE SLEEPING BEAUTY

TO OSBERT SITWELL

I

WHEN we come to that dark house,
Never sound of wave shall rouse
The bird that sings within the blood
Of those who sleep in that deep wood :
For in that house the shadows now
Seem cast by some dark unknown bough.
The gardener plays his old bagpipe
To make the melons' gold seeds ripe ;
The music swoons with a sad sound —
'Keep, my lad, to the good safe ground !
For once, long since, there was a felon
With guineas gold as the seeds of a melon,
And he would sail for a far strand
To seek a waking, clearer land —
A land whose name is only heard
In the strange singing of a bird.
The sea was sharper than green grass,
The sailors would not let him pass,
For the sea was wroth and rose at him
Like the turreted walls of Jerusalem,
Or like the towers and gables seen
Within a deep-boughed garden green.
And the sailors bound and threw him down
Among those wrathful towers to drown.

And oh, far best,' the gardener said,
' Like fruits to lie in your kind bed —
To sleep as snug as in the grave
In your kind bed, and shun the wave,
Nor ever sigh for a strange land
And songs no heart can understand.'

I hunted with the country gentlemen
Who, seeing Psyche fly, thought her a hen

And aimed at her; the mocking wingèd one
Laughed at their wingless state, their crooked gun.

Then on the water — green and jewelled leaves
Hiding ripe fruitage — every sportsman grieves,

Sitting and grumbling in their flat boat edged
With the soft feathers of the foam, scarce fledged.

But I will seek again the palace in the wood,
Where never bird shall rouse our sleepy blood

Within the bear-dark forests, far beyond
This hopeless hunting, or Time's sleepy bond.

.   .   .   .   .

The gardener was old as tongues of nightingales,
That in the wide leaves tell a thousand Grecian tales

And sleep in golden nets of summer light;
' Sweet fig,' he called me, and would stay the flight

Of plums that seemed Jove's golden-feathered rain.
Then, birds like Fortunatus moved again

Among the boughs with silent feathered feet, —
Spraying down dew like jewels amid the sweet

Green darkness ; figs, each like a purse of gold,
Grow among leaves like rippled water green, and cold.

' Beneath those laden boughs,' the gardener sighs,
' Dreaming in endlessness, forgotten beauty lies.

Long since, a wandering and airy nymph
She seemed, when the bright ladies of the court
Came like the sylvan equipage Dian
Leads in her hunting through the deepest woods
And the Dodonian leaves of summer ; only now
We see them smile, an echo through dim leaves.'

Thus spoke the ancient man, wrinkled like old moonlight
Beneath dark boughs. Time dreamed away to night,
And while I heard the leaves like silver cymbals ring
He told me this old tale of Beauty's mournful
    christening :—

Oh the pomp that passed those doors ;
Trains still sweep the empty floors,
Pelongs, bulchauls, pallampores,

Soundless now as any breeze,
Of amber and of orangeries
That sweep from isles in Indian seas ;

While in the floating and mysterious leaves
A silver sound like some forgotten music grieves.

The fairies all received an invitation,
Ordered their sedan-chairs with great elation,

Their richest trains, their plumes, and their bright
    trumps,
Like silver fruits that from dark branches grow in
    clumps.

The fays descend from each dark palanquin
With fanfares and with lute sounds, walk within

The shade ; there, smiling dim as satyr-broods
Hornèd as moons, that haunt our deepest woods,

Are country gentlemen, so countrified
That in their rustic grace they try to hide

Their fingers sprouting into leaves ; we see
Them sweet as cherries growing from a tree —

All fire and snow ; they grow and never move,
Each in the grace of his Pan-haunted grove.

' Her mouth,' the first fay said, ' as fair shall be
As any gentle ripe red strawberry

That grows among the thickest silver leaves ;
Her locks shall be as blond as these — the eve's

Great winds of beauty, fleeces from those flocks
That Dian tends in her deep woods, those locks

Shall seem.' The second fairy said,
' Blessings like dew fall on her lovely head ! '

For lovely as the cherubim's soft breath,
Or Leda's love, whose cold melodious death

Is heavenly music to the sad world lost,
Her skin shall be, as fair as silver frost.'

But now within the dark shade of a deep-dreaming tree
A darker shade and panoply we see,

Drowning the soft sound of the plashing lute,
A great fanfare is heard, like unripe silver fruit.

'Who is this now who comes?'   Dark words reply and
        swoon
Through all the high cold arbours of the moon:

'The slighted Laidronette, the unbidden fay,
Princes of the Pagodas. . . . Shades, make way.'

The sedan-chair that hides her shade is mellow
As the trees' great fruit-jewels glittering yellow,

And round it the old turbaned ladies flock
Like apes that try to pluck an apricock.

The little fawning airs are trembling wan;
And silver as fair Leda's love, the swan,

The moonlight seems; the apricocks have turned to amber,
Cold as from the bright nymph Thetis' chamber,

And far away, the fountains sigh forlorn
As waving rustling sheaves of silver corn.

The wicked fay descended, mopping, mowing
In her wide-hooped petticoat, her water-flowing

Brightly-perfumed silks. . . . 'Ah, ha, I see
You have remembered all the fays but me!'

(She whipped her panthers, golden as the shade
Of afternoon in some deep forest glade.)

'I am very cross because I am old
And my tales are told
And my flames jewel-cold.

I will make your bright birds scream,
I will darken your jewelled dream,
I will spoil your thickest cream.

I will turn the cream sour,
I will darken the bower,
I will look through the darkest shadows and lour —

And sleep as dark as the shade of a tree
Shall cover you. . . . Don't answer me !
For if the Princess prick her finger
Upon a spindle, then she shall be lost

As a child wandering in a glade of thorn,
With sleep like roses blowing soft, forlorn,
Upon each bough.   This, madam, is the cost
Of your dark rudeness.   But I will not linger.'

And with a dark dream's pomp and panoply,
She swept out with her train ; the soft sounds die
Of plumaged revelry bright as her train
Of courtiers ; and all was night again.

Then through the deepest shades went Laidronette,
Princess of the Pagodas ; in a pet
She left the domes, like rich and turbaned fruits
In the great gardens, and she left the lutes ;

Back to her palace in her great sedan
She floats ; worlds turn to snow before her fan.
She sweeps through the dark woods to her vast palace
Where now, at last, she can unleash her malice.

There in her room, an amber orange burned
On the Hesperides' dark trees and spurned
By that gold-peruked conqueror the Sun
(An Alexander whence plumed rivers run,

Fearing his fierceness), Ethiopian shapes
The heat had kissed, with lips like burning grapes,
Unwigged her for the night, while her apes beg
That she will leave uncurtained that Roc's egg,

Her head, a mount of diamonds bald and big
In the ostrich feathers that compose her wig.
Her dwarfs as round as oranges of amber
Among the tall trees of the shadow clamber,

And in Night's deep domain she monstrous lies
With every little wicked dream that flies
And crawls ; with old Bacchantes black with wine,
Whose very hair has changed into a vine,

And ancient satyrs whose wry wig of roses
Nothing but little rotting shames discloses ;
They lie where shadows, cold as the night breeze,
Seem cast by rocks, and never by kind trees.

2

Next dawn, the ancient chamberlain
Came like someone who has lain

For years beneath the deepest water. . . .
He called the housekeeper's young daughter,

Where she sat in her bedgown,
Smoothing the dusky dawn's owl-down,

Until she leaned out through the wet
Leaves in her pale sarcenet.

' Forget the dawn is still owl-dark,
Forget the wet leaves . . . you must hark :

Owing to the fairy's malice,
No spindles must be in the palace.'

In their dark leaf-hid bower the maidens chatter like a bird
Awakening : ' Phoebe, Audrey, have you heard ?

Oh, the dark panic here this very night,
The slighted fairy's anger and our good queen's fright,

And all our spindles banished ! it would seem
That we have naught to do all day but dream ! '

When the dew seems like trembling silver leaves,
Cross Poll Troy looks out through the palace eaves. . . .

' Knot up your butter-yellow satin hair,
You lazy queans. . . . Come quick ! come down the
    stair !

Anne, Anne,
Come draw the milk !

The cream must be as thick as silk
And yellow as the ripest sheen
Of apricock or nectarine.
Beneath the great leaves of that tree
Wicked Goat-foot I can see !
He'll steal the milk and steal the cream
While you lie in a lazy dream.
Fie, the lazy birds, the shames !
Phoebe, you must light the flames ;
They will spring like greenest leaves
Growing round your bower's dim eaves.
Oh the foliage shrill and green
In the fire ! you lazy quean,
Dream not of your heart's desire, —
Phoebe, come and light the fire ! '

3

THEN through the broad green leaves the gardener
    came
With a basket filled with honeyed fruits of dawn
Plucked from the thickest leaves. They heard him sing
As he walked where that pillared avenue
Of tall clear-fruited ripe trees grew
(For so the Palace seemed) ; and sweet
His song fled, soft as wind and fleet :

' Now the dawn lights seem
Ripe yellow fruits in a dream
Among the great green leaves
Of dawn and rustling sheaves.

The vast sun's rays like sheaves of wheat
Are gold and dry,
All bound together, growing yet —
An early offering. I

Heard the old King's lullabies
That his nurse, the South Wind, sighs,
As she heaps the honeycombs
Where he lies ; the fruit-ripe domes

All around him, clear and sweet. . . .
And now the old King's cockscomb crown
Is nodding, falls a-down, a-down. . . .
Till the golden sheaves of the sun shall be mown
He will lie in the palace above the wheat.

The dew all tastes of ripening leaves ;
Dawn's tendril fingers heap
The yellow honeyed fruits whose clear
Sounds flow into his sleep.

Those yellow fruits and honeycomb . . .
" Lulla-lullaby,"
Shrilled the dew on the broad leaves —
" Time itself must die —
                    (— must die)."

Now in the palace the maidens knead
And bake the little loaves of the bread,
Gold as the sun ; they sighing said,
" When will the sun begin to seed
And waken the old Dead —
                    (— cold Dead) ? "

4

Do, do,
Princess, do,
The fairy Chatte Blanche rocks you slow.
Like baskets of white fruit or pearls
Are the fairy's tumbling curls —
Or lattices of roses white
Where-through the snows like doves take flight.
Do, do,
Princess, do,
How furred and white is the fallen snow.

Do, do,
Princess, do,
Like singing blackbirds are the eyes
Of the fairy old and wise.
A honeyed tune, the crystal drops
Of rain that falls, and never stops,
From flowers as white as seraphim's
Breath no winter ever dims. . . .
Do, do,
Princess, do,
Like birds that peck fruit sweet and shrill
With painted bill,
Flies down the snow.

The angels came with footsteps light,
They brushed her hair to make it bright,
They taught her to be sweet and wise
With kisses faint as butterflies.

They said, ' When you go up to heaven
The nursery clock shall ne'er strike seven.
Your boudoir shall be of white satin,
You shall not say your prayers in Latin —

But you shall dance a minuet
On heaven's floors ; frizzed mignonette
Shall seem your curls, of heaven's flowers
Most fair ; and you shall sit in bowers

Of honeysuckle sweet as those pink fires
Whereby the angels dry their locks upon the light's gold
    wires.'

And when the Queen called for her child, they brought
Only her image, formed to please the Court. . . .

An old man with a gardener's hat and red
Poll-parrot nose brought her a tiny bed

Whereon lies folded a small poppet rose
That in her dark leaves like a little babe lies close.

For after Laidronette's wild rage was spent,
The chamberlain to the child's nursery went

And sped her far away, like the East Wind,
To worlds of snow, far from the fairy's mind.

And there the Princess stayed till she was weaned
From milk of doves ; then o'er the snow, bright-preened

By its sharp bill, the wind, the chamberlain,
Whisked the Princess back to the Court again.

5

But the Dowager Queen shook her old head :
' The rose, the peach, and the quince-flower red
And the strawberry flower in the snows are dead.
If none of the rose-tribe can survive
The snow, then how can our poppet live ? '

And in her gown of quilted satin,
As red as quince-flowers, she reads Latin
Missals to the peaches that grow
Gilded with suns, then fade like snow ;

They lie in the nets of dew at leisure.
And this is now her only pleasure —
This and her parrot long ago
Dead, — but none dared tell her so,

And therefore the bird was stuffed and restored
To lifeless immortality ; bored
It seemed, but yet it remained her own ;
And she never knew the bird's soul had flown.

And so indeed seemed Destiny, —
A bird fine-feathered, fair to see
In spite of its condor-wings, fierce beak,
And hooded eyes. . . . Grown old and weak,

Imprisoned now in a gilded cage
In her powder-closet, far from the rage
Of winter, it can only sing
Roulades, and preen its bright clipped wing

Upon her perfumed dressing table
In a cage with a foolish bell-hung gable,
Beneath the portrait of dead Queen Anne
(Whose life was the sweet air blown from a fan),

'Midst brightly perfumed water-flowing
Eighteenth-century silks where growing
Strawberry flowers of the frail frost
Upon the diamond-panes are lost.

6

At Easter when red lacquer buds sound far slow
Quarter-tones for the old dead Mikado,

Through avenues of lime-trees, where the wind
Sounds like a chapeau chinois, shrill, unkind —

The Dowager Queen, a curling Korin wave
That flows for ever past a coral cave,

With Dido, Queen of Carthage, slowly drives
(Her griffin dog that has a thousand lives)

Upon the flat-pearled and fantastic shore
Where curled and turbaned waves sigh, ' Never more.

And she is sunk beneath a clear still lake
Of sleep — so frail with age she cannot wake. . . .

A strange horizon and a soundless sea
Must separate wise age from you and me —

They watch life's movements ripening like fruit
And sigh, knowing the gnarled and twisted root.

Oh, people building castles on the sand,
And taking one another by the hand,

What do you find within each other's eyes ? —
What wisdom unknown of the lonely wise ? —

The promise of what spring, the certainty
Of what eternal life to come — what lie ?

Only the sound of Time's small muffled drum,
The sound of footsteps that will never come,

And little marches all beribboned gay
That lead down the lime avenues away

To the dark grave . . . we for a little weep,
Then pray a little, sinking into sleep.

How far is this wise age from the bright youth
Of Princess Cydalise, a warm wind from the south?

7

In the great nursery where the poppet maids
Seem small round fruits that grow in leafy glades,

The Princess grew in beauty till she seemed
That gentle maid of whom Endymion dreamed.

And in those evenings when the lovely moon
Shone through the smiling woods of deepest June,

Then through the curtains she would play ' Bo-Peep '
With fleecy lamb-tailed clouds when she should sleep.

Sometimes the moon would sing her ancient songs
Of lovely ladies and forgotten wrongs ;

And once she whispered that within the wood
An ancient satyr, wiser than the brood

From which he sprang, within a cloudy cave
Teaches philosophies both old and grave.

The Princess said, ' With my light step I will be gone
To peep within that far cave — but alone ! '

Yet in the darkness her gazelle-light footsteps ran
Far from the cave of that wise satyr-man.

In the great gardens, after bright spring rain,
We find sweet innocence come once again,
White periwinkles, little pensionnaires
With muslin gowns and shy and candid airs,

That under saint-blue skies, with gold stars sown,
Hide their sweet innocence by spring winds blown,
From zephyr libertines that like Richelieu
And d'Orsay their gold-spangled kisses blew ;

And lilies of the valley whose buds blond and tight
Seem curls of little school-children that light
The priests' procession, when on some saint's day
Along the country paths they make their way ;

Forget-me-nots, whose eyes of childish blue,
Gold-starred like heaven, speak of love still true ;
And all the flowers that we call ' dear heart,'
Who say their prayers like children, then depart

Into the dark.   Amid the dew's bright beams
The summer airs, like Weber waltzes, fall
Round the first rose who, flushed with her youth, seems
Like a young Princess dressed for her first ball :

Who knows what beauty ripens from dark mould
After the sad wind and the winter's cold ? —
But a small wind sighed, colder than the rose
Blooming in desolation, ' No one knows.'

THE Princess was young as the innocent flowers
That bloom and love through the bright spring hours
Sometimes she crept through locked doors to annoy
The palace housekeeper, cross Mrs. Troy,
Who kept all the whimpering sad ghosts locked
In a cupboard, was grieved and faintly shocked
If the Princess Jehanne, long since dead,
Whose hair was of costly long gold thread,
Would slip her flat body, like a gleaming
Quivering fish in a clear pool dreaming,
Through the deep mesh of a conversation,
Making some ghostly imputation ;
Or if she frightened the maids till they wince
By stealing a withered gold-crowned quince
Wherewith they make preserves ; in the gloom
She seems, as she glimmers round the room,
Like a lovely milk-white unicorn
In a forestial thicket of thorn.

Life was so still, so clear, that to wake
Under a kingfisher's limpid lake
In the lovely afternoon of a dream
Would not remote or stranger seem.
Everything seemed so clear for a while —
The turn of a head or a deep-seen smile ;
Then a smile seen through wide leaves or deep water,
That beauty seemed to the King's daughter ;
For a flying shadow passed, then gone
Was the gleam, and the Princess was alone.

How sweet seemed the flowers of spring again —
As pink as Susan and Polly and Jane,
Like country maids so sweet and shy
Who bloom and love and wonder not why :
Now when summer comes it seems the door
To the graves that lie under the trivial floor,

And the gardens hard to touch and shining,
Where no mirage dew lies whining.
And the sweet flowers seem for a fading while
Dear as our first love's youthful smile —
Till they bruise and wound the heart and sense
With their lost and terrible innocence.

10

When each clear raindrop holds for flight
A wingless world all plumage-bright,

Like crystal-clear wistaria
After the storm's hysteria,

The Princess visited the farm
Where all the beasts lie, furred as palm

That on the budding Easter boughs
Among the winds of beauty grows.

The farm-pond, fruitish-soft and ripe,
Was smooth as a daguerreotype :

The farm-maid, Rosa, under flimsy
Muslin skies, an angel's whimsy,

Walked. . . . Her daisy-frillèd frock
Was stiff and harder than a rock ;

Frills touch her feet, like plants foam down ;
Her wooden trellised hair is brown.

The grass is furry as a bear
With heat ; the donkey's panniers flare

With fruits whose clear complexions, waxen,
Hide in leaves all hairy-flaxen.

And from the sky, white angels lean
To stroke poor Dobbin's palm-furred skin,

And pluck from the round leaves the pink
Schoolgirlish summer fruits that wink —

Giggle insipidly.   On winding
Roads whose dust seems gilded binding

Made for ' Paul et Virginie '
(So flimsy-tough those roads are), see

The panniered donkey pass !   The ass's
Thoughts, as through the dust he passes,

Where leaves seem parasols of gauze
Shading the stripèd wooden floors,

Seem like this :   ' When long ago
I worked for Balaam, never so

Appeared an angel !   times are stranger
Now,' and, turning to his manger,

He longs — for loads have made him weary —
For gentian stars, all rough and hairy,

And trees that bear white satin streamers
Of lovely flowers to please poor dreamers.

The Princess passed goats, gold as wheat,
With a kind white milky bleat,

Under the wide leaves mild as milk ;
The billowing pigs with ears of silk ;

Maternal cows with a white horn
As hard and dry as rustling corn —

All the poor shadows cast by our sad earthly dress
Of faults and virtues, wavering childishness !

II

WHEN we were young, how beautiful life seemed ! —
The boundless bright horizons that we dreamed,

And the immortal music of the Day and Night,
Leaving the echo of their wonder and their might

Deep in our hearts and minds. How could the dust
Of superstitions taught in schoolrooms, lust

In love's shape, dim our beauty ? What dark lie,
Or cruelty's voice, could drown this God-made harmony ?

For we knew naught of prison-worlds man built
Around us that we may not know man's guilt —

The endless vistas of the goatish faces
Echoing each other, and the basis

Of clay, the plumeless wings of Destiny,
The vistas leading only to the grave where we must lie.

    ·   ·   ·   ·   ·

Then all the beauty of the world lay deep
Mirrored within the beauty water-clear
Of flowering boughs ; Helen and Deirdre, dreamed
And fading, wakened in that loveliness
Of watery branches. In that dead wild spring
Through the bird's shaken voice we heard God sing.

But age has dimmed our innocent paradise
With a faint shadow, shaken dust within our eyes —
And we are one now with the lonely wise,
Knowing the spring is only the clear mirage
Of an eternal beauty that is not.
Those were the days when the fleet summer seemed

The warmth and infinite loveliness of God,
Who cared for us, within a childish heaven.
We could believe then ! Oh, the lips and eyes
That spoke of some far undimmed paradise !
Those were the days. . . .

12

Now that the summer only seems the sad
Mechanical dull action of the light
And shadow playing over a dead world —
Dead as my heart — it seems too long ago
For the remembrance of the beauty and the world we
    used to know ;

When the warm lights of afternoon were mellow
As honeyed yellow pears, the Princess played
At Troy Town in the palace garden, tossed
And through the smiling leaves of summer lost
A round compact gold ball, the smaller image
Of this hard world, grown dry of any love —
Or walked upon the shore, watched the fantastic
Arabesque, the horsemanship of waves.
' Mademoiselle Fantoche, where do they go ? '
A faint cold wind replied, ' I do not know.'

The Princess
' Upon the infinite shore by the sea
The lovely ladies are walking like birds,
Their gowns have the beauty, the feathery
Grace of a bird's soft raiment ; remote
Is their grace and their distinction, — they float
And peck at their deep and honeyed words
As though they were honeyed fruits ; and this
Is ever their life, between sleep and bliss.
Though they are winged for enchanted flight,
They yet remain ever upon the shore
Of Eternity, seeking for nothing more,
Until the cold airs dull their beauty
And the snows of winter load those dazzling
Wings, and no bird-throat can sing ! '

The Governante

' Look not on the infinite wave,
Dream not of the siren cave,
Nor hear the cold wind in the tree
Sigh of worlds we cannot see.

(*She sings*)

The hot muscatelle
Siesta time fell,
And the Spanish belle
Looked out through her shutters.

Under the eglantine
Thorny and lean
A shadow was playing a mandoline, mutters

Only this : " Wave
Your fan . . . siren cave
Never was cold as the wind from the grave."

The governante
Came walking andante, —
Sailed like a brigantine, black of brow.

And the falconette
Who danced a ballette
Sang on the pretty, the brunette bough :

" The ambassade
Of shadows invade
Death's most ultimate, peaceful shade. . . .
Lovely lady, where are you now ? "

   .   .   .   .   .

Come, Madam, you must eat your creamy curd,
Soft as the plumage of a bird, —

Break through the jewelled branches' bird-soft gloom
And find Malinn within the cool still-room.'

77

13

WHERE reynard-haired Malinn
Walks by rock and cave,
The Sun, a Chinese mandarin,
Came dripping from the wave.

' Your hair seems like the sunrise
O'er Persia and Cathay —
A rose-red music strange and dim
As th' embalmèd smile of seraphim.'

He said to her by the white wave
In the water-pallid day
(A forest of white coral boughs
Seemed the delicate sea-spray) :

' In envy of your brighter hair, —
Since, Madam, we must quarrel, —
I've changed the cold flower-lovely spray
To branches of white coral ;

And when, white muslin Madam, you
Coquette with the bright wind,
I shall be but thin rose-dust ;
He will be cold, unkind.'

The flowers that bud like rain and dream
On thin boughs water-clear,
Fade away like a lovely music
Nobody will hear,

And Aeolus and Boreas
Brood among those boughs,
Like hermits haunting the dark caves
None but the wise man knows.

But Malinn's reynard-coloured hair,
Amid the world grown sere
Still seemed the Javanese sunrise
Whose wandering music will surprise
Into cold bird-chattering cries
The Emperor of China
Lying on his bier.

14

THE birds, strange flashing glints of another life,
Peck at the fruits of summer, that too soon
Will fade into a little gilded dust.
Then underneath the dancing, glancing bough
Came Malinn, with her round cheeks dyed as pink
As the insipid empty-tasting fruits
Of summer giggling through the rounded leaves.

Outside the still-room was a cherry-tree,
And through the dancing shadows she could see
Cross ancient Poll Troy come to do her duty. . . .
She had a cold frost-bitten beauty
Like blue moonlight smooth and cold
As amber ; with her trembling old
Hands she tied the boughs aloft
Through the air all creamy soft ;
Then on the sill of the woodland dairy,
Moving as quick and light as a fairy,
She put a bowl of the thickest cream
(As thick as chestnut flowers in a dream).
The gossiping naiad of the water,
In her sprigged gown like the housekeeper's daughter,
Giggles outside the still-room ; she
Plucks at the thick-bustled cherry-tree.
And Poll is cross ; she chases cherried
Country maids like thickest-berried
Cherry-trees in their ruched gown
Till they run from the palace, down,
Like the sprigged muslin waterfalls
Of this clear country, to where calls
Pan, with his satyrs on the rocks
Feeding their wave-weary flocks.
The naiad's giggling irritates
Cross Poll Troy till at last she rates
Her through the thick-leaved cherry-tree :
' My eyes are dim, — I yet can see

You, lazy quean ! Go work ! ' ' I can't.'
' I say you shall ! ' ' I say I shan't ! '
' But when the airs are creamy soft
And candle-flames are quince flowers, oft
Though my heart flutters like a bird,
All dream-dark, though as soft as curd
The moonlight seems still, from my bed
I rise and work, you sleepy head !
Though I am dim and very old,
I wake the flames all jewel-cold,
The flames that seem, when they soar high,
Like waterfalls of jewels ; you sigh,
While I, Miss, churn and make the curd,'
Piped Poll Troy like a small cross bird,
Then shuts the still-room window, goes, for she
Still hears the naiad giggling through the tree.

But Malinn stays where the deep fire's red flowers
Should be as sweet and red as hawthorn bowers.

(*She sings*)
' The purring fire has a bear's dull fur,
Its warmth is sticky, dark as a burr. . . .
Come drowse, for now there is no eye
To watch, no voice to ask me why !
All night I hear my animal blood
Cry to my youth, " Come to the wood ! " . .
But Darkness lumbers like a bear,
Grumbling, cumbers floor and stair. . . .
And on the eightieth step, I know
That on the moon's green lichen stain
I'll slip . . . and his dark breath will blow
My light out. . . . All will be still again ! '

She cried out to the naiad : ' I have torn
My flimsy dress upon a thicket's thorn ;
The petal of a briar-rose lies forlorn

Upon it.' Through the glinting leaves about the dairy
Appeared the cream-smug face of the wicked fairy. . . .
'You've torn your dress, my poppet. . . . I'll come in. . . .
I've brought my spindle with me and I'll spin
A dress for you. . . .

                     Such grey-blue sleeves
Of muslin, like the wind of eve's ;
It shall have frills that flare like leaves ;

The ribbons shall be preened,
Quilled prettily and sheened

As when the courtier-wind plays with a flock
Of birds for battledore and shuttlecock —
Whose feathers stream like ribbons. I will hide
A jewel within each one : you'll seem a bride

For Ariel or some rich water-god. . . . Come, spin ! '
Malinn looked through the leaves. . . . ' Ma'am, please
     come in ! '

Far off, the Martha-coloured scabious
Grew among dust as dry as old Eusebius,

And underneath the cotton-nightcap trees
Wanders a little cold pig-snouted breeze.

Then in a gown all frilled with foliage like hell's fires,
And quilled like nests of cockatrices, with the light's gold
     wires

Sewing it stiff, old Laidronette the fairy
Crept through the window of the woodland dairy.

Butter and cream
Turn hard as a jewel,
The shrill flames scream,
The leaves mutter ' Cruel ! '

Through the dark jewelled leaves
See the Princess peep
As lovely as eve's
Soft wind of sleep.

She picks up the spindle. ' Oh, the curious bliss ! . . .
It pricks my finger now. How strange this is, —
For I am like that lovely fawn-queen, dead
Long since, — pierced through the pool-clear heart,' she
    said.

Her room now seems like some pale cave
Haunted by a goatish wave.

Through the curtains — waves of water —
Comes the housekeeper's young daughter,

Where like coral-branches seem
The candles' light, the candles' gleam.

' Does Echo mourn her lost love there ? '
Echo is a courtly air

Sighing the name of Cydalise
Beside clear pools of sleep ; she sees

Her like a nymph in some deep grot
(Where the wave whispers not),

Like a rose-bush in that cave
Haunted by a goatish wave.

Do, do,
Princess, do,
Like a tree that drips with gold you flow.
Soon beneath that peaceful shade
The whole world dreaming will be laid.
Do, do,
Princess, do,
The years like soft winds come and go.

Do, do,
Princess, do,
How river-thick flow your fleeced locks
Like the nymphs' music o'er the rocks. . . .
From satyr-haunted caverns drip
These lovely airs on brow and lip.
Do, do,
Princess, do,
Like a tree that drips with gold you flow.

But far from snow-soft sleep, the country Fair
Spangled like planets the bucolic air
Under hot Capricorn, with gold goat-legs,
Rough satyr hands, that in the sunburnt hay
Pulled the long wind-blown hair of Susans, Megs,
And under great trees dark as water lay.

It seemed a low-hung country of the blind, —
A sensual touch upon the heart and mind,
Like crazy creaking chalets hanging low
From the dark hairiness of bestial skies
The clouds seem, like a potting-shed where grow
The flower-like planets for the gay flower-show :
Gold-freckled calceolarias,
Marigolds, cinerarias,
African marigolds, coarse-frilled,
And cherries, apricots, all chilled
With dew, for thus the bright stars seemed
To cottage windows where none dreamed.
But country gentlemen who from their birth,
Like kind red strawberries, root deep in earth
And sleep as in the grave, dream far beyond
The sensual aspects of the hairy sky
That something hides, they have forgotten why !
And so they wander, aiming with their gun
At mocking feathered creatures that have learnt
That movement is but groping into life, —
Under rough trees like shepherds' goatish tents.

And only Midsummer's wide country Fair
Seems to them heaven and hell, and earth and air.

The people ride in roundabouts ; their hair
Is like the gardens of the Pleiades,
Or the first impulse from which music sprung,
And the dark sound in the smooth growth of trees ;

They sparkle like the sea ; their love is young
For ever, they are golden as the boy
Who gave an apple smoother than the breeze
To Lady Venus, lovely as the seas ;
Their lips are like the gold fires burning Troy.

Like harsh and crackling rags of laughter seems
The music, bright flung as an angel's hair —
Yet awful as the ultimate despair
Of angels and of devils. . . . Something dreams
Within the sound that shrieks both high and low
Like some ventriloquist's bright-painted show
On green grass, shrill as anger, dulled as hate :
It shrieks to the dulled soul, ' Too late, too late ! '
Sometimes it jangles thin as the sharp wires
Whereon the poor half-human puppets move ;
Sometimes it flares in foliage like hell's fires,
Or whispers insincerities for love.
A little hurdy-gurdy waltz sounds hollow
And bright-husked as the hearts of passing people,
Whose talk is only of the growth of plums
And pears : ' Life goes, Death never comes,'
They sigh, while the bright music like a wave
Sings of far lands and many a siren cave.

And there are terrible and quick drum-taps
That seem the anguished beat of our own heart
Making an endless battle without hope
Against materialism and the world.
And sometimes terrible lumbering Darkness comes
Breaking the trivial matchboard floors that hide
From us the Dead we dare not look upon :
O childish eyes, O cold and murdered face —
Dead innocence and youth that were our own !

But age has brought a little subtle change
Like the withdrawal caused by the slow dropping

Of cold sad water on some vast stone image :
A slow withdrawal, a sad, gradual change
O'er tragic masks through which strange gods have
    cried —
Till seen through death-cold rents in saturnine leaves
They seem, almost, to echo in their form
The saturnine cold laughter of the water.
And this, too, is the fate of country masks
Of Comedy, as fresh as smiling fruits
Of summer seen, vermilion, through deep leaves.

Now from the countrysides where people know
That Destiny is wingless and bemired,
With feathers dirty as a hen's, too tired
To fly — where old pig-snouted Darkness grovels
For life's mired rags among the broken hovels
The country bumpkins come, with faces round
And pink as summer fruits, with hair as gold,
Sharp-pointed, as the summer sun (that old
Bucolic mime, whose laughing pantomime
Is rearing pink fruits from the sharp white rime).
They come from little rooms, each a poor booth
(Seen through the summer leaves, all smiling smooth).
There, for all beauty, is the badly painted
Ancestral portrait of their grey-beard God ;
In that poor clownish booth it is so cold
That small airs prick like grass, a wooden sword.

They pass along the country roads as thick
With walls and gardens as a childish heaven,
Where all the flowers seem a pink fleshly heart
And mirage-dews sigh, ' We will never part.'

And there are young Princesses at each inn,
And poor young people poverty makes wise,
With eyes like maps of the wide summer heaven ;
And on the country roads there is a shrine,
As blue and sparkling as the sea-god's wine,

For country gods and goddesses of gardens,
Where every fruit and flower to old songs hardens :
Pomona, tinsel-pink as that bright pear,
The moon — she seems a poor bucolic clown
With dry and gilded foliage for her hair, —
Where branches cast a shallow melancholy,
An owl-soft shadow falling over folly.
The pink schoolgirlish fruits hang in bright sheaves
Between the rounded and the negroid leaves. . . .
And we remember nursery afternoons
When the small music-box of the sweet snow
Gave half-forgotten tunes, and our nurse told
Us tales that fell with the same tinkling notes. . . .
' Once on a time,' she said, ' and long ago.'
Her voice was sweet as the bright-sparkling rime,
The fruits are cold as that sweet music's time —
Yet all those fruits like the bright snow will fade.

The country bumpkins travel to the Fair,
For Night and Day, and Hell and Heaven, seem
Only a clown's booth seen in some bad dream,
Wherefrom we watch the movements of our life
Growing and ripening like summer fruits
And dwindling into dust, a mirage lie :
Hell is no vastness, it has naught to keep
But little rotting souls and a small sleep.
It has the same bright-coloured clarity we knew
In nursery afternoons so long ago,
Bright as our childish dreams ; but we are old,
This is a different world ; the snow lies cold
Upon our heart, though midsummer is here. . . .

17

Bʊᴛ in the Court, the little people know
That Sleep is bright as fruit and soft as snow.

The sunlight seems like warm brocade
In the courtyard through the great arcade ;

And golden as a Sultan's turban
The ripened medlars hang ; the urban

Maids of the ladies at the palace
Talked like birds, with a gentle malice,

And on the wall, light-motes take shapes
Of vines, with showers of emerald grapes.

' Queen Venus is a toothless crone
Blackened with age ; all night alone

She lies, and no bird ever cries
For the wild starlight of her eyes.

' Once Helen was Prince Paris' doxy ;
She meets her lovers now by proxy,

And wrinkled as the gold sea-sand
Are the breasts that once seemed heaven's land.'

Look at that little shadow . . . oh, the joy,
As black as any jewelled Negro boy.

O little shade — see, I will call him Zambo !
Look where he silent sits and plays dumbcrambo,

There at the doors, with ghosts . . . and his
  mentero,
Half in brocaded sunlight, points to Zero !

Black fingers stretched to pluck the fruits of gold
Through the great leaves. . . . I feel a sudden cold

Sweet air from the arcade. . . . Again it goes.
The scented darkness seems as rich as snows,

Like cornucopias with ostrich plumes
And great gold fruits the clouds seem from these glooms.'

Down in the great arcade of the courtyard
The fairies' coachmen, tawny as a pard,

Are talking of those feathered July eves
When all these dames desert their country leaves

(Though still as lovely as those moonlight maids
Juno and Dian, haunting their deep glades)

And in their coach, with maids and footmen, drive
Up to the great town houses where they live ;

No longer they seem fairies, but we see
Them named as the old Duchess of Bohea,

And Madam Cards, the Marchioness of Gout ;
Though they are old, they still enjoy a rout,

And through the dark leaves of the shadow-grove,
As wickedly as ever, eyes still rove

That dealt death from behind a fluttered fan
In Pompeii, Athens, before Time began.

In courtyards stained with the black night like wine,
Strange figures with hair lifted like a vine

Listen. . . . Who is it hearkens at their doors,
In the vast rooms and endless corridors ?

It is goat-footed, mincing Death, who presses
His muzzle at the keyhole, hears their dresses

Rustling like rose-leaves. . . . They hit him with their fan,
Through scented moonlight move to their sedan.

When the hot gilded day will reach
A restful close,
A Japanese dwarf forest on the beach,
With dark trees of the shadow, the street grows.
How sand-like quivers the gold light
Under the large black leaves of shadow ; mirage-bright
It lies, that dusty gold,
Untouched of any air ;
Like Dead Sea fruit carved in cornelian, bold,
The faces of a man and Pleasure's mournful daughter

Show lovely in the light, a moment flare,
Then shadows fall again — dark agates through clear water.

Then these Chinoiseries, old ghosts of red and white
Smooth lacquer, in their palanquins take flight

For tea, and the last esoteric rage
Whose plumes may soften age, that harpy's cage.

Their smile is like Death's trap . . . a little gilded dust
Of valueless beauty from the sun soon must

Brush, for a fading while, each feathered cheek
That paradisal airs will never sleek —

And round them, as they move, the unfading sea, Eternity,
With its cool feathered airs of beauty, sighs of no horizons
    they can see.

What would these ghosts do, if the truths they know,
That were served up like snow-cold jewelled fruits
And the enfeathered airs of lutes,
Could be their guests in cold reality ?

91

They would be shivering,
Wide-eyed as a Negro king
Seeing the evanescent mirage snow —
They would be silenced by the cold
That is of the spirit, endlessly
Unfabled and untold.

The swan's-breath winter these have known is finer
Fading than the early snows of China,

The poems of Queen Marguerite of Navarre
(Narcissus-petalled, perfumed like a star),

Or the Pleiades' citron-scented poems, fading like the snows,
Perfuming their long fingers till their eyelids close.

The winters these have known have been too kind,
With skies that seemed the bitter gilded rind

Of unattainable fruits ; small women go
As white as ermines, and small winds are slow

As tunes upon a lute ; the point-lace on the trees
And the pearl-berries of the snow upon dark bushes freeze,

And the snow falls, as sharp and bright, unripe and sour,
As the budding grapes' bright perfume or the sweet grape-
        flower.

The daughters of the Silence now are dead,
And these Chinoiserie ghosts,
These mummies in dim hosts,
Tread the long mournful avenues instead ;
Alarm the soul by their cold interest —
For what can be the purpose of their quest ?

When spring begins, in China and Tibet
Through bell'd lime-avenues a springe is set
To catch the softly-smiling wind,
The cherubim to catch and blind

As cruel men blind a singing-bird;
They trap them with the sound of lutes
And the softest smiles of fruits,
That these old ghosts may prove the feathered creatures real
    to hold,
And make them sing upon a perch of gold
In cages with a foolish bell-hung gable,
Amid the powders on their dressing table;
Till, trapped by our mortality, they die, and their small
    bones,
Sounding as sweetly as the west wind's tones,
Are sold because they sound like a small music-box;
Their slayers sell for silver the bright plumes in flocks,
To make the pillows for a sleepy head
That never dreams of heaven, but the lonely Dead.

And still they dwindle the bright world down to the
    gilded glooms
Of dust, these mummies, hieing, harrying fast
The Soul, their quarry, through the deserted tombs —
Or lying, lotus-eaters in a dreamful ease,
Perfuming their cold lips with silence and the past
Beneath the Asian darkness of smooth trees. . . .
Thus spoke the men; then sleep came colder than the rose
Blooming in desolation. . . . No one knows
The end there is to dust — it is the soul that shall survive
    them at the last.

18

BENEATH a wan and sylvan tree,
Whose water-flowing beauty our tired eyes
Can feel from very far, two travellers lie ;
And one is swarthy as the summer wind —
A man who travelled from a far country ;
The other Soldan in his pomp and panoply
Seems like le Roi Soleil in all his pride
When his gold periwig is floating wide.
They talked together, those dark kings beneath the bough,
And their songs mingled with soft winds that flow.

The Soldan (sings)
' When green as a river was the barley,
Green as a river the rye,
I waded deep and began to parley
With a youth whom I heard sigh.
" I seek," said he, " a lovely lady,
A nymph as bright as a queen,
Like a tree that drips with pearls her shady
Locks of hair were seen ;
And all the rivers became her flocks
Though their wool you cannot shear,
Because of the love of her flowing locks.
The kingly sun like a swain
Came strong, unheeding of her scorn,
Wading in deeps where she has lain,
Sleeping upon her river lawn
And chasing her starry satyr train.
She fled, and changed into a tree, —
That lovely fair-haired lady. . . .
And now I seek through the sere summer
Where no trees are shady."

They say that Daphne never was more fair
With all the shaken pearls of her long hair —
The lovely tree that was Apollo's love,
To whom he brought his richest spoils — than she !

94

And oh, that other Soldan, the hot sun
Burns not with love as I, with my dark pomp,
My helmet thick-plumed as a water-god's,
Whose cornucopia filled with dripping jewels
Is not so rich as treasuries I bear —
Dark spices, nard and spikenard, ambergris. . . .
No maid will change into a tree before my kiss ! '

The Man from a Far Countree
' But I will be content with some far-lesser maid,
Who feeds her flocks beneath a fair-haired tree
And listens to the wind's song ; she shall be
My soldanesse and rule my far countree.

(*He sings*)
Rose and Alice,
Oh, the pretty lassies,
With their mouths like a calice
And their hair a golden palace —
Through my heart like a lovely wind they blow.

Though I am black and not comely,
Though I am black as the darkest trees,
I have swarms of gold that will fly like honey-bees,
By the rivers of the sun I will feed my words
Until they skip like those fleecèd lambs
The waterfalls, and the rivers (horned rams) ;
Then for all my darkness I shall be
The peacefulness of a lovely tree —
A tree wherein the golden birds
Are singing in the darkest branches, O ! '

Thus sang those plumed Kings, and the winds that flow
Whispered of lands no waking heart may know.

Now from the silk pavilions of the seas
The nymphs sing, gold and cold as orange-trees.

    ' Through gilded trellises
    Of the heat, Dolores,
    Inez, Manuccia,
    Isabel, Lucia,
    Mock Time that flies.
    " Lovely bird, will you stay and sing,
    Flirting your sheenèd wing, —
    Peck with your beak, and cling
    To our balconies ? "
    They flirt their fans, flaunting —
    " O silence, enchanting
    As music ! " then slanting
    Their eyes,
    Like gilded or emerald grapes,
    They take mantillas, capes,
    Hiding their simian shapes.
    Sighs
    Each lady, " Our spadille
    Is done. . . . Dance the quadrille
    From Hell's towers to Seville ;
    Surprise
    Their siesta," Dolores
    Said. Through gilded trellises
    Of the heat, spangles
    Pelt down through the tangles
    Of bell-flowers ; each dangles
    Her castanets, shutters
    Fall while the heat mutters,
    With sounds like a mandoline
    Or tinkled tambourine. . . .
    Ladies, Time dies ! '

And petals of the foam, like perfumed orange-blossom,
Pelt the nymphs singing in their bowers — cold as their
    bosom.

In the hot noon — like glowing muscadine
The light seems, and the shade like golden wine —

Beneath the deep shade of the trees' arcade,
All foppish in his dressing-gown's brocade

And turban, comes the great Magnifico,
And hearkens not where the beccafico

Time taps at the lovely sylvan trees.
Now underneath the shadows fallen from these

The queen sits with her court, and through the glade
The light from their silks casts another silver shade.

Home goes the great Magnifico ; his dressing-gown
Is changed for water-rustling silks that drown

The shades, and walking proudly as the breeze
Now he advances through the sylph-slim trees.

' Madam, the Soldan and the King of Ethiop's land
Approach as suitors for your daughter's hand.'

The day grew water-pale and cool as the long eves. . .
A lady sang through water-rippling leaves :

       ' The mauve summer rain
       Is falling again —
       It soaks through the eaves
       And the ladies' sleeves —
       It soaks through the leaves

       That like silver fish fall
       In the fountains, recall
       Afternoons when I
       Was a child small and shy
       In the palace. . . . Fish lie

On the grass with lives darkling.
Our laughter falls sparkling
As the mauve raindrops bright
When they fall through the light
With the briefest delight.

The pavilions float
On the lake like a boat. . . .
Mauve rains from trees fall
Like wistaria flowers . . . all
My life is like this
And drifts into nothingness !

The strange ladies sigh
" The autumn is nigh " . . .
The King bows and mutters. . . .
His eyelids seem shutters
Of a palace pavilion
Deserted a million

Echoing years ago.
Oh, but the rain falls slow.'

    .   .   .   .   .

But no one heard the great Magnifico
Or this pale song, for underneath the low
Deep bough the queen slept, while the flowers that fall
Seemed Ariadne's starry coronal.

In the great room above the orangery
The old queen's dwarfs are drinking their bohea

While the thin flames seem gold and whispering leaves
Of trees in the Hesperides, whose faint sound grieves.

So small, they could be hid in a pomander,
Miss Ellen and Sir Pompey Alexander

Seem. . . . The tea is gold as evening,
The perfumes in the orangery sing,

And, flashing like exotic-plumaged birds,
The lovely shadows whisper unknown words.

Upon the wall, the portrait of Queen Anne
Frowned at them and waved a languid fan —

Queen Anne, whose white wig glittering in the net
Of gold light seems a florid bergerette,

Sheep-floury underneath the powder. . . .
Her lips' small strawberry said ' Louder '

To the shadows' fluttering bird. . . .
But the lovely one scarce heard. . . .

The zephyrs' lips like ruffled roses sleek
Caressingly each faintly upturned cheek ;

And now the shutters like blue water
Fall. . . . Where is the king's daughter ?

The candle-flames seem orange-flowers
Whose pale light falls in perfumed showers ;

But Queen Anne, sleeping on the wall,
Long dead, would answer not at all.

THE little golden lights like Chinese ladies peep
Through the old queen's curtains, then like sleep

Their gentle footsteps fade again and fail,
And once again the world is ghostly pale.

In the queen's powder-closet, Mrs. Troy
Teases the flames to wake them and annoy. . . .

So pale are those thin ghostly flames that yet
They seem like the old notes of a spinet

That sometimes sounds a courante or gavotte
By Mozart or Scarlatti — sometimes not —

While the pale silken ribbons of the rain,
Knotted, are fluttering down the window-pane.

But suddenly the flames turn green and red
As unripe fruit ; their shrilling fills her head

With noises like a painted puppet-show ;
And in that music, shrieking high and low,

Dead is the pointed flames' small minuet —
And from the shrilling fire leaps Laidronette.

The ghostly apparition that appeared
Wagged from her chin a cockatrice's beard ;

She crouches like a flame, the adder-sting
Of her sharp tongue is ready ; hear her sing :

' The candle flames bob
Like strawberries low,
Bob-cherry, bob-cherry,
See them go

In the hands of the queen's maids
Under the trees
Of the shadow, flickering in the breeze.
Crept a starved and a humble air
From the hovels, grunting with low pig-snout —
Starved thin, creeping
Everywhere, weeping,
It blew the queen's strawberry candle-flames out.

The maids in long chequered gowns,
Hunting for these,
Find but the shadows'
Flickering trees.'

The humble ghosts like poppet maids
Walk tiptoe in the shadow glades.

Their mouths seem small red strawberries ;
Their naïve naiad-titterings freeze

The airs in the long corridors
Where they must hark at hopeless doors.

And Mrs. Troy rose up like a thin shriek
Or pointed flame. . . . ' Oh, my poor head is weak !

Oh dear,
Oh dear,
Whatever shall I do ?
In the flames' shrill rout
Laidronette slipped through.
I forget the Latin
For my prayer !
My quilted satin
Is beyond repair !
I must tell the queen
But I dare not be seen !

Oh dear, oh dear,
I tremble with fear,
Like a nectarine bough
When the sun shines through.

How harmless has been my poor life —
Yet when a young girl I had strife !
Out, alas ! how I remember
That dawn, when, to light the ember,
I must steal and I must creep
In the kitchen half asleep.
Noises from the sharp green wood
Burnt and bit my satyr blood,
And my cockscomb hair raised ire
In parrot-whistlers in the fire !

Now the ember as it dozes
Seems lattices of bunchèd roses,
Fuchsias and fat strawberries,
Dahlias, cherries, and one sees
Through those lattices' gold wire
The parrot-whistlers in the fire,
Pecking cherries every one.
" Polly, put the kettle on,"
Scream they ; " scratch poor pretty Polly "
(Kettles hissing at their folly !).
From the wood they spring and scream,
Scald the milk, upset the cream. . . .
Oh, the feathers jewel-bright !
Alas ! my life was never light.'

The shrill flames nodded, beckoned, then lay dead ;
Her wig awry, cross Poll Troy nods her head.

The long dark corridors seem shadow-groves
Wherein a little courtier air still roves. . . .

Pale rose-leaves, wet and scented, seems the rain,
Whose bright drops cease, as soft as sleep again.

Her gown seems like a pale and tuneful rose.

.   .   .   .   .

Hours passed ; the soft melodious moonlight grows. . . .
A murmurous sound of far-off Circean seas
And old enchantments and the growth of trees.

.   .   .   .   .

Across the silver grass the powdered ghosts
Are wandering in dim and scattered hosts

Among the woods and fields, and they forget
Everything but that their love's hand yet
Is touching theirs ; the ribbons of the moon are blue
And pink ; those ghosts pick bunches from the dew

Of ghostly flowers, all poignant with spring rain,
Smelling of youth that will not come again.

23

THE public Scribe, noctambulo,
Where moonlight, cold as blades of grass,
Echoes upon deserted walls,
Turned his dusty folio. . . .
Dry grass that cackles thin in Hell
The spires of fire . . . his nightcap fell. . . .

Doctor Gradus
Mounts Parnassus
On that dusty ass the Law ;
His hair is grey
As asses' ears,
The cold wind's bray
He never hears. . . .
O'er donkey's hide-grass the attorney
Still continues on his journey

With the dusty Law's proceedings
Through the old forestial readings
For the Town of Troy
Prince Paris lost when yet a boy.

Il Dottore in the long grass
Culls the simples — cold henbane,
Nettles that make fevers pass,
Wood-spurge that will cure a blain.

He walks where weeds have covered all. . . .
The moon's vast echoes die
Across the plain where weeds, grown tall,
Pearled treasuries of Asia seem,
Sunk in an endless dream.
And the mandarins in Asia,
In the silken palace of the moon,
Are all who are left to drink this physic
That will restore them from a swoon.

24

NIGHT passed, and in that world of leaves
The Dawn came, rustling like corn-sheaves;

And a small wind came like little Boy Blue
Over the cornfield and rustling through
The large leaves. . . . Oh, how very deep
The old queen is sighing in her sleep:

' Alas, blue wind,
Bluebeard unkind,
Why have you blown so far from me,
Through the jewelled blue leaves that sound
      like the sea,

The lady Margotte,
The goosegirl Gargotte
Agog with curiosity?

They played Troy Town on the palace wall. . . .
Like small grape hyacinths were their curls
And thin as the spring wind were those girls —
But now they never come if I call.'

The kingly cock with his red-gold beard,
And his red-gold crown had crowed unheard

While his queens ruffled down
Each feathered gown
Beside the waterfall's crystal town;

The cock, the dawn-fruits, the gold corn,
Sing this aubade, cold, forlorn:

' Jane, Jane,
Forget the pain
In your heart. Go work again.

Light is given that you may
Work till owl-soft dusk of day.

The morning light whines on the floor. . . .
No one e'er will cross the door,

No one ever cares to know
How ragged flowers like you do grow.

Like beaux and belles about the Court
King James the Second held, athwart

The field the sheep run — foolish graces,
Periwigs, long Stuart faces,

While ragged-robin, cockscomb flowers
Cluck beneath the crystal showers.

A far-off huntsman sounds his horn
That sounds like rain, harsh and forlorn ;

Pink as his coat, poor-robin seems. . . .
Jane, no longer lie in dreams.

The crude pink stalactites of rain
Are sounding from the boughs again.

Each sighs the name of Harriet, Mary,
Susan, Anne, grown cold and wary —

Never your name. Bright and gay,
They used to whisper, " Come away,"

But now they have forgotten why.
Come, no longer sleeping lie.

Jane, Jane,
Forget the pain
In your heart. Go work again ! '

No answer came. No footsteps now will climb
Down from Jane's attic. She forgets the time,
Her wages, plainness, and how none could love
A maid with cockscomb hair, in Sleep's dark grove.

25

AND now the brutish forests close around
The beauty sleeping in enchanted ground.

All night the harsh bucolic winds that grunt
Through those green curtains, help me in my hunt.

Oh the swinish hairy beasts
Of the rough wind
(Wild boars tearing through the forests)!
Nothing they will find

But stars like empty wooden nuts,
In leaves green and shrill.
Home they go to their rough stye
The clouds . . . and home go I.

Above the wooden shutters
Of my room at morn,
Like bunches of the country flowers
Seem the fresh dawn hours.

And the young dawn creeps
Tiptoe through my room, . . .
Never speaks of one who sleeps
In the forest's gloom.

26

THE gardener played his old bagpipe
To make the melons and the peaches ripe. . . .
The threads are mixed in a tartan sound. . . .
' Keep, my lad, to the good safe ground.
For Jonah long since was a felon,
With guineas gold as a grape or melon.
He always said his prayers in Latin
To peaches like red quilted satin ;
And he had four and twenty daughters,
As lovely as the thick-fleeced waters
Or the Hesperides' thick-leaved trees —
And they were lovely as the evening breeze.
One Sabbath roamed that godless man
Beneath the great trees sylvan wan
And met an ancient satyr crone,
Cold as the droning wind the drone
Hears when the thickest gold will thrive,
Summer-long, in the combs of the honey-hive.
She said, " You must sail, as I understand,
Across the sea to a Better Land."
The sea was sharper than green grass,
The sailors would not let him pass,
And the sea was wroth and rose at him
Like the turreted walls of Jerusalem.
Or like the towers and gables seen
In the midst of a deep-boughed garden green.
If my old bagpipe I blew
It would not blow those great towers down.
The sailors took and bound him, threw
Him in among those towers to drown.
And oh, far best,' the gardener said,
' Like fruits to lie in your kind bed,
To sleep as snug as in the grave
In your kind bed, and shun the wave,
Nor ever sigh for a strange land
And songs no heart can understand.'

FAÇADE

TO SACHEVERELL SITWELL

ঌ

1. The Drum

(The Narrative of the Demon of Tedworth)

In his tall senatorial,
Black and manorial,
House where decoy-duck
Dust doth clack —
Clatter and quack
To a shadow black, —
Said the musty Justice Mompesson,
' What is that dark stark beating drum
That we hear rolling like the sea ? '
' It is a beggar with a pass
Signed by you.' ' I signed not one.'
They took the ragged drum that we
Once heard rolling like the sea ;
In the house of the Justice it must lie
And usher in Eternity.

   .   .   .   .   .

Is it black night ?
Black as Hecate howls a star
Wolfishly, and whined
The wind from very far.

In the pomp of the Mompesson house is one
Candle that lolls like the midnight sun,

Or the coral comb of a cock ; . . . it rocks. . . .
Only the goatish snow's locks
Watch the candles lit by fright
One by one through the black night.

Through the kitchen there runs a hare —
Whinnying, whines like grass, the air ;
It passes ; now is standing there
A lovely lady . . . see her eyes —
Black angels in a heavenly place,
Her shady locks and her dangerous grace.

' I thought I saw the wicked old witch in
The richest gallipot in the kitchen ! '
A lolloping galloping candle confesses.
' Outside in the passage are wildernesses
Of darkness rustling like witches' dresses.'

Out go the candles one by one
Hearing the rolling of a drum !

What is the march we hear groan
As the hoofèd sound of a drum marched on
With a pang like darkness, with a clang
Blacker than an orang-outang ?
' Heliogabalus is alone, —
Only his bones to play upon ! '

The mocking money in the pockets
Then turned black . . . now caws
The fire . . . outside, one scratched the door
As with iron claws, —

Scratching under the children's bed
And up the trembling stairs . . . ' Long dead '
Moaned the water black as crape.
Over the snow the wintry moon
Limp as henbane, or herb paris,
Spotted the bare trees ; and soon

Whinnying, neighed the maned blue wind
Turning the burning milk to snow,
Whining it shied down the corridor —
Over the floor I heard it go
Where the drum rolls up the stair, nor tarries.

2. *Clowns' Houses*

BENEATH the flat and paper sky
The sun, a demon's eye,
Glowed through the air, that mask of glass ;
All wand'ring sounds that pass

Seemed out of tune, as if the light
Were fiddle-strings pulled tight.
The market-square with spire and bell
Clanged out the hour in Hell ;

The busy chatter of the heat
Shrilled like a parokeet ;
And shuddering at the noonday light
The dust lay dead and white

As powder on a mummy's face,
Or fawned with simian grace
Round booths with many a hard bright toy
And wooden brittle joy :

The cap and bells of Time the Clown
That, jangling, whistled down,
Young cherubs hidden in the guise
Of every bird that flies ;

And star-bright masks for youth to wear,
Lest any dream that fare
— Bright pilgrim — past our ken, should see
Hints of Reality.

Upon the sharp-set grass, shrill-green.
Tall trees like rattles lean,
And jangle sharp and dizzily ;
But when night falls they sigh

Till Pierrot moon steals slyly in,
His face more white than sin,

Black-masked, and with cool touch lays bare
Each cherry, plum, and pear.

Then underneath the veilèd eyes
Of houses, darkness lies, —
Tall houses ; like a hopeless prayer
They cleave the sly dumb air.

Blind are those houses, paper-thin ;
Old shadows hid therein,
With sly and crazy movements creep
Like marionettes, and weep.

Tall windows show Infinity ;
And, hard reality,
The candles weep and pry and dance
Like lives mocked at by Chance.

The rooms are vast as Sleep within :
When once I ventured in,
Chill Silence, like a surging sea,
Slowly enveloped me.

3. Père Amelot

THE stars like quaking-grass grow in each gap
Of air (ruined castle wall). . . .
Père Amelot in his white nightcap
Peered through . . . saw nothing at all.

Like statues green from the verdigris
Of the moon, two shadows join
His shade, that under that castle wall sees
The moon like a Roman coin.

Out of his nightcap he drew three pence. . . .
Marie and Angélique pass
The knife through Père Amelot's back — in the dense
Bushes fly . . . he nods on the grass.

The man with the lanthorn, a moment after,
Picks up the moon that fell
Like an Augustan coin when laughter
Shook the hen-cackling grass of Hell ;

And the Public Writer, inscribing his runes
Beneath that castle wall, sees
Three Roman coins as blackened as prunes —
And Père Amelot slain for these !

The stars like quaking-grass grow in each gap
Of air — ruined castle wall. . . .
Père Amelot nods in his white nightcap . . .
He knows there is nothing at all !

4. *Ass-Face*

Ass-FACE drank
The asses' milk of the stars . . .
The milky spirals as they sank
From heaven's saloons and golden bars,
Made a gown
For Columbine,
Spirting down
On sands divine
By the asses' hide of the sea
(With each tide braying free).
And the beavers building Babel
Beneath each tree's thin beard,
Said, ' Is it Cain and Abel
Fighting again we heard ? '
It is Ass-Face, Ass-Face,
Drunk on the milk of the stars,
Who will spoil their houses of white lace —
Expelled from the golden bars !

5. Said King Pompey

SAID King Pompey, the emperor's ape
Shuddering black in his temporal cape
Of dust, ' The dust is everything —
The heart to love and the voice to sing,
Indianapolis
And the Acropolis,
Also the hairy sky that we
Take for a coverlet comfortably.'
Said the Bishop, ' The world is flat. . . .'
But the see-saw Crowd sent the Emperor down
To the howling dust — and up went the Clown
With his face that is filched from the new young Dead. . . .
And the Tyrant's ghost and the Low-Man-Flea
Are emperor-brothers, cast shades that are red
From the tide of blood — (Red Sea, Dead Sea),
And Attila's voice or the hum of a gnat
Can usher in Eternity.

6. The Bat

CASTELLATED, tall,
From battlements fall
Shades on heroic
Lonely grass,
Where the moonlight's echoes die and pass.
Near the rustic boorish,
Fustian Moorish
Castle wall of the ultimate Shade,
With his cloak castellated as that wall, afraid,
The mountebank doctor,
The old stage quack,
Where decoy-duck dust
Began to clack,
Watched Heliogabalusene the Bat
In his furred cloak hang head down from the flat
Wall, cling to what is convenient,
Lenient.
' If you hang upside down with squeaking shrill,
You will see dust, lust, and the will to kill,
And life is a matter of which way falls
Your tufted turreted Shade near these walls.
For muttering guttering shadow will plan
If you're ruined wall, or pygmy man,'
Said Heliogabalusene, ' or a pig,
Or the empty Caesar in tall periwig.'
And the mountebank doctor,
The old stage quack,
Spread out a black membraned wing of his cloak
And his shuffling footsteps seem to choke,
Near the Castle wall of the ultimate Shade
Where decoy-duck dust
Quacks, clacks, afraid.

7. *Lullaby for Jumbo*

JUMBO asleep !
Grey leaves thick-furred
As his ears, keep
Conversations blurred.
Thicker than hide
Is the trumpeting water ;
Don Pasquito's bride
And his youngest daughter
Watch the leaves
Elephantine grey :
What is it grieves
In the torrid day ?
Is it the animal
World that snores
Harsh and inimical
In sleepy pores ? —
And why should the spined flowers
Red as a soldier
Make Don Pasquito
Seem still mouldier ?

8. Trio for Two Cats and a Trombone

LONG steel grass —
The white soldiers pass —
The light is braying like an ass.
See
The tall Spanish jade
With hair black as nightshade
Worn as a cockade !
Flee
Her eyes' gasconade
And her gown's parade
(As stiff as a brigade).
Tee-hee !
The hard and braying light
Is zebra'd black and white,
It will take away the slight
And free
Tinge of the mouth-organ sound,
(Oyster-stall notes) oozing round
Her flounces as they sweep the ground.
The
Trumpet and the drum
And the martial cornet come
To make the people dumb —
But we
Won't wait for sly-foot night
(Moonlight, watered milk-white, bright)
To make clear the declaration
Of our Paphian vocation,
Beside the castanetted sea,
Where stalks Il Capitaneo
Swaggart braggadocio
Sword and moustachio —
He
Is green as a cassada
And his hair is an armada.
To the jade ' Come kiss me harder '

He called across the battlements as she
Heard our voices thin and shrill
As the steely grasses' thrill,
Or the sound of the onycha
When the phoca has the pica
In the palace of the Queen Chinee !

9. *Madam Mouse Trots*

'Dame Souris trotte grise dans le noir.'—Verlaine

MADAME MOUSE trots,
Grey in the black night !
Madame Mouse trots :
Furred is the light.
The elephant-trunks
Trumpet from the sea . . .
Grey in the black night
The mouse trots free.
Hoarse as a dog's bark
The heavy leaves are furled . . .
The cat's in his cradle,
All's well with the world !

10. Four in the Morning

CRIED the navy-blue ghost
Of Mr. Belaker
The allegro Negro cocktail-shaker,
' Why did the cock crow,
Why am I lost,
Down the endless road to Infinity toss'd ?
The tropical leaves are whispering white
As water ; I race the wind in my flight.
The white lace houses are carried away
By the tide ; far out they float and sway.
White is the nursemaid on the parade.
Is she real, as she flirts with me unafraid ?
I raced through the leaves as white as water . . .
Ghostly, flowed over the nursemaid, caught her,
Left her . . . edging the far-off sand
Is the foam of the sirens' Metropole and Grand.
And along the parade I am blown and lost,
Down the endless road to Infinity toss'd.
The guinea-fowl-plumaged houses sleep . . .
On one, I saw the lone grass weep,
Where only the whimpering greyhound wind
Chased me, raced me, for what it could find.'
And there in the black and furry boughs
How slowly, coldly, old Time grows,
Where the pigeons smelling of gingerbread,
And the spectacled owls so deeply read,
And the sweet ring-doves of curded milk,
Watch the Infanta's gown of silk
In the ghost-room tall where the governante
Gesticulates lente, and walks andante.
' Madam, Princesses must be obedient ;
For a medicine now becomes expedient, —
Of five ingredients, — a diapente,'
Said the governante, fading lente . . .
In at the window then looked he,
The navy-blue ghost of Mr. Belaker,

The allegro Negro cocktail-shaker, —
And his flattened face like the moon saw she, —
Rhinoceros-black (a flowing sea !).

11. *Black Mrs. Behemoth*

In a room of the palace
Black Mrs. Behemoth
Gave way to wroth
And the wildest malice.
Cried Mrs. Behemoth,
' Come, court lady,
Doomed like a moth,
Through palace rooms shady ! '
The candle flame
Seemed a yellow pompion,
Sharp as a scorpion ;
Nobody came . . .
Only a bugbear
Air unkind,
That bud-furred papoose,
The young spring wind,
Blew out the candle.
Where is it gone ?
To flat Coromandel
Rolling on !

12. *Came the Great Popinjay*

CAME the great Popinjay
Smelling his nosegay :
In cages like grots
The birds sang gavottes.
' Herodiade's flea
Was named sweet Amanda,
She danced like a lady
From here to Uganda.
Oh, what a dance was there !
Long-haired, the candle
Salome-like tossed her hair
To a dance tune by Handel.' . . .
Dance they still ?   Then came
Courtier Death,
Blew out the candle flame
With civet breath.

13. *The Wind's Bastinado*

THE wind's bastinado
Whipt on the calico
Skin of the Macaroon
And the black Picaroon
Beneath the galloon
Of the midnight sky.
Came the great Soldan
In his sedan
Floating his fan —
Saw what the sly
Shadow's cocoon
In the barracoon
Held.   Out they fly.
' This melon,
Sir Mammon,
Comes out of Babylon :
Buy for a patacoon —
Sir, you must buy ! '
Said Il Magnifico
Pulling a fico —
With a stoccado
And a gambado,
Making a wry
Face : ' This corraceous
Round orchidaceous
Laceous porraceous
Fruit is a lie !
It is my friend King Pharaoh's head
That nodding blew out of the Pyramid . . .'
The tree's small corinths
Were hard as jacinths,
For it is winter and cold winds sigh . . .
No nightingale
In her farthingale
Of bunchèd leaves let her singing die.

14. En Famille

In the early spring-time, after their tea,
Through the young fields of the springing Bohea,
Jemima, Jocasta, Dinah, and Deb
Walked with their father Sir Joshua Jebb —
An admiral red, whose only notion
(A butterfly poised on a pigtailed ocean)
Is of the peruked sea whose swell
Breaks on the flowerless rocks of Hell.
Under the thin trees, Deb and Dinah,
Jemima, Jocasta, walked, and finer
Their black hair seemed (flat-sleek to see)
Than the young leaves of the springing Bohea ;
Their cheeks were like nutmeg-flowers when swells
The rain into foolish silver bells.
They said, ' If the door you would only slam,
Or if, Papa, you would once say " Damn " —
Instead of merely roaring " Avast "
Or boldly invoking the nautical Blast —
We should now stand in the street of Hell
Watching siesta shutters that fell
With a noise like amber softly sliding ;
Our moon-like glances through these gliding
Would see at her table preened and set
Myrrhina sitting at her toilette
With eyelids closed as soft as the breeze
That flows from gold flowers on the incense-trees.'

    .   .   .   .   .

The Admiral said, ' You could never call —
I assure you it would not do at all !
She gets down from table without saying " Please,"
Forgets her prayers and to cross her T's,
In short, her scandalous reputation
Has shocked the whole of the Hellish nation ;
And every turbaned Chinoiserie,
With whom we should sip our black Bohea,

Would stretch out her simian fingers thin
To scratch you, my dears, like a mandoline
For Hell is just as properly proper
As Greenwich, or as Bath, or Joppa ! '

15. *Country Dance*

THAT hobnailed goblin, the bob-tailed Hob,
Said, 'It is time I began to rob.'
For strawberries bob, hob-nob with the pearls
Of cream (like the curls of the dairy girls),
And flushed with the heat and fruitish-ripe
Are the gowns of the maids who dance to the pipe.
Chase a maid?
She's afraid!
'Go gather a bob-cherry kiss from a tree,
But don't, I prithee, come bothering me!'
She said —
As she fled.
The snouted satyrs drink clouted cream
'Neath the chestnut-trees as thick as a dream;
So I went,
And I leant,
Where none but the doltish coltish wind
Nuzzled my hand for what it could find.
As it neighed,
I said,
'Don't touch me, sir, don't touch me, I say!
You'll tumble my strawberries into the hay.'
Those snow-mounds of silver that bee, the spring,
Has sucked his sweetness from, I will bring
With fair-haired plants and with apples chill
For the great god Pan's high altar . . . I'll spill
Not one!
So, in fun,
We rolled on the grass and began to run
Chasing that gaudy satyr the Sun;
Over the haycocks, away we ran
Crying, 'Here be berries as sunburnt as Pan!
But Silenus
Has seen us. . . .
He runs like the rough satyr Sun.
                                    Come away!

16. Mariner Man

' WHAT are you staring at, mariner man,
Wrinkled as sea-sand and old as the sea ? '
' Those trains will run over their tails, if they can,
Snorting and sporting like porpoises !   Flee
The burly, the whirligig wheels of the train,
As round as the world and as large again,
Running half the way over to Babylon, down
Through fields of clover to gay Troy town —
A-puffing their smoke as grey as the curl
On my forehead as wrinkled as sands of the sea ! —
But what can that matter to you, my girl ?
(And what can that matter to me ?) '

17. One O'Clock

GREAT SNORING and Norwich
A dish of pease porridge !
The clock of Troy town
Sounds one o'clock ; brown
Honey-bees in the clover
Are half the seas over,
And Time is a-boring
From Troy to Great Snoring.
But Time, the grey mouse,
Can't wake up the house,
For old King Priam
Is sleepy as I am !

18. The Octogenarian

THE octogenarian
Leaned from his window,
To the valerian
Growing below
Said, ' My nightcap
Is only the gap
In the trembling thorn
Where the mild unicorn
With the little Infanta
Danced the lavolta
(Clapping hands : molto
Lent' eleganta).'
The man with the lanthorn
Peers high and low ;
No more
Than a snore
As he walks to and fro. . . .
Il Dottore the stoic
Culls silver herb
Beneath the superb
Vast moon azoic.

19. Rain

BESIDE the smooth black marble sea
You and I drift aimlessly.

Each blade of grass springs pale, alone,
Tuneless as a quartertone. . . .

Remote your face seems, far away,
Beneath the ghostly water, Day,

That laps across you, as again
We move across the endless plain.

We are two ghosts today, each ghost
For ever wandering and lost ;

No yesterday and no tomorrow
Know we, neither joy nor sorrow,

For this is the hour when like a swan
The silence floats, so still and wan

That bird-songs, silver masks to hide
Strange faces, now all sounds have died,

Find but a curdled sheepskin flower
Embodied in this ghostly hour.

20. *Bells of Grey Crystal*

BELLS of grey crystal
Break on each bough —
The swans' breath will mist all
The cold airs now.
Like tall pagodas
Two people go,
Trail their long codas
Of talk through the snow.
Lonely are these
And lonely am I. . . .
The clouds, grey Chinese geese
Sleek through the sky.

21. *When Cold December*

WHEN cold December
Froze to grisamber
The jangling bells on the sweet
    rose-trees —
Then fading slow
And furred is the snow
As the almond's sweet husk —
And smelling like musk.
The snow amygdaline
Under the eglantine
Where bristling stars shine
Like a gilt porcupine —
The snow confesses
The little Princesses
On their small chioppines
Dance under the orpines.
See the casuistries
Of their slant fluttering eyes —
Gilt as the zodiac
(Dancing Herodiac).
Only the snow slides
Like gilded myrrh —
From the rose-branches — hides
Rose-roots that stir.

22. *Fox Trot*

OLD

Sir

Faulk,

Tall as a stork,

Before the honeyed fruits of dawn were ripe, would walk,

And stalk with a gun

The reynard-coloured sun,

Among the pheasant-feathered corn the unicorn has torn,
 forlorn the

Smock-faced sheep

Sit

  And

     Sleep ;

Periwigged as William and Mary, weep . . .

' Sally, Mary, Mattie, what's the matter, why cry ? '

The huntsman and the reynard-coloured sun and I sigh ;

' Oh, the nursery-maid Meg

With a leg like a peg

Chased the feathered dreams like hens, and when they
 laid an egg

In the sheepskin

Meadows

Where

The serene King James would steer

Horse and hounds, then he

From the shade of a tree

Picked it up as spoil to boil for nursery tea,' said the
 mourners. In the

Corn, towers strain,

Feathered tall as a crane,

And whistling down the feathered rain, old Noah goes
 again —

An old dull mome

With a head like a pome,

Seeing the world as a bare egg,

Laid by the feathered air ; Meg

Would beg three of these
For the nursery teas
Of Japhet, Shem, and Ham ; she gave it
Underneath the trees,
Where the boiling
Water
   Hissed,
Like the goose-king's feathered daughter — kissed
Pot and pan and copper kettle
Put upon their proper mettle,
Lest the Flood — the Flood — the Flood begin again
    through these !

23. *Polka*

' " TRA la la la —
            See me dance the polka,"
Said Mr. Wagg like a bear,
" With my top-hat
And my whiskers that —
(Tra la la la) trap the Fair.

Where the waves seem chiming haycocks
I dance the polka ; there
Stand Venus' children in their gay frocks, —
Maroon and marine, — and stare

To see me fire my pistol
Through the distance blue as my coat ;
Like Wellington, Byron, the Marquis of Bristol,
Buzbied great trees float.

While the wheezing hurdy-gurdy
Of the marine wind blows me
To the tune of 'Annie Rooney', sturdy,
Over the sheafs of the sea ;

And bright as a seedsman's packet
With zinnias, candytufts chill,
Is Mrs. Marigold's jacket
As she gapes at the inn door still,

Where at dawn in the box of the sailor,
Blue as the decks of the sea,
Nelson awoke, crowed like the cocks,
Then back to the dust sank he.

And Robinson Crusoe
Rues so
The bright and foxy beer, —
But he finds fresh isles in a Negress' smiles, —
The poxy doxy dear,

As they watch me dance the polka,"
Said Mr. Wagg like a bear,
" In my top-hat and my whiskers that, —
Tra la la la, trap the Fair.

Tra la la la la —
Tra la la la la —
Tra la la la la la la la
              La
              La
              La ! " '

24. Mazurka

'God Pluto is a kindly man ; the children ran :
" Come help us with the games our dames ban."
He drinks his beer and builds his forge ; as red as George
The Fourth his face is that the flames tan.
Like baskets of ripe fruit the bird-songs' oaten flutes
All honeyed yellow sound in air, where
Among the hairy leaves fall trills of dew and sheaves
Are tasting of fresh green anew. Flare
His flames as tall
As Windsor Castle, all
Balmoral was not higher ;
Like feathered masks and peas in pots and castled trees
Walled gardens of the seas, the flames seemed all of these.
As red and green as
Petticoats of queans
Among the flowering
Beans they
Bloom. . . . " Come rest and be !
I care for nobody, not I, the world can be and no one
        cares for me ! "
In the lane, Hattie
Meddlesome Mattie,
Suddenly quarrel.
Flames like Balmoral
From feathered doxies
Blow up like boxes,
Cram full of matches —
Each yells and scratches.
Flames green and yellow spirt from lips and eyes and skirt,
The leaves like chestnut horses' ears rear.
Ladies, though my forge has made me red as George
The Fourth, such flames we know not here, dear ! '

25. Jodelling Song

'WE bear velvet cream,
Green and babyish
Small leaves seem; each stream
Horses' tails that swish,

And the chimes remind
Us of sweet birds singing,
Like the jangling bells
On rose-trees ringing.

Man must say farewell
To parents now,
And to William Tell,
And Mrs. Cow.

Man must say farewells
To storks and Bettes,
And to roses' bells,
And statuettes.

Forests white and black
In spring are blue
With forget-me-nots,
And to lovers true

Still the sweet bird begs
And tries to cozen
Them: " Buy angels' eggs
Sold by the dozen."

Gone are clouds like inns
On the gardens' brinks,
And the mountain djinns, —
Ganymede sells drinks;

While the days seem grey
And his heart of ice,

Grey as chamois, or
The edelweiss,

And the mountain streams
Like cowbells sound —
Tirra lirra, drowned
In the waiter's dreams

Who has gone beyond
The forest waves,
While his true and fond
Ones seek their graves.'

26. Waltz

DAISY and Lily,
Lazy and silly,
Walk by the shore of the wan grassy sea, —
Talking once more 'neath a swan-bosomed tree.
Rose castles,
Tourelles,
Those bustles
Where swells
Each foam-bell of ermine,
They roam and determine
What fashions have been and what fashions will be, —
What tartan leaves born,
What crinolines worn.
By Queen Thetis,
Pelisses
Of tarlatine blue,
Like the thin plaided leaves that the castle crags grew;
Or velours d'Afrande :
On the water-gods' land
Her hair seemed gold trees on the honey-cell sand
When the thickest gold spangles, on deep water seen,
Were like twanging guitar and like cold mandoline,
And the nymphs of great caves,
With hair like gold waves,
Of Venus, wore tarlatine.
Louise and Charlottine
(Boreas' daughters)
And the nymphs of deep waters,
The nymph Taglioni, Grisi the ondine,
Wear plaided Victoria and thin Clementine
Like the crinolined waterfalls ;
Wood-nymphs wear bonnets, shawls,
Elegant parasols
Floating are seen.
The Amazons wear balzarine of jonquille
Beside the blond lace of a deep-falling rill ;

Through glades like a nun
They run from and shun
The enormous and gold-rayed rustling sun ;
And the nymphs of the fountains
Descend from the mountains
Like elegant willows
On their deep barouche pillows,
In cashmere Alvandar, barège Isabelle,
Like bells of bright water from clearest wood-well.
Our élégantes favouring bonnets of blond,
The stars in their apiaries,
Sylphs in their aviaries,
Seeing them, spangle these, and the sylphs fond
From their aviaries fanned
With each long fluid hand
The manteaux espagnols,
Mimic the waterfalls
Over the long and the light summer land.

    .   .   .   .

So Daisy and Lily,
Lazy and silly,
Walk by the shore of the wan grassy sea,
Talking once more 'neath a swan-bosomed tree.
Rose castles,
Tourelles,
Those bustles !
Mourelles
Of the shade in their train follow.
Ladies, how vain, — hollow, —
Gone is the sweet swallow, —
Gone, Philomel !

27. *Popular Song*

FOR CONSTANT LAMBERT

LILY O'GRADY,
Silly and shady,
Longing to be
A lazy lady,
Walked by the cupolas, gables in the
Lake's Georgian stables,
In a fairy tale like the heat intense,
And the mist in the woods when across the fence
The children gathering strawberries
Are changed by the heat into Negresses,
Though their fair hair
Shines there
Like gold-haired planets, Calliope, Io,
Pomona, Antiope, Echo, and Clio.
Then Lily O'Grady,
Silly and shady,
Sauntered along like a
Lazy lady:
Beside the waves' haycocks her gown with tucks
Was of satin the colour of shining green ducks,
And her fol-de-rol
Parasol
Was a great gold sun o'er the haycocks shining,
But she was a Negress black as the shade
That time on the brightest lady laid.
Then a satyr, dog-haired as trunks of trees,
Began to flatter, began to tease,
And she ran like the nymphs with golden foot
That trampled the strawberry, buttercup root,
In the thick gold dew as bright as the mesh
Of dead Panope's golden flesh,
Made from the music whence were born
Memphis and Thebes in the first hot morn,
— And ran, to wake
In the lake,

Where the water-ripples seem hay to rake.
And Adeline,
Charlottine,
Round rose-bubbling Victorine,
And the other fish
Express a wish
For mastic mantles and gowns with a swish ;
And bright and slight as the posies
Of buttercups and of roses,
And buds of the wild wood-lilies
They chase her, as frisky as fillies.
The red retriever-haired satyr
Can whine and tease her and flatter,
But Lily O'Grady,
Silly and shady,
In the deep shade is a lazy lady ;
Now Pompey's dead, Homer's read,
Heliogabalus lost his head,
And shade is on the brightest wing,
And dust forbids the bird to sing.

28. By the Lake

Across the flat and the pastel snow
Two people go. . . . 'And do you remember
When last we wandered this shore?' . . . 'Ah no!
For it is cold-hearted December.'
'Dead, the leaves that like asses' ears hung on the trees
When last we wandered and squandered joy here;
Now Midas your husband will listen for these
Whispers — these tears for joy's bier.'
And as they walk, they seem tall pagodas;
And all the ropes let down from the cloud
Ring the hard cold bell-buds upon the trees — codas
Of overtones, ecstasies, grown for love's shroud.

29. *Dark Song*

THE fire was furry as a bear
And the flames purr . . .
The brown bear rambles in his chain
Captive to cruel men
Through the dark and hairy wood.
The maid sighed, ' All my blood
Is animal.   They thought I sat
Like a household cat ;
But through the dark woods rambled I . . .
Oh, if my blood would die ! '
The fire had a bear's fur ;
It heard and knew. . . .
The dark earth furry as a bear,
Grumbled too !

30. The Cat

His kind velvet bonnet
Warmly lies upon
My weary lap, and on it
My tears run.

The black and furry fire
Sinks low, and like the dire
Sound of charring coal, the black
Cat's whirring back.

On the bare bough
A few blue threadbare leaves,
A few blue plaided leaves grow
Like mornings and like eves.

Scotch bonnet, bonny,
Lying on my gown,
The fire was once, hey nonny,
A battelmented town;

And every morn I build
Those steep castles there,
And every night they're ruined
Like the boughs bare.

And nothing doth remain,
Kind bonny, but my pain,
And night and morn, like boughs
    they're bare,
With nobody to care.

31. *Water Party*

Rose Castles
Those bustles
Beneath parasols seen !
Fat blondine pearls
Rondine curls
Seem. Bannerols sheen
The brave tartan
Waves' Spartan
Domes (Crystal Palaces)
Where like fallacies
Die the calices
Of the water-flowers green.
Said the Dean
To the Queen,
On the tartan wave seen :
' Each chilly
White lily
Has her own crinoline,
And the seraphs recline
On divans divine
In a smooth seventh heaven of
        polished pitch-pine.'
Castellated,
Related
To castles the waves lean
Balmoral-like ;
They quarrel, strike
(As round as a rondine)
With sharp towers
The water-flowers
And, floating between,
Each châtelaine
In the battle slain —
Laid low by the Ondine.

32. *The Satyr in the Periwig*

THE Satyr Scarabombadon
Pulled periwig and breeches on :
' Grown old and stiff, this modern dress
Adds monstrously to my distress.
The gout within a hoofen heel
Is very hard to bear ; I feel
When crushed into a buckled shoe
The twinge will be redoubled, too.
And when I walk in gardens green
And, weeping, think on what has been,
Then wipe one eye — the other sees
The plums and cherries on the trees.
Small bird-quick women pass me by
With sleeves that flutter airily,
And baskets blazing like a fire
With laughing fruits of my desire :
Plums sunburnt as the King of Spain,
Gold-cheeked as any Nubian,
With strawberries all goldy-freckled,
Pears fat as thrushes and as speckled.
Pursue them ? . . . Yes, and squeeze a tear !
" Please spare poor Satyr one, my dear ! "
" Be off, sir ! Go and steal your own ! "
— Alas, poor Scarabombadon,
Trees rend his ruffles, stretch a twig,
Tear off a satyr's periwig ! '

33. I Do Like to be Beside the Seaside

WHEN

Don

Pasquito arrived at the seaside
Where the donkey's hide tide brayed, he
Saw the banditto Jo in a black cape
Whose slack shape waved like the sea —
Thetis wrote a treatise noting wheat is silver
    like the sea; the lovely cheat is sweet as
    foam; Erotis notices that she
              Will
              Steal
              The
Wheat-king's luggage, like Babel
Before the League of Nations grew —
So Jo put the luggage and the label
In the pocket of Flo the Kangaroo.
Through trees like rich hotels that bode
Of dreamless ease fled she,
Carrying the load and goading the road
Through the marine scene to the sea.
' Don Pasquito, the road is eloping
With your luggage, though heavy and large;
You must follow and leave your moping
Bride to my guidance and charge ! '

When

Don

Pasquito returned from the road's end,
Where vanilla-coloured ladies ride
From Sevilla, his mantilla'd bride and young
    friend
Were forgetting their mentor and guide.
For the lady and her friend from Le Touquet
In the very shady trees upon the sand

Were plucking a white satin bouquet
Of foam, while the sand's brassy band
Blared in the wind.   Don Pasquito
Hid where the leaves drip with sweet . . .
But a word stung him like a mosquito . . .
For what they hear, they repeat !

34. *Hornpipe*

SAILORS come
To the drum
Out of Babylon ;
　Hobby-horses
Foam, the dumb
Sky rhinoceros-glum

Watched the courses of the breakers' rocking-horses and
　　with Glaucis,
Lady Venus on the settee of the horsehair sea !
Where Lord Tennyson in laurels wrote a gloria free,
In a borealic iceberg came Victoria ; she
Knew Prince Albert's tall memorial took the colours of
　　the floreal
And the borealic iceberg ; floating on they see
New-arisen Madam Venus for whose sake from far
Came the fat and zebra'd emperor from Zanzibar
Where like golden bouquets lay far Asia, Africa, Cathay,
All laid before that shady lady by the fibroid Shah.
Captain Fracasse stout as any water-butt came, stood
With Sir Bacchus both a-drinking the black tarr'd grapes'
　　blood
Plucked among the tartan leafage
By the furry wind whose grief age
Could not wither — like a squirrel with a gold star-nut.
Queen Victoria sitting shocked upon the rocking-horse
Of a wave said to the Laureate, ' This minx of course
Is as sharp as any lynx and blacker-deeper than the drinks
　　and quite as
Hot as any hottentot, without remorse !
　　　　　　　For the minx,'
　　　　　　　　　　Said she,
　　　　　' And the drinks,
　　　　　　　　　　You can see
Are hot as any hottentot and not the goods for me ! '

35. Scotch Rhapsody

' Do not take a bath in Jordan,

                              Gordon,

On the holy Sabbath, on the peaceful day ! '
Said the huntsman, playing on his old bagpipe,
Boring to death the pheasant and the snipe —
Boring the ptarmigan and grouse for fun —
Boring them worse than a nine-bore gun.
Till the flaxen leaves where the prunes are ripe
Heard the tartan wind a-droning in the pipe,
And they heard MacPherson say :
' Where do the waves go ?   What hotels
Hide their bustles and their gay ombrelles ?
And would there be room ? — Would there be *room* ?
    Would there be room for me ? '
There is a hotel at Ostend
Cold as the wind, without an end,
Haunted by ghostly poor relations
Of Bostonian conversations
(Bagpipes rotting through the walls).
And there the pearl-ropes fall like shawls
With a noise like marine waterfalls.
And ' Another little drink wouldn't do us any harm '
Pierces through the Sabbatical calm.
And that is the place for me !
So do not take a bath in Jordon,

                              Gordon,

On the holy Sabbath, on the peaceful day —
Or you'll never go to heaven, Gordon MacPherson,
And speaking purely as a private person
That is the place — *that* is the place — that is the *place* for
    me !

36. Something Lies Beyond the Scene

SOMETHING lies beyond the scene, the encre de chine
    marine obscene
Horizon
  In
    Hell
Black as a bison
See the tall black Aga on the sofa in the alga mope, his
Bell-rope
Moustache (clear as a great bell !)
Waves in eighteen-eighty
Bustles
Come
Late with tambourines of
Rustling
Foam.
They answer to the names
Of ancient dames and shames, and
Only call horizons their home.
Coldly wheeze (Chinese as these black-armoured fleas
    that dance) the breezes
Seeking for horizons
Wide ; from her orisons
In her wide
Vermilion
Pavilion
By the seaside
The doors clang open and hide
Where the wind died,
Nothing but the Princess
Cockatrice
Lean
Dancing a caprice
To the wind's tambourine.

37. Sir Beelzebub

WHEN
Sir
Beelzebub called for his syllabub in the hotel in Hell
   Where Proserpine first fell,
Blue as the gendarmerie were the waves of the sea,
   (Rocking and shocking the barmaid).

Nobody comes to give him his rum but the
Rim of the sky hippopotamus-glum
Enhances the chances to bless with a benison
Alfred Lord Tennyson crossing the bar laid
With cold vegetation from pale deputations
Of temperance workers (all signed In Memoriam)
Hoping with glory to trip up the Laureate's feet,
   (Moving in classical metres) . . .

Like Balaclava, the lava came down from the
Roof, and the sea's blue wooden gendarmerie
Took them in charge while Beelzebub roared for his rum.
  . . . None of them come !

MARINE

∽

1. *Why?*

Noah's granddaughter
Sat on his knee ;
Her questions like water
Gushed ceaselessly.

Her hair's gilded wool
Seems the sun's tent ;
Her mouth, a grape golden-cool,
Shows through the rent.

Noah's replies
Are all one hears ;
And the small ripples rise
Like listening ass-ears.

' That young giraffe ?
His proud elevation
Raises a laugh
To the height of quotation.' . . .

' The camel's face
Is like Mrs. Grundy's ;
He makes that grimace
At working on Sundays.'

' The kangaroo, chaste,
Of Victorian complexion,
Wears at her waist
Each pledge of affection.'

' The trunk of the elephant
Is not a box,
The cock's gilded crown can't
Frighten the fox.'

    .   .   .   .

The sea-gods talk Greek . . .
But they learn the word ' why '!
Like leaves of the palm,
Their beards, gilded and dry,

Are spreading upon
The blue marble Pompeii
Whose temples are gone
(So the sea seems) ; Aglae

Asks ' What for ? ' . . . The waves' door
Begins to slam.
Like water the questions pour.
Noah said, ' Damn ! '

2. *Fireworks*

PINK faces (worlds or flowers or seas or stars) —
You all alike are patterned with hot bars

Of coloured light ; and, falling where I stand,
The sharp and rainbow splinters from the band

Seem fireworks, splinters of the Infinite
(Glitter of leaves the echoes).   And the night

Will weld this dust of bright Infinity
To forms that we may touch and call and see :

Pink pyramids of faces : tulip-trees
Spilling night perfumes on the terraces.

The music, blond airs waving like a sea,
Draws in its vortex of immensity

The new-awakened flower-strange hair and eyes
Of crowds beneath the floating summer skies.

And against the silk pavilions of the sea
I watch the people move incessantly

Vibrating, petals blown from flower-hued stars
Beneath the music-fireworks' waving bars ;

So all seems indivisible, at one :
The flow of hair, the flowers, the seas that run —

A coloured floating music of the night
Through the pavilions of the Infinite.

3. Switchback

By the blue wooden sea,
Curling capriciously,
Coral and amber grots
(Cherries and apricots),
Ribbons of noisy heat,
Binding them head and feet,
Horses as fat as plums
Snort as each bumpkin comes :
Giggles like towers of glass
(Pink and blue spirals) pass ;
Oh, how the Vacancy
Laughed at them rushing by !
' Turn again, flesh and brain,
Only yourselves again !
How far above the Ape,
Differing in each shape,
You with your regular,
Meaningless circles are ! '

4. *Minstrels*

BESIDE the sea, metallic bright
And sequined with the noisy light,
Duennas slowly promenade
Each like a patch of sudden shade ;

While colours like a parokeet
Shrill loudly to the chattering heat,
And gowns as white as innocence
With sudden sweetness take the sense.

Those crested paladins the waves
Are sighing to their tawny slaves
The sands, where, orange-turban'd, stand, —
Opaque black gems — the Negro band !

While in the purring greenery
The crowd moves like a tropic sea —
The people, sparkles from the heat
That dies from ennui at our feet.

The instruments that snore like flies
Seem mourners at Time's obsequies.
The sun, a pulse's beat, inflates
And with the band coagulates :

' A thousand years seem but a day —
Time waits for no man, yet he'll stay
Bewildered when we cross this bar
Into the Unknown — there we are ! '

Eternity and Time commence
To merge amid the somnolence
Of winding circles, bend on bend,
With no beginning and no end,

Down which they chase queer tunes that gape
Till they come close, — then just escape !
But though Time's barriers are defied
They never seem quite satisfied.

The crowds, bright sparks struck out by Time,
Pass, touch each other, never chime :
Each soul a separate entity —
Some past, some present, some to be :

But now, an empty blot of white,
Beneath the senseless shocks of light
Flashed by the tunes that cannot thrill
The nerves. Oh ! Time is hard to kill !

5. Pedagogues

THE air is like a jarring bell
That jangles words it cannot spell,
And black as Fate, the iron trees
Stretch thirstily to catch the breeze.

The fat leaves pat the shrinking air;
The hot sun's patronising stare
Rouses the stout flies from content
To some small show of sentiment.

Beneath the terrace shines the green
Metallic strip of sea, and sheen
Of sands, where folk flaunt parrot-bright
With rags and tags of noisy light.

The brass band's snorting stabs the sky
And tears the yielding vacancy —
The imbecile and smiling blue
Until fresh meaning trickles through;

And slowly we perambulate
With spectacles that concentrate,
In one short hour, Eternity,
In one small lens, Infinity.

With children, our primeval curse,
We overrun the universe —
Beneath the giddy lights of noon,
White as a tired August moon.

The air is like a jarring bell
That jangles words it cannot spell,
And black as Fate, the iron trees
Stretch thirstily to catch the breeze.

6. *Portrait of a Barmaid*

METALLIC waves of people jar
Through crackling green toward the bar,

Where on the tables, chattering white,
The sharp drinks quarrel with the light.

Those coloured muslin blinds, the smiles,
Shroud wooden faces ; and at whiles

They splash like a thin water (you
Yourself reflected in their hue).

The conversations, loud and bright,
Seem spinal bars of shunting light

In firework-spirting greenery.
O complicate machinery

For building Babel ! Iron crane
Beneath your hair, that blue-ribbed mane

In noise and murder like the sea
Without its mutability !

Outside the bar, where jangling heat
Seems out of tune and off the beat,

A concertina's glycerine
Exudes and mirrors in the green

Your soul, pure glucose edged with hints
Of tentative and half-soiled tints.

7. *Fantasia for Mouth-Organ*

' I HAD a mother-in-
Law ; no other kin
Could be so kind,' said
He.
' She wrung me on the mangle
When the hot sun's jangle
Bent the North Pole to South, and
The
Wind hyperborean
Dried the marmorean
Wash for a nominal
Fee.
But the wheezing wind's harmonium
Seemed an encomium
Of life when one is
Free,
And as life was getting barrener
I set out as a mariner —
The hero of this epopee.
I sailed on botanic
Gardens oceanic
Where siren-birds sip Bohea —
Past the lodging-houses lean
Where like oozing glycerine
The ozone drips ; and the wee
Horses age had tattered
Flap along the battered
Platform grasses (green as tea).
But the ship and the narrator
Had traversed the equator
Before I knew that Fate's decree
Saw fit to decide
The mother of my bride
To companion the refugee.
The South Pole floating past
Was taller than a mast —

The North Pole and the South congree
O'er the ocean of red horsehair
(Unknown to any corsair)
In the snow's cold ivory —
All smooth as a japonica,
In sound like a harmonica,
Where the humming-bird quick lights flee
To the polar sea's pavilion.
We paid for twenty million
Red velvet drinks with one rupee,
And in the central hulk
My mother-in-law's bulk
Sat reared upon the snow's settee.
Her jangling jet bonnet
(With the polar lights upon it)
A cathedral seemed, whose key
Was her nose, a horny cockatrice
Goggling out to mock at these
Sights ; for each degree
Of the North Pole and the South
Had for bonnet, seas uncouth —
Electric fish a-curl like a trochee
Are their lithe and writhing locks.
The redskins came in flocks
And pelted hairy fruitage from the tree.
Then we floated back toward
The equator ; flat as sward
And green as grass the water seemed to be.
Like a dulcimer or zither
Was the tinkling and the glitter
Of the icebergs as they floated aerily,
For on water soft as calices
That open, Crystal Palaces
Those bergs of ice seemed ; in their apogee
Were the queerest, brightest pictures —
Exhibitions with the strictures
Vanished from the Infinite ; and we
Then traversed the equator.

And it was either Fate or
Whatever other Power is our pawnee —
But when natives with smooth joints
And features like gilt points
Of the starfish moon came dancing a boree,
When they saw
My mother-in-law
They decided not to tackle
Me !
She is tough as the armorian
Leather that the saurian
Sun spreads over the
Sea —
So she saved my life,
Did the mother of my wife —
Who is more than a mother to
Me ! '

8. *Myself in the Merry-Go-Round*

THE giddy sun's kaleidoscope,
The pivot of a switchback world,
Is tied to it by many a rope :
The people (flaunting streamers), furled
Metallic banners of the seas,
The giddy sun's kaleidoscope
Casts colours on the face of these :
Cosmetics of Eternity,
And powders faces blue as death ;
Beneath the parasols we see
Gilt faces tarnished by sea-breath,
And crawling like the foam, each horse
Beside the silken tents of sea
In whirlpool-circles takes his course.
Huge houses, humped like camels, chase
The wooden horses' ceaseless bound ;
The throbbing whirring sun that drags
The streets upon its noisy round,
With tramways chasing them in vain,
Projects in coloured cubes each face —
Then shatters them upon our brain.
The house-fronts hurl them back ; they jar
Upon cross-currents of the noise :
Like atoms of my soul they are,
They shake the body's equipoise —
A clothes-line for the Muse to fly
(So thin and jarred and angular)
Her rags of tattered finery.
Beneath the heat the trees' sharp hue —
A ceaseless whirr, metallic-green —
Sounds like a gimlet shrilling through
The mind, to reach the dazzling sheen
Of meanings life can not decide :
Then words set all awry, and you
Are left upon the other side.
Our senses, each a wooden horse

We paint, till they appear to us
Like life, and then queer strangers course
In our place on each Pegasus.
The very heat seems but to be
The product of some man-made force —
Steam from the band's machinery.
The heat is in a thousand rags
Reverberant with sound, whose dry
Frayed ends we never catch, like tags
Of an unfinished entity ;
And like a stretched accordion
The houses throb with heat, and flags
Of smoke are tunes light plays upon.
The band's kaleidoscopic whirr
Tears up those jarring threads of heat,
The crowds : plush mantles seem to purr ;
Crustacean silk gowns take the beat
From houses ; each reverberates
From this vitality and stir
The giddy heat still acerbates.
And in the swirling restaurant
Where liqueurs at perpetual feud
Dispute for sequined lights and taunt
Hot leaves, our dusty souls exude
Their sentiments, while scraps of sense
Float inward from the band and flaunt —
Disturb the general somnolence.

THE DRUNKARD

THIS black tower drinks the blinding light.
Strange windows, livid white,

Tremble beneath the curse of God.
Yet living weeds still nod

To the huge sun, a devil's eye
That tracks the souls that die.

The clock beats like the heart of Doom
Within the narrow room ;

And whispering with some ghastly air
The curtains float and stir.

But still she never speaks a word ;
I think she hardly heard

When I with reeling footsteps came
And softly spoke her name.

But yet she does not sleep.   Her eyes
Still watch in wide surprise

The thirsty knife that pitied her ;
But those lids never stir,

Though creeping Fear still gnaws like pain
The hollow of her brain.

She must have some sly plan, the cheat,
To lie so still.   The beat

That once throbbed like a muffled drum
With fear to hear me come

Now never sounds when I creep nigh.
Oh, she was always sly!

And if, to spite her, I dared steal
Behind her bed and feel

With fumbling fingers for her heart . . .
Ere I could touch the smart,

Once more wild shriek on shriek would tear
The dumb and shuddering air. . . .

Yet still she never speaks to me.
She only smiles to see

How in dark corners secret-sly
New-born Eternity,

All spider-like, doth spin and cast
Strange threads to hold Time fast.

COLONEL FANTOCK

TO OSBERT AND SACHEVERELL SITWELL

THUS spoke the lady underneath the trees :
I was a member of a family
Whose legend was of hunting — (all the rare
And unattainable brightness of the air) —
A race whose fabled skill in falconry
Was used on the small song-birds and a winged
And blinded Destiny. . . . I think that only
Winged ones know the highest eyrie is so lonely.
There in a land, austere and elegant,
The castle seemed an arabesque in music ;
We moved in an hallucination born
Of silence, which like music gave us lotus
To eat, perfuming lips and our long eyelids
As we trailed over the sad summer grass,
Or sat beneath a smooth and mournful tree.

And Time passed, suavely, imperceptibly.

But Dagobert and Peregrine and I
Were children then ; we walked like shy gazelles
Among the music of the thin flower-bells.
And life still held some promise, — never ask
Of what, — but life seemed less a stranger, then,
Than ever after in this cold existence.
I always was a little outside life —
And so the things we touch could comfort me ;
I loved the shy dreams we could hear and see —
For I was like one dead, like a small ghost,
A little cold air wandering and lost.

All day within the straw-roofed arabesque
Of the towered castle and the sleepy gardens wandered
We ; those delicate paladins the waves
Told us fantastic legends that we pondered.

And the soft leaves were breasted like a dove,
Crooning old mournful tales of untrue love.

When night came, sounding like the growth of trees,
My great-grandmother bent to say good-night,
And the enchanted moonlight seemed transformed
Into the silvery tinkling of an old
And gentle music-box that played a tune
Of Circean enchantments and far seas ;
Her voice was lulling like the splash of these.
When she had given me her good-night kiss,
There, in her lengthened shadow, I saw this
Old military ghost with mayfly whiskers, —
Poor harmless creature, blown by the cold wind,
Boasting of unseen unreal victories
To a harsh unbelieving world unkind :
For all the battles that this warrior fought
Were with cold poverty and helpless age —
His spoils were shelters from the winter's rage.
And so for ever through his braggart voice,
Through all that martial trumpet's sound, his soul
Wept with a little sound so pitiful,
Knowing that he is outside life for ever
With no one that will warm or comfort him. . . .
He is not even dead, but Death's buffoon
On a bare stage, a shrunken pantaloon.
His military banner never fell,
Nor his account of victories, the stories
Of old apocryphal misfortunes, glories
Which comforted his heart in later life
When he was the Napoleon of the schoolroom
And all the victories he gained were over
Little boys who would not learn to spell.

All day within the sweet and ancient gardens
He had my childish self for audience —
Whose body flat and strange, whose pale straight hair
Made me appear as though I had been drowned —
(We all have the remote air of a legend) —
And Dagobert my brother whose large strength,
Great body and grave beauty still reflect
The Angevin dead kings from whom we spring ;
And sweet as the young tender winds that stir
In thickets when the earliest flower-bells sing
Upon the boughs, was his just character ;
And Peregrine the youngest with a naïve
Shy grace like a faun's, whose slant eyes seemed
The warm green light beneath eternal boughs.
His hair was like the fronds of feathers, life
In him was changing ever, springing fresh
As the dark songs of birds . . . the furry warmth
And purring sound of fires was in his voice
Which never failed to warm and comfort me.

And there were haunted summers in Troy Park
When all the stillness budded into leaves ;
We listened, like Ophelia drowned in blond
And fluid hair, beneath stag-antlered trees ;
Then, in the ancient park the country-pleasant
Shadows fell as brown as any pheasant,
And Colonel Fantock seemed like one of these.
Sometimes for comfort in the castle kitchen
He drowsed, where with a sweet and velvet lip
The snapdragons within the fire
Of their red summer never tire.
And Colonel Fantock liked our company ;
For us he wandered over each old lie,
Changing the flowering hawthorn, full of bees,
Into the silver helm of Hercules,
For us defended Troy from the top stair
Outside the nursery, when the calm full moon
Was like the sound within the growth of trees.

But then came one cruel day in deepest June,
When pink flowers seemed a sweet Mozartian tune,
And Colonel Fantock pondered o'er a book.
A gay voice like a honeysuckle nook —
So sweet, — said, ' It is Colonel Fantock's age
Which makes him babble.' . . . Blown by winter's rage
The poor old man then knew his creeping fate,
The darkening shadow that would take his sight
And hearing ; and he thought of his saved pence
Which scarce would rent a grave. . . . That youthful voice
Was a dark bell which ever clanged ' Too late ' —
A creeping shadow that would steal from him
Even the little boys who would not spell —
His only prisoners. . . . On that June day
Cold Death had taken his first citadel.

THREE RUSTIC ELEGIES

∽

1. The Little Ghost Who Died for Love

Deborah Churchill, born in 1678, was hanged in 1708 for shielding her lover in a duel. His opponent was killed, her lover fled to Holland, and she was hanged in his stead, according to the law of the time. The chronicle said, ' Though she died at peace with God, this malefactor could never understand the justice of her sentence, to the last moment of her life.'

' FEAR not, O maidens, shivering
As bunches of the dew-drenched leaves
In the calm moonlight . . . it is the cold sends quivering
My voice, a little nightingale that grieves.

Now Time beats not, and dead Love is forgotten . . .
The spirit too is dead and dank and rotten,

And I forget the moment when I ran
Between my lover and the sworded man —

Blinded with terror lest I lose his heart.
The sworded man dropped, and I saw depart

Love and my lover and my life . . . he fled
And I was strung and hung upon the tree.
It is so cold now that my heart is dead
And drops through time . . . night is too dark to see

Him still. . . . But it is spring ; upon the fruit-boughs
        of your lips,
Young maids, the dew like India's splendour drips ;

Pass by among the strawberry beds, and pluck the berries
Cooled by the silver moon ; pluck boughs of cherries

That seem the lovely lucent coral bough
(From streams of starry milk those branches grow)
That Cassiopeia feeds with her faint light,
Like Æthiopia ever jewelled bright.

Those lovely cherries do enclose
Deep in their sweet hearts the silver snows,

And the small budding flowers upon the trees
Are filled with sweetness like the bags of bees.

Forget my fate . . . but I, a moonlight ghost,
Creep down the strawberry paths and seek the lost

World, the apothecary at the Fair.
I, Deborah, in my long cloak of brown
Like the small nightingale that dances down
The cherried boughs, creep to the doctor's bare
Booth . . . cold as ivy is the air,

And, where I stand, the brown and ragged light
Holds something still beyond, hid from my sight.

Once, plumaged like the sea, his swanskin head
Had wintry white quills . . . " Hearken to the Dead . . .
I was a nightingale, but now I croak
Like some dark harpy hidden in night's cloak,
Upon the walls ; among the Dead, am quick ;
Oh, give me medicine, for the world is sick ;
Not medicines, planet-spotted like fritillaries,
For country sins and old stupidities,
Nor potions you may give a country maid
When she is lovesick . . . love in earth is laid,

Grown dead and rotten " . . . so I sank me down,
Poor Deborah in my long cloak of brown.
Though cockcrow marches, crying of false dawns,
Shall bury my dark voice, yet still it mourns
Among the ruins, — for it is not I
But this old world, is sick and soon must die ! '

2. *The Hambone and the Heart*

TO PAVEL TCHELITCHEW

A Girl speaks :

HERE in this great house in the barrack square,
The plump and heart-shaped flames all stare
Like silver empty hearts in wayside shrines.
No flame warms ever, shines,
Nor may I ever tire.

Outside, the dust of all the dead
Thick on the ground is spread,
Covering the tinsel flowers
And pretty dove-quick hours.

O dust of all the dead, my heart has known
That terrible Gehenna of the bone
Deserted by the flesh, — with Death alone !

Could we foretell the worm within the heart,
That holds the households and the parks of heaven,
Could we foretell that land was only earth,
Would it be worth the pain of death and birth,
Would it be worth the soul from body riven ?

For here, my sight, my sun, my sense,
In my gown white as innocence,
I walked with you. Ah, that my sun
Loved my heart less than carrion !

Alas ! I dreamed that the bare heart could feed
One who with death's corruption loved to breed, —
This Dead, who fell, that he might satisfy
The hungry grave's blind need, —

That Venus stinking of the Worm !
Deep in the grave, no passions storm :

181

The worm's a pallid thing to kiss !
She is the hungering grave that is

Not filled, that is not satisfied !
Not all the sunken Dead that lie
Corrupt there, chill her luxuries.

And fleet, and volatile her kiss,
For all the grave's eternities !
And soon another Dead shall slake
Her passion, till that dust, too, break.

Like little pigeons small dove-breasted flowers
Were cooing of far-off bird-footed showers,
My coral neck was pink as the young rose
Or like the sweet pink honey-wax that grows,
Or the fresh coral beams of clear moonlight,
Where leaves like small doves flutter from our sight.

Beneath the twisted rose-boughs of the heat
Our shadows walked like little foreigners,
Like small unhappy children dressed in mourning —
But could not understand what we were saying,
Nor could we understand their whispered warning.
There by the waterfalls we saw the Clown,
As tall as Heaven's golden town,
And in his hands, a Heart, and a Hambone
Pursued by loving vermin ; but deserted, lone,
The Heart cried to my own :

The Heart speaks :
Young girl, you dance and laugh to see
The thing that I have come to be.
Oh, once this heart was like your own !
Go, pray that yours may turn to stone.

This is the murdered heart of one
Who bore and loved an only son.

For him, I worked away mine eyes:
My starved breast could not still his cries.

My little lamb, of milk bereft . . .
My heart was all that I had left.
Ah, could I give thee this for food,
My lamb, thou knowest that I would.

Yet lovely was the summer light
Those days . . . I feel it through this night.
Once Judas had a childish kiss,
And still his mother knows but this.

He grew to manhood. Then one came,
False-hearted as Hell's blackest shame
To steal my child from me, and thrust
The soul I loved down to the dust.

Her hungry wicked lips were red
As that dark blood my son's hand shed;
Her eyes were black as Hell's own night;
Her ice-cold breast was winter-white.

I had put by a little gold
To bury me when I was cold.
That fangèd wanton kiss to buy,
My son's love willed that I should die.

The gold was hid beneath my bed, —
So little, and my weary head
Was all the guard it had. They lie
So quiet and still who soon must die.

He stole to kill me while I slept,
The little son who never wept,
But that I kissed his tears away
So fast, his weeping seemed but play.

So light his footfall.   Yet I heard
Its echo in my heart and stirred
From out my weary sleep to see
My child's face bending over me.

The wicked knife flashed serpent-wise,
Yet I saw nothing but his eyes
And heard one little word he said
Go echoing down among the Dead.

.   .   .   .   .

They say the Dead may never dream.
But yet I heard my pierced heart scream
His name within the dark.   They lie
Who say the Dead can ever die.

For in the grave I may not sleep,
For dreaming that I hear him weep.
And in the dark my dead hands grope
In search of him.   O barren hope !

I cannot draw his head to rest,
Deep down upon my wounded breast :
He gave the breast that fed him well
To suckle the small worms of Hell !

The little wicked thoughts that fed
Upon the weary helpless Dead,
They whispered o'er my broken heart, —
They struck their fangs deep in the smart.

' The child she bore with bloody sweat
And agony has paid his debt.
Through that bleak face the stark winds play,
The crows have chased his soul away, —

His body is a blackened rag
Upon the tree, — a monstrous flag,'

Thus one worm to the other saith.
Those slow mean servitors of Death,

They chuckling said : ' Your soul grown blind
With anguish, is the shrieking wind
That blows the flame that never dies
About his empty lidless eyes.'

I tore them from my heart, I said :
' The life-blood that my son's hand shed —
That from my broken heart outburst,
I'd give again to quench his thirst.

He did no sin.   But cold blind earth
The body was that gave him birth.
All mine, all mine the sin.   The love
I bore him was not deep enough.'

.   .   .   .   .

The Girl speaks :
O crumbling heart, I too, I too have known
The terrible Gehenna of the bone
Deserted by the flesh. . . . I too have wept
Through centuries, like the deserted bone,
To all the dust of all the Dead to fill
That place. . . . It would not be the dust I loved !

For underneath the lime-tree's golden town
Of Heaven, where he stood, the tattered Clown
Holding the screaming Heart and the Hambone,
You saw the Clown's thick hambone, life-pink carrion,
That Venus perfuming the summer air.
Old pigs, starved dogs, and long worms of the grave
Were rooting at it, nosing at it there :
Then you, my sun, left me and ran to it
Through pigs, dogs, grave-worms' ramparted tall waves.

.   .   .   .   .

I know that I must soon have the long pang
Of grave-worms in the heart. . . . You are so changed,
How shall I know you from the other long
Anguishing grave-worms ? I can but foretell
The worm where once the kiss clung, and that last less
    chasm-deep farewell.

3. *The Ghost Whose Lips were Warm*

FOR GEOFFREY GORER

' T. M., Esq., an old acquaintance of mine, hath assured me, that . . . after his first wife's death, as he lay in bed awake . . . his wife opened the Closet Door, and came into the Chamber by the Bed side, and looked upon him and stooped down and kissed him ; her Lips were warm, he fancied they would have been cold. He was about to have Embraced her, but was afraid it might have done him hurt. When she went from him, he asked her when he should see her again ? She turned about and smiled, but said nothing.' — *Miscellanies collected by John Aubrey, Esq. F.R.S.*, 1696.

' THE ice, weeping, breaks.
But my heart is underground.
And the ice of its dead tears melts never. Wakes
No sigh, no sound,

From where the dead lie close, as those above —
The young — lie in their first deep night of love,

When the spring nights are fiery with wild dew, and rest
Leaves on young leaves, and youthful breast on breast.

The dead lie soft in the first fire of spring
And through the eternal cold, they hear birds sing,

And smile as if the one long-treasured kiss
Had worn away their once-loved lips to this

Remembered smile — for there is always one
Kiss that we take to be our grave's long sun.

Once Time was but the beat of heart to heart ;
And one kiss burnt the imperfect woof apart

Of this dead world, and summer broke from this :
We built new worlds with one immortal kiss.

Sun of my life, she went to warm the dead,
And I must now go sunless in their stead.

They clothed a dead man in my dress. By day
He walks the earth, by night he rots away ;

So walks a dead man, waning, in my dress,
By black disastrous suns of death grown less,

Grown dim and shrunken, wax before a fire,
A shrunken apeish thing, blackened and dire.

This black disastrous sun yet hath no heat.
How shall I bear my heart without its beat,

My clay without its soul, my eternal bone
That cries to its deserting flesh, alone,

More cold than she is in her grave's long night,
That hath my heart for covering, warmth, and light !

.   .   .   .   .

But when she had been twelve months in her grave
She came where I lay in my bed : she gave

Her kiss. And oh, her lips were warm to me.
And so I feared it, dared not touch and see

If still her heart were warm . . . dust-dun, death-cold
Lips should be from death's night. I dared not hold

That heart that came warm from the grave . . . afraid,
I tore down all the earth of death, and laid

Its endless cold upon her heart. For this
Dead man in my dress dared not kiss

Her who laid by death's cold, lest I
Should feel it when she came to lie

Beside my heart. My dead love gave
Lips warm with love though in her grave.

I stole her kiss, the only light
She had to warm her eternal night.'

Note.—For later version of this, see 'One Day in Spring,' page 326.

THE MADNESS OF SAUL

Fragment

Semichorus I of Ethiopian Women

O VINEYARDS of the world, cry to the Dawn —
Great streams of light that water all the world
And flow like music in our veins, bring life
To those unborn. Fresh founts and waterways
Of the young light, flow down and lie like peace
Upon the upturned faces of the blind.
For all the winds and wings of the wide dark
Fan us to flame, and, Mother of the world,
I stand with hands upraised to the young Day.

Semichorus II

The Sun's wide wings have fanned our bodies black :
With eyelids like the flashing of a sword,
And lips like fire of flowers or frankincense,
We builded Day with our immortal kiss.
We bring thee flowers, some pale with unshed tears,
All lustrous with the echoes of the dawn
And perfumed with the light, or flame of flowers
As yellow as the hair of Iacchus —
They grew in palace portals of the Sun.
And these shall touch the eyelids of the moon
With slumber, fill with music the chill air.

Semichorus I

Oh, we are black because the heat hath kissed
Our lips, those heavy grapes, and laid a kiss
On eyelids like the chambers of the south
Wherefrom the sweet light drips for frankincense.

And we have brought you flowers — mounds of silver,
And full of chilly bubbles for the bees.

Semichorus II

We sat beside the rivers and we wept,
For we are black beneath the Sun's hot kiss.
The Sun hath left his tent and kissed our breasts
Till they were sweeter than the budding grapes.
The savour of our eyelids seemed the morn.
And then She came, the music of the air,
And all the old worlds died away like dew.

Semichorus I

We are the perfumed portals of the dawn,
We are the flowering vineyards of the Sun
That break in music, glorify the Lord.
Our heartstrings like the music of the suns
Echo across the splendour of the earth,
And Time, a fiery dew, upon our hair
Is shed and fades ; with lips and veins I cry —
Light fills me, light invades me, light is life.

(Enter Saul)

Semichorus II

I heard a cry that rustled through the day :
Broad rivers fanned by wings of many winds
Have such a sound. But then it died again.
And all night long I heard the tread of Doom.

Saul

Why have you slain the Sun ? He was my brother ;
He kills the one he loves. So brothers do.

Semichorus I

The Sun hath golden feet to crush our grapes :
But all the grapes of joy grew ripe too soon.

Saul

Flesh is but dew, it falls like summer rains.
She came, a fiery sun, to drain my life,
And she hath kissed me, melted up my veins.

(*Enter Atarah, Mother of Saul*)

Atarah

Behold me, broken on the wheel of light;
My footsteps are the tread of blinded Doom.

Chorus

Thy body reels as though some unheard wind,
Broken from Hell, blew on thee. What is this?

Atarah

Slain, slain, and by the hand of his own brother.

Chorus

Thy lips are red, but not with blood of fruits.

Atarah

I kissed my son. My lips shall wither now.

Chorus

And thou art clothed with trembling like the grass.

Atarah

My name is Madness, I whose face was light.
Thus I exhale from all the chasms of life,
Till heaven is broken into dust and dies.

Chorus

Queen, old age, clear and terrible as noon,
Thy face hath gathered darkness from the heavens.

Atarah

Pull down the heavens, seal mine eyes with night.
Oh, emptiness sifts endlessly, they rock, come down.

I had two eyes, and she has blinded them —
Two breasts to feed the world : she hacked them off.
These were my sons, twin-born, my roots of life :
And she has torn my roots ; I drift through space.

Saul

Ay, there is nothing left but silence now.
A cry went up, the weft of the world was riven,
Then silence filled my veins instead of blood.
She came, a snake, and stabbed my veins with love.
Her fangs grew in my blood. I killed my brother.

Atarah

You should have stabbed my womb, Saul, my son Saul.

Saul

Oh, that my tired body could find sleep
Once more within your dark womb, O my mother.

Atarah

The earth is drunken with my lamentation,
And night invades my veins and flows within
My face grown blind and featureless as heaven.
I would Time were a dew that fades away,
And life, a veil the hate of God has riven,
And this sad house of clay wherein I dwell
Were broken like the earth — were spilt as rain.
My tongue is changed to dust. I fain would weep,
Only mine eyelids withered when he died.

Chorus

Nay, thou art veiled with tears like some sad river.

Atarah

Bountiful Death, with lips and veins I cry
Come to my breast that I may give you suck.

I had two sons, they clung upon my breast —
But, oh, they never need my breast-milk now —
My breasts will wither for the want of them.

Amasa

Nay, sit a little, warming in the sun ;
We have such withered hands that soon grow cold.
I bore men, too, and then the old grey men,
The old grey hungry men said one word, 'war' —
And wrung my children's bodies dry of blood
And hid them in a hole lest I should kiss them.
We are so old we should be gone — too old
To die, too weak to creep into the grave,
Two poor old women : for these strong young men
Have taken all the grave-room, and we're left !

Atarah

The lips that kissed my sons are changed to dust,
But I've one prayer still left, one prayer, O God !
Seal up her eyes that she may never weep ;
Seal up her tongue upon the Judgment Day ;
Seal up the earth that she may never creep
To hide her face from thee within the grave :
Seal up her breast that she may never feed
Those children of her womb, the worms of death !

Saul

Crush down the beat of Time, O mighty God —
The pulse of youth, the veins of love and hate,
That I may hear the crying of her soul.
With those lips, red as hell, she burned the world.
The light is dead, for with her long black hair
That twists and writhes like hell's long hissing river
She quenched the light. Oh, she is very pale :
White with the dust of aeons is her face —
Things ground to powder by the mills of lust.

And I will sift her dust like whitened ash
From craters of my hate. She looked at me . . .
My bones were water, and the world lay dead.

Atarah

My body is broken as the form of night.
I gave these light, and they have blinded me.

Chorus

Our heartstrings were the music of the suns
When their strong youth comes freshened from deep seas ;
We were the perfum'd portals of the dawn —
The singing gardens of the Pleiades.
The vineyards of the world, our heavy locks,
When all the fruits of summer shout for joy ;
Our eyelids were the chambers of the south,
The gold light drips therefrom like frankincense.
Then madness blew on us, a mighty wind :
The palaces of light are overthrown,
And broken lie the rainbows, their great harps,
With burning music muted by the dust.
Our thoughts, strong horses that unfettered ran
Within the golden pastures of the Day ;
Then madness reined them ; she has drunk their strength
As summer drains the strongest rivers' pride.
We built new worlds with our immortal kiss,
Then madness swept like Time across our worlds.
And when we spoke, all space broke into flower
Till madness came like winter withering ;
And Time was but the beat of heart to heart,
Till madness sealed the heartbeat of the world.
Bull-throated now the fires of madness blast :
The world's vast walls reel blindly, then collapse.

Semichorus

Pull down the heavens like a sackcloth pall
To spread upon our faces sealed with night ;

Crush out the dawn-spring from the ruined heaven,
The fabric of the air is torn apart :
The world is dead.   There is no world at all.
The light is dead.   There shall be no more light.
Pull down the heavens like a sackcloth pall.
Crush down the beat of Time.   It was my heart.

ELEGY ON DEAD FASHION

FOR THOMAS BALSTON

Queen Venus' old historians seem like bees
That suck their honey from the thick lime-trees ;
Behind their honeyed lattices all day,
As murmurous as thick-leaved lime-trees, they

Dream cells of Time away in murmuring o'er
The talk of little people gone before,
Within their palaces until gold eves
Bring them to windows in the tree-tops' leaves.

Manteaux espagnols by the water's sheen,
Where trees resemble a great pelerine,
Are spread about the groups upon the lawns
Smooth as an almond's husk, or coats of fawns.

And cavaliers and ladies on the grass
Watch Chloe and young Damon as they pass, —
The shepherdess that runs from her swain's kiss,
Through leafy nets in a gown à l'Amadis

That rustles like the trembling evening,
Which falling on the lawns and brakes will bring
Roucoulement of doves, and veilèd belles
Preening their cloaks of cashmere tourterelles.

Oh, voices speaking by the waterfall !
Heroic statues cast a shadow tall,
And rustic faces where long water runs
Are now transformed to gold five-petalled suns.

But the historians murmur still like bees :
' How old is Venus ? older than the trees,
Does she remember still the ancient bliss,
Grown dead and rotten, of Adonis' kiss ? '

197

Through mulberry-trees a candle's thick gold thread, —
So seems the summer sun to the sad Dead ;
That cackling candle's loud cacophonies
Will wake not Plato, Aristophanes,

For all their wisdom.   There in the deep groves
They must forget Olympus and their loves,
Lying beneath the coldest flower we see
On the young green-blooming strawberry.

The nymphs are dead like the great summer roses ;
Only an Abyssinian wind dozes —
Cloyed with late honey are his dark wings' sheens,
Yet, once on these lone crags, nymphs bright as queens

Walked with elegant footsteps through light leaves,
Where only elegiac air now grieves, —
For the light leaves are sere and whisper dead
Echoes of elegances lost and fled.

Queen Thetis wore pelisses of tissue
Of marine blue or violet, or deep blue,
Beside the softest flower-bells of the seas.
In winter, under thick swan-bosomed trees

The colours most in favour were marine,
Blue Louise, gris bois, grenate, myrtle green ;
Beside the ermine bells of the lorn foam —
Those shivering flower-bells — nymphs light-footed roam

No more, nor walk within vast, bear-furred woods
Where cross owls mocked them from their leafy hoods,
And, once, the ermine leaves of the cold snow
Seemed fashion leaves of eighty years ago. —

When first as thin as young Prince Jamie's plaid
The tartan leaves upon the branches laid
Showed feathered flowers as brown as any gannet,
And thin as January or as Janet, —

Chione, Cleopatra, Boreas' daughters
Walked beside the stream's drake-plumaged waters
In crinolines of plaided sarsenet,
Scotch caps, where those drake-curling waters wet

Their elegant insteps. — Household nymphs must wear
For humble tasks the ponceau gros d'hiver, —
(Tisiphone the Fury, like a dire
Wind raising up Balmoral towers of fire).

Another wind's small drum through thin leaves taps,
And Venus' children wearing their Scotch caps
Or a small toque hongroise that is round-brimmed,
And with a wing from Venus' pigeons trimmed,

Run now with hoops and dolls they call ' cher cœur,'
Chase Cupid in his jacket artilleur,
Play on the cliffs where like the goats' thick locks
The coarse grass grows, and clamber on the rocks.

Above the forest, whence he shot the does,
Was Jupiter's vast shooting-box of snows —
His blunderbuss's ancient repercussions
Fired but pears and apples, furred as Russians.

He threw his gun down and began to curse,
When up ran Venus' children with their nurse :
' See, Grandpapa, rocks like Balmoral's towers
Held still these brown and gannet-plumaged flowers.'

Then underneath the hairy and the bestial
Skies of winter ripening, a celestial
Bucolic comedy of subtle meaning
Grew with rough summer suns, until with preening

Of soft bird-breasted leaves, again we knew
The secret of how hell and heaven grew.
Where walked great Jupiter, and like a peasant
Shot the partridge, grouse, and hare, and pheasant.

In the gods' country park there was a farm
Where all the gentle beasts came to no harm,
Left to run wild.   And there in that great wood
Was Juno's dairy, cold as any bud,

With milk and cream, as sweet and thick as yellow
Apricots and melons, in the mellow
Noon when dairymaids must bear it through
Lanes full of trilling flowers and budding dew.

And then beside the swanskin pool where pansies
And strawberries and other pretty fancies
With the wild cherries sing their madrigals,
The goddesses walked by the waterfalls ;

But now beside the water's thin flower-bells
No bustles seem rose castles and tourelles
Beside the little lake that seems of thin
And plumeless and too delicate swanskin ;

Nor sparks and rays from calèche wheels that roll
Mirror the haycocks with gilt rays like Sol
Where trees seemed icebergs, — rose and green reflections
Of the passing nymphs and their confections. —

In summer, when nymph Echo was serene
On these lone crags walked many a beauteous queen,
As lovely as the light and spangled breeze
Beside the caves and myrtle groves and trees.

One wood-nymph wore a deep black velvet bonnet
With blackest ivy leaves for wreaths upon it, —
Shading her face as lovely as the fountains
While she descended from deep-wooded mountains,

And with the wood-gods hiding, Charlottine,
Boreas' daughter, wore a crinoline.
So fair with water-flowing hair was she,
That crinoline would shine from crag and tree.

When the gold spangles on the water seen
Were like the twanging of a mandoline,
And all the ripples were like ripest fruits
That grow from the deep water's twisted roots,

The water-nymph, dark Mademoiselle Persane,
On blond sands wore an Algerine turbane ;
Of blue velours d'Afrique was the pelisse
Of Grisi the ondine, and like the fleece

Of water gods, or gold trees on the strand,
Her gold hair fell like fountains on the sand, —
The thick gold sand beside the siren waves, —
Like honey-cells those sands and fountain caves.

Dream of the picnics where trees, sylvan, wan,
Shaded our feasts of nightingale and swan,
With wines as plumed as birds of paradise,
Or Persian winds, to drown the time that flies !

Then, on the shaven ice-green grass one sees
Roses and cherries and ripe strawberries
Bobbing at our lips like scarlet fire
Between the meshes of the light's gold wire,

And the bacchantes with their dew-wet hair,
Like velvety dark leaves of vineyards, wear
Great bunchèd tufts of African red coral
Whose glints with sheen of dew and leaves now quarrel.

Here in a sheep-thick shade of tree and root
Nymphs nurse each fawn whose pretty golden foot
Skipped there. They, milk of flaxen lilies, sip
From a sweet cup that has a coral lip,

In that green darkness. Melons dark as caves
Held thick gold honey for their fountain waves,
And there were gourds as wrinkled dark as Pan,
Or old Silenus, — figs whence jewels ran.

There in the forest, through the green baize leaves,
Walked Artemis, and like the bound-up sheaves
Of gilt and rustling-tressèd corn, her arrows
Through greenhouses of vegetable marrows

She aimed ; like the vast serres-chaudes of the lake,
Those greenhouses her arrows then did break !
Her dress was trimmed with straw, her hair streamed bright
And glittering as topaz, chrysolite.

Among their castles of gold straw entwined
With blackest ivy buds and leaves, and lined
With lambs' wool, and among the cocks of hay,
The satyrs danced the sheep-trot all the day,

In wooded gardens where the green baize leaves
Hid fruit that rustled like Ceres' gilt sheaves
They danced the gallopade and the mazurka,
Cracoviak, cachucha, and the turka,

With Fauna and the country deities,
Pan's love Eupheme, and the Hyades, —
Phaola and Ambrosia and Eudora,
Panope and Eupompe with great Flora,

Euryale, the Amazonian queen
Whose gown is looped above the yellow sheen
Of her bright yellow petticoat, — the breeze
Strewed wild flowers on her straw hat through the trees :

And country nymphs with round straw hats deep-brimmed,
And at one side with pheasants' feathers trimmed, —
With gowns of green mohair, and high kid boots
Wherewith they trample radish, strawberry, roots.

But far are we from the forests of our rest
Where the wolf Nature from maternal breast
Fed us with strong brown milk . . . those epochs gone,
Our eyeless statues weep from blinded stone.

And far are we from the innocence of man,
When Time's vast sculptures from rough dust began,
And natural law and moral were but one, —
Derived from the rich wisdom of the sun.

In those deep ages the most primitive
And roughest and uncouthest shapes did live
Knowing the memory of before their birth,
And their soul's life before this uncouth earth.

We could remember in that ancient time
Of our primeval innocence, a clime
Divined deep in the soul, in which the light
Of vaster suns gave wisdom to our sight;

Now, days like wild beasts desecrate each part
Of that forgotten tomb that was our heart;
There are more awful ruins hanging there
Than those which hang and nod at empty air.

Yet still our souls keep memories of that time
In sylvan wildernesses, our soul's prime
Of wisdom, forests that were gods' abode,
And Saturn marching in the Dorian mode.

But all the nymphs are dead.   The sound of fountains
Weeps swan-soft elegies to the deep mountains, —
Repeats their laughter, mournful now and slow,
To the dead nymph Echo.   Long ago

Among the pallid roses' spangled sheens
On these lone crags nymphs that were bright as queens
Walked with elegant footsteps through light leaves
Where now a dark-winged southern wind soft grieves,

So cloyed with honey he must close his wing.
No ondine Grisi now may rise to sing,
For the light leaves are sere and whisper dead
Echoes of elegances lost and fled.

The nymphs are dead. And yet when spring begins
The nation of the Dead must feel old sins
Wake unremembering bones, eternal, old
As Death. Oh, think how these must feel the cold

In the deep groves ! But here these dead still walk
As though they lived, and sigh awhile, and talk.
O perfumed nosegay brought for noseless Death!
This brightest myrrh can not perfume that breath.

The nymphs are dead, — Syrinx and Dryope
And that smooth nymph that changed into a tree.
But though the shade, that Æthiopia, sees
Their beauty make more bright its treasuries,

Their amber blood in porphyry veins still grows ·
Deep in the dark secret of the rose,
Though dust are their bright temples in the heat,
The nymph Parthenope with golden feet.

My glittering fire has turned into a ghost,
My rose is now cold amber and is lost ;
Yet from that fire you still could light the sun,
And from that amber, bee-winged motes could come ;

Though grown from rocks and trees, dark as Saint Anne,
The little nun-like leaves weep our small span,
And eyeless statues in the garden weep
For Niobe who by the founts doth sleep,

In gardens of a fairy aristocracy
That lead downhill to mountain peaks of sea,
Where people build like beavers on the sand
Among life's common movements, understand

That Troy and Babylon were built with bricks ;
They engineer great wells into the Styx
And build hotels upon the peaks of seas
Where the small trivial Dead can sit and freeze.

Still ancient fanfares sound from mountain gorges
Where once Prometheus lit enormous forges :
' Debout les morts ! ' No key when the heart closes :
The nymphs are dead like the great summer roses.

But Janet, the old wood-god Janus' daughter,
All January-thin and blond as water,
Runs through the gardens, sees Europa ride
Down to the great Swiss mountains of the tide,

Though in the deep woods, budding violets
And strawberries as round as triolets
Beneath their swanskin leaves feel all alone. . . .
The golden feet that crushed them now are gone.

Beside the Alps of sea, each crinoline
Of muslin and of gauze and grenadine
Sweeps by the Mendelssohnian waterfall,
O'er beaver-smooth grass, by the castle wall,

Beside the thick mosaic of the leaves.
Left by the glamour of some huger eves
The thick gold spangles on those leaves are seen
Like the sharp twanging of a mandoline ;

And there, with Fortune, I too sit apart
Feeling the jewel turn flower, the flower turn heart,
Knowing not goddess's from beggar's bones,
Nor all death's gulf between those semitones.

We who were proud and various as the wave, —
What strange companions the unreasoning grave
Will give us . . . wintry Prudence's empty skull
May lie near that of Venus the dead trull !

There are great diamonds hidden in the mud
Waiting Prometheus' fire and Time's vast flood ;
Wild glistening flowers that spring from these could know
The secret of how hell and heaven grow.

But at a wayside station near the rock
Where vast Prometheus lies, another bock
Is brought by Ganymede . . . why dream the Flood
Would save those diamonds hidden in the mud?

The farmer on his donkey now rides down
The mountain side, with angels' eggs the town
Will buy, beside the mountain peaks of sea
And gardens of the fairy aristocracy,

And ladies in their carriages drive down
The mountain to the gardens of the town,
And the hot wind, that little Savoyard,
Decked them with wild flowers à la montagnarde.

The wood-nymphs Nettie, Alexandrine, tear
Balmoral gowns made for this mountain wear, —
White veils; each Fauchon-émigré bonnet
Bears coronets of berries wild upon it;

Huge as the great gold sun, each parasol
That hides it; fluid zephyrs now extol
Antiope's short bell-shaped pelerine
Worn lest gauze ribbons of the rain be seen.

'Oh the blond hair of Fortune in the grove!
Lean from your carriage, hold her lest she rove.'
'Her face is winter, wrinkled, peaceless, mired,
Black as the cave where Cerberus was sired. —

O soul, my Lazarus! There was a clime
Deep in your tomb of flesh, defying time,
When a god's soul played there, began to dance
Deep in that tomb with divine, deathless Chance.

But that huge god grew wearied of our game
And all the lion-like waterfalls grew tame.
Venus, a statue mouldering on the wall,
Noiseless and broken now, forgetting all

The fanfares, knows that Phoebus gilds her still
On pastoral afternoons ; but she is chill.
Venus, you too have known the anguished cold,
The crumbling years, the fear of growing old !

Here in this theatre of redistributions,
This old arena built for retributions,
We rose imperial from primeval slime
Through architecture of our bones by Time ;

Now Night like lava flows without a chart
From unremembering craters of the heart,
Anguished with their dead fires. — Beneath the caves
And crags the Numidean Sibyl raves ;

We hear the Sibyl crying Prophecy.
" There where the kiss seems immortality
I prophesy the Worm . . . there, in the kiss,
He'll find his most imperial luxuries." '

    .   .   .   .   .

Where mountains, millers' dusty bags, seem full
Of Priam's gold, and all the black sheep's wool
Of thunderstorms, and grass in forests floats
As green as Tyrolean peasants' petticoats,

Dead Venus drove in her barouche, her shawl
As mauve as mountain distance covering all,
As she swept o'er the plain with her postillions
That were black and haughty as Castillians.

There, high above the thickest forests were
The steepest high-walled castles of the air ;
And paths led to those castles that were bordered
With great gardens, neat and walled and ordered,

With rivers, feathered masks, and pots of peas
Mournful beneath the vast and castled trees,
Where gardeners clip the strange wind's glittering fleece.
Oh, how that wind can blow through a pelisse !

Miss Ellen and Miss Harriet, the ondines,
Bore baskets full of velvet nectarines
And walnuts, over wooden trellised bridges
That cross the streams and the steep mountain ridges.

They wore straw-coloured crinolines of faille
Beneath their shady bonnets made of paille, —
Their melancholy laughter ever sounds
Through castled trees and over castle grounds.

But I am sad, and by the wrinkled lake,
Where the great mauve flowers will never wake,
But drip with sleep and dew, I read this thin,
Dry, withered book of delicate swanskin,

And find a tale of an Olympian glade
Where Psyche has become a kitchenmaid ;
The world, that pitiful old catchpenny,
Whines at her booth for pence, and finds too many

Showing the gods no larger than ourselves,
And twittering bird-like from the rocky shelves
Of this Olympus, and no prophecy
They roar, but whisper triviality.

The ancient castle wall of Chaos nods.
Through gaps of ruined air and withered pods
A showman came ; he smiles like Time and mocks
Me, takes his marionettes from their small box —

The gods, Time-crumbled into marionettes.
Death frays their ageless bodies, hunger frets
Them, till at last, like us, they dance
Upon the old dull string pulled now by Chance.

This is the game the apeish shuddering dust
Plays for the market and the house of lust ;
There are a thousand deaths the spirit dies
Unknown to the sad Dead that we despise.

Still ladies in their carriages drive down
The mountain to the gardens of the town,
And the hot wind, that little Savoyard,
Decked them with wild flowers à la montagnarde.

Rich as a tomb each dress ! oh, pity these !
I think the rich died young, and no one sees
The young loved face show for a fading while
Through that death-mask, the sad and cynic smile.

   .   .   .   .   .

These living skeletons blown by the wind
Were Cleopatra, Thaïs . . . age unkind
Has shrunken them so feeble and so small
That Death will never comfort them at all.

They are so poor they seem to have put by
The outworn fashion of the flesh ! They lie
Naked and bare in their mortality
Waiting for Death to warm them, childishly.

Do these Dead, shivering in their raggedness
Of outworn flesh, know us more dead, and guess
How day rolls down, that vast eternal stone,
Shuts each in his accustomed grave, alone ?

Round the eternal skeleton their dress
Is rags ; our mountain-high forgetfulness
Through centuries is piled above the Dead,
Waiting in vain for some remembered tread

Upon this rock-bound march that all we made
To the eternal empire of the shade, —
To the small sound of Time's drum in the heart.
The sound they wait for dies, the steps depart.

Come not, O solemn and revengeful Dead, —
Most loving Dead, from your eternal bed
To meet this living ghost, lest you should keep
Some memory of what I was, and weep.

METAMORPHOSIS
(*First Version*, 1929)

THE coral-cold snow seemed the Parthenon,
Huge peristyle of temples that are gone,
And dark as Asia, now, is Beauty's daughter,
The rose, once clear as music o'er deep water.

Now the full moon her fire and light doth spill
On turkey-plumaged leaves and window-sill,

On leaves that seem the necks and plumes of urban
Turkeys, each a Sultan in a turban,

And strawberries among the beavers' wool
(So grass seemed where that ruined temple's cool

Shade fell). When first the dew with golden foot
Makes tremble every leaf and strawberry root,

The rainbow gives those berries light above,
The dark rose gives them all her secret love,

Until those coral tears of the rich light
Hold roses, rubies, rainbows for the sight.

My ancient shadow nods a turbaned head ;
One candle through thick leaves throws a gold thread ;

The dark green country temple of the snows
Hides porphyry bones of nymphs whence grew the rose,

And dark green dog-haired leaves of strawberries,
All marked with maps of unknown lands and seas,

And that small Negro page, the cross dark quail,
Chasing the ghosts of dairymaids that fail

In butter-yellow dew by Georgian stables
(The snow, dark green as strawberry leaves, has gables).

But Time, a heavy ghost, groans through thick leaves ;
Time is a weary bell which ever grieves ;

It is not Death which is the skeleton —
But Time ; Death merely strikes the hour of one,

Night's creeping end ere light begins again.
Oh, Death has never worm for heart and brain

Like that which Time conceives to fill his grave,
Devouring the last faith, the word love gave,

Changing the light in eyes to heavy tears,
Changing the beat in heart to empty years

Wherein we listen for that little sound
Of footsteps that come never to our ground.

How terrible these winter nights must be
To the deserted Dead . . . if we could see

The eternal anguish of the skeleton,
So fleshless even the dog leaves it alone,

Atridae-like devouring its own blood
With hopeless love beneath the earth's blind hood ;
For warmth, the rags of flesh about the bone
Devoured by black disastrous dreams, alone

The worm is their companion, vast years
Pile mountain-high above, and the last tears

Freeze to gigantic polar nights of ice
Around the heart through crumbling centuries.

O Dead, your heart is gone, it cannot weep !
From decency the skeleton must sleep ;

O heart, shrink out of sight, you have no flesh
For love or dog or worm to court afresh,

Only your youthful smile is mirrored lone
In that eternity, the skeleton.

For never come they now, nor comes the hour
When your lips spoke, and winter broke in flower,

The Parthenon was built by your dead kiss.
What should they seek, now you are changed to this

Vast craggy bulk, strong as the prophet's rock ?
No grief tore waters from that stone to mock
Death's immobility, and, changed to stone,
Those eyelids see one sight and one alone.

What do they see ?   Some lost and childish kiss
In summers ere they knew that love was this,

The terrible Gehenna of the bone
Deserted by the flesh, tears changed to stone ?

Or do they blame us that we walk this earth,
Who are more dead than they, nor seek rebirth

Nor change ? The snowflake's six-rayed star can see
Rock-crystal's cold six-rayed eternity —

Thus light grief melts in craggy waterfalls ;
But mine melts never, though the last spring calls :

The polar night's huge boulder hath rolled this,
My heart, my Sisyphus, in the abyss.

Do the Dead know the nights wherein we grope
From our more terrible abyss of hope
To soft despair? The nights when creeping Fear
Crumples our hearts, knowing when age appear,

Our sun, our love, will leave us more alone
Than the black mouldering rags about the bone?

Age shrinks our hearts to ape-like dust . . . that ape
Looks through the eyes where all death's chasms gape

Between ourself and what we used to be.
My soul, my Lazarus, know you not me?

Am I so changed by Time's appalling night?
'Tis but my bone that cannot stand upright,

That leans as if it thirsted . . . for what spring,
The ape's bent skeleton foreshadowing,

With head bent from the light, its only kiss?
Do the Dead know that metamorphosis,

When the appalling lion-claws of age
With talons tear the cheek and heart, yet rage

For life devours the bone, a tigerish fire?
But quenched in the vast empire of the mire

These craters cry not to the eternal bone:
The Dead may hide the changing skeleton.

So quench the light, my Lazarus, nor see
The thing we are, the thing that we might be:

In mouldering cerements of that thick grave,
Our flesh, we lose the one light that could save.

But yet it shall avail that grass shall sing
From loveless bones in some foreshadowed spring,

And summer break from a long-shadowed kiss,
Though our dry bones are sunless grown as this,

And eyeless statues, broken and alone
In shadeless avenues, the music gone,
We stand . . . the leaves we knew are black as jet,
Though the light scatters feathers on them yet,

Remembering sylvan nymphs. . . . Death is our clime,
And, among heavy leaves, our bell to chime —

Death is our sun, illumining our old
Dim-jewelled bones — Death is our winter cold,

Yet sighs of voyages and landing stages
From unknown seas, and sylvan equipages,

And of a clime where Death's light on the eyes
Could make each shapeless lump of clay grow wise ;

The topaz, sapphires, diamonds of the bone,
That mineral in our earth's dark mine, alone
Leap to the eastern light. . . . Death-blinded eyes
See beyond wild bird-winged discoveries.

Death is the Sun's heat making all men black :
O Death, the splendours die in the leaves' track :

All men are Ethiopian shades of thee :
The wild and glittering fleece Parthenope

Loosened, more rich than feathers of bright birds,
Though rich and thick as Ethiopian herds

Died like the wave, or early light that grew
In eastern quarries ripening precious dew.[1]

Though lovely are the tombs of the dead nymphs
On the heroic shore, the glittering plinths
Of jacynth, hyacinthine waves profound
Sigh of the beauty out of sight and sound

And many a golden foot that pressed the sand :
The panoply of suns on distant strand.

Panope walking like the pomp of waves
With plumaged helmet near the fountain caves

Is only now an arena for the worm ;
Her golden flesh lies in the dust's frail storm,

And beauty water-bright for long is laid
Deep in the empire of eternal shade ;

Only the sighing waves know now the plinth
Of those deep tombs that were of hyacinth.

Still echoes of that helmeted bright hair
Are like the pomp of tropic suns, the blare

That from the inaccessible horizon runs,
The eternal music of heroic suns
When their strong youth comes freshened from deep seas,
And the first music heard among the trees.

By elephant trunks of the water, showers
Now change to cornucopias of flowers ;

Panope with her dark majestic train
Of nymphs walked like the pomp of waves, the main

[1] Dryden's 'Annus Mirabilis.'

Sees Asia, Parthenope, Eunomia,
Euphrosyne, Urania, Ausonia,

In feathered head-dresses as bright as sleep,
As onward with the pomp of waves they sweep

In pelongs, chelloes, and great pallampores,
Gaze d'Ispahan and bulchauls, sallampores,

In plumaged turbans, sweeping gros des Indes,
That the long golden fingers of the winds

Pull by the waters paler than a pearl.
The airs like rain-wet shrinking petals curl

And waves are freckled with gold ripples, these
Seem golden spangles on the strawberries ;
And black Bacchantes with their panached feathers
Wear mittens with gold fringe bright as the weathers,

Where elephant trunks of the water rear
As the great pomp and train of nymphs draws near —

An ambassade of Amazons ; rich trees
And Abyssinian glooms have fostered these.

But now Melpomene, Zenobia,
The Amazons black as Ethiopia,

In Pan's huge forests seem like statues tall,
Where the thick jewels from the rich figs fall

In this vast empire of eternal shade
Where leaves seem Memphis, Thebes, from music made.

In wooded gardens by each gardener's frame
Dark wrinkled satyrs with long straw beards came,

Dark honey from rough cups of straw to sip,
And every straw cup has an amber lip.

The gardener, wrinkled, dark, beside a cave
Sways branches gold-mosaic'd as the wave

And finds these are with satyrs' straw beards twined
By that gold-fingered arborist, the wind.

And there beside the greenest, shaggiest caves,
As green as melons hiding honey waves,

The rose that shone like the first light of tears
Was once a buskined bright nymph in lost years,

And from the amber dust that was a rose
In the green heat Parthenope still grows.

In this green world the melons' dogskin flowers,
Leaves green as country temples, snare the hours,

And dew seems butter-yellow, the bright mesh
Of dear and dead Panope's golden flesh

Where grapes and apples boom like emerald rain
In green baize forests, and the sylvan train

Of country nymphs wear yellow petticoats
Looped over leathern gaiters ; long hair floats,
Cream-coloured and as thick as ponies' manes,
Through swan-soft great mauve leaves where Jove's gold
    rains

Still fly ; rich strawberries are honeyed cold
By all Pan's honey and Palmyra's gold,

And in the laughing green the rich fruits ran
With gilded honeyed blood of Phoebus, Pan.

But now the branches droop their melancholy
And owl-soft dusk upon this summer folly ;

And under trees that were as fresh and green
As laughing nymphs' guitar and mandoline

(When country nymphs wear yellow petticoats
Looped over leathern gaiters, long hair floats

From straw hats trimmed with pheasants' feathers twined
By the long golden fingers of the wind),

The broken country statue Corydon,
Gilded by Phoebus, with his straw flute gone,

Stands in the cocks of snow (once cocks of hay
Gilded and rustling o'er that green land lay) ;

And shadows brush the statue, not the snowy
Winged bees Sylvia and Thisbe, Chloe,

That sang sweet country songs in owl-dusked leaves :
' Poor Rose Is Dying ' and ' Sweet Sultan Grieves.'

But Time drifts owl-dusk o'er the brightest eyes
And dulls the sleepy gods and the sad wise,

And shall despoil our woods and monuments
And make them like the small bees' cerements . . .

And heavy is dark Time, that ever moans
Among thick leaves his mournful overtones.

Now the snow lies upon my rose-shaped heart,
And on the years, and many a glittering chart

The dog-furred strawberry leaves bear — maps from dream
To dream — and berries with Orion's gleam.

This dark-green country temple of the snows
Hides still the amber dust of nymph and rose,

The melons' dogskin flowers where the mellow,
Whining early dew is butter-yellow,

And the nymphs' smooth-eared hound, far from the light,
When early dew whines hound-like as in fright.

I looked out from my window where the urban
Leaves seemed turkeys (Sultans in a turban)
Across the lake where, cupolas and gables,
The ripples seemed deserted Georgian stables ;

And my old shadow nods a turbaned head,
The full moon sees one candle's thick gold thread

Pierce through the thick leaves near the window-sill,
Where she her lovely fire and light doth spill.

The rose that shone like the first light of tears
Is faded, and its leaves, bright as the years

When we knew life and love and youth, are wet
With tears beneath the shady winter.   Yet

Although the small immortal serpent cries,
' I, only, know if Plato still be wise,

Great golden Hector had the pomp and pride
Of waves, but like the strength of these, he died ;

And the first soundless wrinkles fall like snow
On many a golden cheek, and none may know,

Seeing your ancient wrinkled shadow-shape,
If this be long-dead Venus or an ape ' —

To patience with the apeish dust I came,
Seeing this mimicry of death a game ;

Since all things have beginnings ; the bright plume
Was once thin grass in shady winter's gloom,

And the furred fire is barking for the shape
Of hoarse-voiced animals ; cold air agape

Whines to be shut in water's shape and plumes ;
All this is hidden in the winter's glooms.

I, too, from ruined walls hung upside down
And, bat-like, only saw Death's ruined town

And mumbling crumbling dust. . . . I saw the people
Mouthing blindly for the earth's blind nipple.

Their thick sleep dreams not of the infinite
Wild strength the grass must have to find the light

With all the bulk of earth across its eyes
And strength, and the huge weight of centuries.

Hate-hidden by a monk's cowl of ape's pelt,
Bear-clumsy and appalling, mine own self
Devouring, blinded by the earth's thick hood
I crouched, Atridae-like devoured my blood

And knew the anguish of the skeleton
Deserted by the flesh, with Death alone.

Then my immortal Sun rose, Heavenly Love,
To rouse my carrion to life and move

The polar night, the boulder that rolled this,
My heart, my Sisyphus, in the abyss.

Come then, my Sun, to melt the eternal ice
Of Death, and crumble the thick centuries,
Nor shrink, my soul, as dull wax owlish eyes
In the sun's light, before my sad eternities.

METAMORPHOSIS

(Second Version, 1946)

THE coral-cold snow seemed the Parthenon —
Huge peristyle of temples that are gone —

And in the winter's Æthiopian shade —
The time of the cold heart and the world's winter —
Death seemed our only clime —
And Death our bell to chime

The passing tears among the heavy leaves
Where black as a Negress in the winter night
Is the face of Beauty in the great moon's light.

But all the nations and the centuries
And weight of Death press down upon mine eyes
In this deep-perfumed dwelling of the Dead;

The dark green country temple of the snows
Hides the porphyry bones of nymphs whence grew the
      rose

And dark green dog-haired leaves of strawberries
All marked with maps of unknown lands and seas,

Among the grass that seemed like beaver's wool,
In winter, where that ruined temple's cool

Shade fell.   Here, once in Spring, the dew with a golden
      foot
Made tremble every leaf and hidden root,

And the rainbow gave those berries light above —
The dark rose gave them all her secret love

Until those coral tears of the rich light
Changed the dark earth into a starry sky,
With those great berries, bright as Sirius' pomp and
      empery.

But lost in the climate of the winter shade
And the immensity of the long cold,

We must lie down in darkness, have no light
But from the ashes of the outworn heart
Wherein we have no warmth, nor any part —

For we are our own ghost, and our own Death
That has no tears to flow, that has no breath.

While Time, a heavy ghost, groans through thick
      leaves . . .
Time is a weary bell which ever grieves :

It is not Death which is the skeleton —
But Time . . . Death merely strikes the hour of one —

Night's creeping end ere light begins again . . .
O Death has never worm for heart and brain

Like that which Time conceives to fill his grave —
Devouring the last faith, the word Love gave,

Changing the light in the eyes to heavy tears,
Changing the beat of the heart to Time's — the years

Wherein we listen for that little sound
Of footsteps that come never to our ground.

And Time, like Echo, sounds in the winter air
And speaks with the dull voice of our despair —

Sighs ' Terrible these winter nights must be
To the deserted Dead . . . if we could see

The eternal anguish of the skeleton —
So fleshless even the dog leaves it alone !

Not theirs the sleep of love . . . alone they lie
While the spring heats, the fevers of the world, pass by :

For warmth, they have the rags about the bone ;
Devoured by black disastrous dreams, alone

The worm is their companion . . . vast years
Pile mountain-high above, and the last tears

Freeze to gigantic polar nights of ice
Around the heart, through crumbling centuries.'

O mortal eyes !   O beat of the mortal heart
That measures all Death's grandeurs by the part

You have in Time. . . . Not theirs the Gehenna of
        the bone
Deserted by the flesh, with Death alone :

But like a small child, close to their mother's breast
They sleep in the arms of Earth with a blind trust —
Forgetting all their hungers and the lust
For life.   In their lost innocence they rest,

Not envying the old loves and the old sins,
The maelstrom of the blood, the secrecy
Of Spring, the instinct of blind lust from which a world
        begins —

But knowing the birth of a great flower among a million
Flowers, the extinction of a far-off sun
And its many-hued perihelion and aphelion —
The extinction of a heart — all these are one.

For what should they know of lesser loves and fears
From their long aeons, — or of the passing years,

And nights more dark than theirs, wherein we grope
From the more terrible abyss of hope

To soft despair . . . the nights when creeping Fear
Crumples our hearts, knowing when Age appear

Our sun, our love, will leave us more alone
Than the black mouldering rags about the bone !

Age shrinks our hearts to ape-like dust . . . that Ape
Looks through the eyes where all Death's chasms gape

Between ourself and what we used to be . . .
My soul, my Lazarus, know you not me ?

What gap of Death is there ?   What has Time done
That I should be unworthy of the Sun ? . . .

Time is the worm, but Death our Sun, illumining our old
Dim-jewelled bones.   Death is our winter cold

Before the rising of the sap . . . Death's light upon the
     eyes
Could make each shapeless lump of clay grow wise :

The topaz, diamonds, sapphires of the bone,
That mineral in our earth's dark mine, alone
Leap to the eastern light . . . Death-blinded eyes
See beyond wild bird-winged discoveries.

Death is the Sun's heat making all men black !
. . . O Death, the splendours die in the leaves'
     track. . . .

All men are Æthiopian shades of thee.
The wild and glittering fleece Parthenope

Loosened, more rich than feathers of bright birds —
Though rich and thick as Æthiopian herds

Died like the wave, or early light that grew
In eastern quarries ripening precious dew.

Though lovely are the tombs of the dead nymphs
On the heroic shore, the glittering plinths
Of jacynth, hyacinthine waves profound
Sigh of the beauty out of sight and sound ;

And many a golden foot that pressed the sands —
The panoply of suns on distant strands

Are only now an arena for the worm —
The golden flesh lies in the dust's frail storm

And beauty water-bright for long is laid
Deep in the empire of eternal shade ;

Only the sighing waves know now the plinth
Of those deep tombs that were of hyacinth.

The myths of Earth are dead.   Yet with an infinite
Wild strength the grass of spring still finds the light

With all the weight of earth upon its eyes
And strength, and the huge bulk of centuries.

Like Saturn's cincture, or the condensation
Of nebulae to suns, the whole spring nation

Of flowers begin . . . the lights of faith and nature,
With a hairy stalk, and with an Angel's face,
They speak of the innocent dark that gave them birth —
And of how a sun can be born from a clod of earth.

So, out of the dark, see our great Spring begins
— Our Christ, the new Song, breaking out in the fields
    and hedgerows,
The heart of Man !   O the new temper of Christ, in
    veins and branches !

He comes, our Sun, to melt the eternal ice
Of Death, the crusts of Time round the sunken soul —
Coming again in the spring of the world, clothed with
    the scarlet-coloured
Blood of our martyrdoms, — the fire of spring.

ROMANCE

FOR RÉE GORER

SHE grew within his heart as the flushed rose
In the green heat of the long summer grows
Deep in the sorrowful heaven of her leaves.
And this song only is the sound that grieves
When the gold-fingered wind from the green veins
Of the rich rose deflowers her amber blood,
The sharp green rains.
Such is the song, grown from a sleepy head,
Of lovers in a country paradise, —
You shall not find it where a song-bird flies,
Nor from the sound that in a bird-throat grieves ;
— Its chart lies not in maps on strawberry leaves.

Green were the pomp and pleasure of the shade
Wherein they dwelt ; like country temples green
The huge leaves bear a dark-mosaic'd sheen
Like gold on forest temples richly laid.

In that smooth darkness, the gourds dark as caves
Hold thick gold honey for their fountain waves,

Figs, dark and wrinkled as Silenus, hold
Rubies and garnets, and the melons cold
Waves dancing . . .

When the day first gleaned the sun's corn-sheaves
They walked among those temples of the leaves ;
And the rich heat had made them black as cloud
Or smooth-leaved trees ; they lay by waters loud,
And gold-stringed citherns of loud waters made
A madrigal, a country serenade.

But Time drifts by as the long-plumaged winds
And the dark swans whose plumes seem weeping leaves
In the shade's richest splendour, — these drift by.
And sometimes he would turn to her and sigh :

' The bright swans leave the wave . . . so leave not me,
With Æthiopæa, smooth Aërope :
Amid the pomp and splendour of the shade
Their rich and leafy plumes a lulling music made.

Dark are their plumes, and dark the airs that grew
Amid those weeping leaves.
Plantations of the East drop precious dew
That, ripened by the light, rich leaves perspire,
Such are the drops that from the bright swans' feathers
     flew.

Come then, my pomp and pleasure of the shade,
Most lovely cloud that the hot sun made black
As dark-leaved swans.
                    Come then, O precious cloud,
Lean to my heart.   No shade of some rich tree
Shall pour such splendour as your heart to me.'

So these two lovers dreamed the time away
Beside smooth waters like the honey waves
In the ripe melons that are dark as caves ;
Eternity seemed but a summer day.

And they forgot, seeing the Asian train
Of waves upon the glittering wide sea main
And rich gold waves from fountain caverns run,
That all the splendour of the eastern sun,

And many a rose-shaped heart, must lie beneath
The maps on strawberry leaves dark green as snows,
With amber dust that was a nymph or rose —

And worlds more vast lie ruined by sad Time
That is the conqueror of our green clime.
For even the beasts eschew the shrunken heart
That dieth of itself, small deaths devour —
Or that worm mightier than death's — the small
    corroding hour.

How ancient is the Worm, companionless
As the black dust of Venus ? Dulled to this
And loathèd as the Worm, she is alone
Though all the morbid suns lay in her kiss.

How old, the small undying snake that wreathes
Round lips and eyes, now that the kiss has gone ?
In that last night, when we, too, are alone
We have, for love that seemed eternity
The old unchanging memory of the bone —
That porphyry whence grew the summer rose.

Most ancient is the Worm, — more old than Night
Or the first music heard among the trees
And the unknown horizons' harmonies
Where the huge suns come freshened. Shrunk and cold
Is he, like Venus blackened, noseless, old.

Yet all immensities lie in his strong
Embrace, horizons that no sight hath known,
The veins whose sea had heard the siren song
And worlds that grew from an immortal kiss.

And still their love amid this green world grieves :
' The gold light drips like myrrh upon the leaves
And fills with gold those chambers of the South
That were your eyes, that honeycomb your mouth.

And now the undying Worm makes no great stir,
His tight embrace chills not our luxuries
Though the last light perfumes our bones like myrrh
And Time's beat dies.

Come, with your kiss renew
The day, till all the old worlds die like dew.

When the green century of summer rains
Lay on the leaves, then like the rose I wept.
For I had dwelt in sorrow as the rose
In the deep heaven of her leaves lies close.
Then you, my gardener, with green fingers stroked my
    leaves
Till all the gold drops turned to honey.   Grieves
This empire of green shade when honeyed rains
And amber blood flush all the sharp green veins
Of the rich rose ?
             So doth my rose-shaped heart
Feel the first flush of summer ; love's first smart
Seemed no more sorrowful than the deep tears
The rose wept in that green and honeyed clime.

The green rains drip like the slow beat of Time
That grows within the amber blood, green veins
Of the rich rose, and in the rose-shaped heart,
— Changing the amber flesh to a clay wall.
Then comes the endless cold
At last, that is the Zero, mighty, old,
Huge as the heart, but than the worm more small —
Our final structure, the heart's ragged dress
That rose from Nothing, fell to Nothingness.

For the vast universal Night shall cover
The earth from Pole to Pole, and like a lover
Invade your heart that changed into my stone,
And I your Sisyphus.   We two shall lie
Like those within the grave's eternity
And dream our arms hold the horizons deep
Where the strong suns come freshened from deep
    seas,
The continents beyond discoveries,
Eternal youth, and the gods' wisdom, sleep.

How should I dream that I must wake alone
With a void coffin of sad flesh and bone : —
You, with the small undying serpent's kiss,
You, the dull rumour of the dust's renown —
The polar night, a boulder rolling down
My heart, your Sisyphus, to that abyss
Where is nor light, nor dark, nor soul, nor heart to eat —
Only the dust of all the dead, the sound of passing feet.'

So winter fell; the heart shaped like the rose
Beneath the mountain of oblivion lies
With all death's nations and the centuries.
And this song ending fades like the shrill snows,

Dim as the languid moon's vast fading light
That scatters sparkles faint and dim and chill
Upon the wide leaves round my window-sill
Like Æthiopæa ever jewelled bright . . .

So fading from the branches the snow sang
With a strange perfume, a melodious twang
As if a rose should change into a ghost —
A ghost turn to a perfume on the leaves.

NOTE.—For a later variation of the song, and certain lines in 'Metamorphosis,'
see 'Most Lovely Shade,' page 321.

FIVE SONGS

TO GEORGIA SITWELL

∽

1. *Daphne*

Heat of the sun that maketh all men black, —
They are but Æthiopian shades of thee —
Pour down upon this wild and glittering fleece
That is more rich than feathers of bright birds,
The ripening gems, the drops of the still night.
I parch for that still shade, my heat of love
That parched those ripening gems hath withered me.

Come with the African pomp and train of waves,
Give me your darkness, my immortal shade,
Beside the waterwells my heart hath known!
The shepherds hairy-rough as satyrs come,
Bring up their fleeces that are waterfull
With freshness clear as precious gums of trees
Where weep the incense-trees from some deep smart.
So the fresh water from your fleece flows in
To fill with richness all my desert heart.

2. *The Peach Tree*

BETWEEN the amber portals of the sea
The gilded fleece of heat hangs on my tree ;
My skin is bright as this . . .
Come, wind, and smooth my skin, bright as your kiss

Less bright, less bright than Fatima's gold skin,
My gilded fleece that sighs
' She is the glittering dew born of the heat,
She is that young gazelle, the leaping Sun of Paradise.'

Come, Nubian shade, smooth the gilt fleece's curl,
Until your long dark fluid hands unfold
My peach, that cloud of gold,
Its kernel, crackling amber water-cold.

Shine, Fatima, my Sun, show your gold face
Through panached ostrich plumes of leaves, then from
    above
My ripening fruits will feel the bright dew fall apace,
Till at your feet I pour my golden love.

3. The Strawberry

BENEATH my dog-furred leaves you see
The creeping strawberry
In a gold net
The footprints of the dew have made more wet.

Mahomet resting on a cloud of gold
Dreamed of the strawberry
Made of the purpling gauzy heat
And jasper dust trod by his golden feet. —

The jasper dust beside
The fountain tide,
The water jacynth-cold,
The water-ripples like mosaics gold
Have made my green leaves wide and water-cold.

From palaces among the widest leaves
My Sun, my Fatima,
Shows her gold face and sighs,
And darkness dies.

At noon my Fatima, my bright gazelle,
Walks by each gauzy bell
Of strawberries made of such purpling air
As the heat knows, and there

When Fatima, my dew with golden foot,
Comes like all the music of the air
Then shine my berries till those golden footsteps
        die —
Like all the glittering desert of the air when the
        hot sun goes by.

4. *The Greengage Tree*

FROM gold-mosaic'd wave
And from the fountain cave
Grew my dark-plumaged leaves all green and fountain-
    cold,
My minarets of gold,

Mosaic'd like the tomb,
Far in the forest gloom,
Of water-lovely Fatima in forests far away.
The gardener doth sway

The branches and doth find
(As wrinkled dark and kind
As satyrs) these with satyrs' straw beards twined
By that gold-fingered arborist the wind.

Among thick leaves the shade
Seems like a cavalcade,
Or Artemis plume-helmeted from a sylvan serenade,
Or Amazon's ambassade.

A Caliph plays a lute,
A gardener plays a flute,
Then from my feathered stem a most delightful gust,
    a glittering sea
Grows in my rich fruit.

And each bird-angel comes
To sip dark honey from my plums,
My rich green amber gums
That make puffed feather sleeves, long feathered
    skirts all gold,
And sticky from the dew my golden net doth hold.

5. The Nectarine Tree

THIS rich and swan-skin tree has grown
From the nymphs' amber blood and bone.

What laughter falls like rain or tears
Among my boughs, what golden shears ?

Come, gardener, and tie
With your long beard of bass
(So like the winds' fair hair)
The pillars of my tree, and win
The wind to me.

Smooth as the amber skin
Of fair Parthenope,
And that smooth nymph that changed into a tree
Each swan-soft silver skin,
Or like Parthenope's smooth voice that falls like amber,
Or moonlight falling in her deep sea-tinselled chamber.

GOLD COAST CUSTOMS

TO HELEN ROOTHAM

In Ashantee, a hundred years ago, the death of any rich or important person was followed by several days of national ceremonies, during which the utmost licence prevailed, and slaves and poor persons were killed that the bones of the deceased might be washed with human blood.   These ceremonies were called Customs.

ONE fantee wave
Is grave and tall
As brave Ashantee's
Thick mud wall.
Munza rattles his bones in the dust,
Lurking in murk because he must.

Striped black and white
Is the squealing light ;
The dust brays white in the market-place,
Dead powder spread on a black skull's face.

Like monkey-skin
Is the sea — one sin
Like a weasel is nailed to bleach on the rocks
Where the eyeless mud screeched fawning, mocks

At a Negro that wipes
His knife . . . dug there,
A bugbear bellowing
Bone dared rear —
A bugbear bone that bellows white
As the ventriloquist sound of light,

It rears at his head-dress of felted black hair
The one humanity clinging there —

His eyeless face whitened like black and white bones
And his beard of rusty
Brown grass cones.

Hard blue and white
Cowrie shells (the light
Grown hard) outline
The leopard-skin musty
Leaves that shine
With an animal smell both thick and fusty

One house like a rat-skin
Mask flaps fleet
In the sailor's tall
Ventriloquist street
Where the rag houses flap —
Hiding a gap.

Here, tier on tier
Like a black box rear
In the flapping slum
Beside Death's docks.
I did not know this meaner Death
Meant this : that the bunches of nerves still dance
And caper among these slums, and prance.

' Mariners, put your bones to bed ! '
But at Lady Bamburgher's parties each head,
Grinning, knew it had left its bones
In the mud with the white skulls . . . only the grin
Is left, strings of nerves, and the drum-taut skin.

When the sun in the empty
Sky is high
In his dirty brown and white
Bird-skin dress —
He hangs like a skull
With a yellow dull
Face made of clay

(Where tainted, painted, the plague-spots bray)
To hide where the real face rotted away.

So our worm-skin and paper masks still keep,
Above the rotting bones they hide,
The marks of the Plague whereof we died :
The belief,
The grief,
The love,
Or the grin
Of the shapeless worm-soft unshaping Sin —
Unshaping till no more the beat of the blood
Can raise up the body from endless mud
Though the hell-fires cold
As the worm, and old,
Are painted upon each unshaped form —
No more man, woman, or beast to see —
But the universal devouring Worm.

When the sun of dawn looks down on the shrunken
Heads, drums of skin, and the dead men drunken,
I only know one half of my heart
Lies in that terrible coffin of stone,
My body that stalks through the slum alone.
And that half of my heart
That is in your breast
You gave for meat
In the sailor's street
To the rat that had only my bones to eat.

But those hardened hearts
That roll and sprawl,
In a cowl of foul blind monkey-skin,
Lest the whips of the light crash roaring in —
Those hearts that roll
Down the phantom street
They have for their beat
The cannibal drums
And the cries of the slums,
And the Bamburgher parties — they have them all!

One high house flaps . . . taps
Light's skin drum —
Monkey-like shrunk
On all fours now come
The parties' sick ghosts, each hunting himself —
Black gaps beneath an ape's thick pelt,

Chasing a rat,
Their soul's ghost fat
Through the Negro swamp,
Slum hovel's cramp,
Of Lady Bamburgher's parties above
With the latest grin, and the latest love,
And the latest game :
To show the shame
Of the rat-fat soul to the grinning day
With even the rat-skin flayed away.

Now, a thick cloud floating
Low o'er the lake,
Millions of flies
Begin to awake,
With the animation
Of smart conversation :
From Bedlam's madness the thick gadflies
Seek for the broken statue's eyes.

Where the mud and the murk
Whispering lurk :
' From me arises everything,
The Negro's louse,
The armadillo,
Munza's bone and his peccadillo ' —

Where flaps degraded
The black and sated
Slack macerated
And antiquated
Beckoning Negress
Nun of the shade,

And the rickety houses
Rock and rot,
Lady Bamburgher airs
That foul plague-spot
Her romantic heart.
From the cannibal mart,
That smart Plague-cart,
Lady Bamburgher rolls where the foul news-
    sheet
And the shambles for souls are set in the
    street.

And stuck in front
Of this world-tall Worm,
Stuck in front
Of this world's confession —
Like something rolled
Before a procession,
Is the face, a flimsy worm-skin thing
That someone has raked
From the low plague-pit
As a figure-head
For Corruption dead,
And a mask for the universal Worm.

Her ape-skin yellow
Tails of hair
Clung about her bone-white bare
Eyeless mask that cackled there :

The Worm's mask hid
Her eyeless mud,
Her shapeless love,
The plot to escape
From the God-ordained shape

And her soul, the cannibal
Amazon's mart,

Where in squealing light
And clotted black night
On the monkey-skin black and white striped dust they
Cackle and bray to the murdered day.

And the Amazon queen
With a bone-black face
Wears a mask with an ape-skin beard ; she grinds
Her male child's bones in a mortar, binds
Him for food, and the people buy.   For this

Hidden behind
The Worm's mask grown
White as a bone
Where eyeholes rot wide
And are painted for sight,
And the little mouth red as a dead Plague-spot
On that white mask painted to hide Death's rot,

For this painted Plague-cart's
Heart, for this
Slime of the Worm that paints her kiss
And the dead men's bones round her throat and wrist,
The half of my heart that lay in your breast
Has fallen away
To rot and bray
With the painted mud through the eyeless day.

The dust of all the dead can blow
Backwards and forwards, to and fro
To cover the half of my heart with death's rot,
Yet the dust of that other half comes not
To this coffin of stone that stalks through the slum ;
Though love to you now is the deaf Worm's lust
That, cloven in halves, will re-unite
Foulness to deadness in the dust
And chaos of the enormous night.

How far is our innocent paradise,
The blue-striped sand,
Bull-bellowing band
Of waves, and the great gold suns made wise
By the dead days and the horizons grand.

Can a planet tease
With its great gold train,
Walking beside the pompous main —
That great gold planet the heat of the Sun
Where we saw black Shadow, a black man, run,
So a Negress dare
Wear long gold hair?
The Negress Dorothy one sees
Beside the caverns and the trees,
Where her parasol
Throws a shadow tall
As a waterfall —
The Negress Dorothy still feels
The great gold planet tease her brain.

And dreaming deep within her blood
Lay Africa like the dark in the wood;
For Africa is the unhistorical,
Unremembering, unrhetorical,
Undeveloped spirit involved
In the conditions of nature — Man,
That black image of stone hath delved
On the threshold where history began.

Now under the cannibal
Sun is spread
The black rhinoceros-hide of the mud
For endlessness and timelessness . . . dead
Grass creaks like a carrion-bird's voice, rattles,
Squeaks like a wooden shuttle.   Battles
Have worn this deserted skeleton black
As empty chain armour . . . lazily back

With only the half of its heart it lies
With the giggling mud devouring its eyes,
Naught left to fight
But the black clotted night
In its heart, and ventriloquist squealing light.

But lying beneath the giggling mud
I thought there was something living, the bray
Of the eyeless mud can not betray —
Though it is buried beneath black bones
Of the fetiches screeching like overtones
Of the light, as they feel the slaves' spilt blood.

In tiers like a box
Beside the docks
The Negro prays,
The Negro knocks.
' Is Anyone there ? '
His mumblings tear
Nothing but paper walls, and the blare
Of the gaping capering empty air.
The cannibal drums still roll in the mud
To the bones of the king's mother laved in blood
And the trophies with long black hair, shrunken heads
That drunken, shrunk upon tumbled beds.

The Negro rolls
His red eyeballs,
Prostrates himself.
The Negro sprawls :
His God is but a flat black stone
Upright upon a squeaking bone.

The Negro's dull
Red eyeballs roll . . .
The immortality of the soul
Is but black ghosts that squeak through the hole
That once seemed eyes in Munza's skull.

This is his god :
The cannibal sun
On bones that played
For evermore,
And the dusty roar
Of the ancient Dead,
And the squealing rat,
The soul's ghost fat.

But Lady Bamburgher's Shrunken Head,
Slum hovel, is full of the rat-eaten bones
Of a fashionable god that lived not
Ever, but still has bones to rot :
A bloodless and an unborn thing
That cannot wake, yet cannot sleep,
That makes no sound, that cannot weep,
That hears all, bears all, cannot move —
It is buried so deep
Like a shameful thing
In that plague-spot heart, Death's last dust-heap.

  . . . . .

A tall house flaps
In the canvas street,
Down in the wineshop
The Amazons meet

With the tall abbess
Of the shade. . . .
A ghost in a gown
Like a stiff brigade

Watches the sailor
With a guitar
Lure the wind
From the islands far.

O far horizons and bright blue wine
And majesty of the seas that shine,

Bull-bellowing waves that ever fall
Round the god-like feet and the goddess tall !

A great yellow flower
With the silence shy
To the wind from the islands
Sighs ' I die.'

At the foot of the steps
Like the navy-blue ghost
Of a coiling Negro,
In dock slums lost,

(The ghost haunting steamers
And cocktail bars,
Card-sharpers, schemers,
And Pullman cars)

A ripple rose
With mud at its root
And weeping kissed
A statue's foot.

In the sailor's tall
Ventriloquist street
The calico dummies
Flap and meet :
Calculate : ' Sally go
Pick up a sailor.'
Behind that façade
The worm is a jailer.

' I cannot stiffen . . . I left my bones
Down in the street : no overtones
Of the murdered light can join my dust
To my black bones pressed in the House of **Lust**.
Only my feet still walk in the street ;
But where is my heart and its empty beat ?

" Starved silly Sally, why dilly and dally ? "
The dummies said when I was a girl.
The rat deserts a room that is bare,
But Want, a cruel rat gnawing there
Ate to the heart, all else was gone,
Nothing remained but Want alone.
So now I'm a gay girl, a calico dummy,
With nothing left alive but my feet
That walk up and down in the Sailor's Street.

Behind the bawdy hovels like hoardings
Where harridans peer from the grovelling boarding
House, the lunatic
Wind still shakes
My empty rag-body, nothing wakes ;
The wind like a lunatic in a fouled
Nightgown, whipped those rags and howled.

Once I saw it come
Through the canvas slum,
Rattle and beat what seemed a drum,
Rattle and beat it with a bone.
O Christ, that bone was dead, alone.
Christ, who will speak to such ragged Dead
As me, I am dead, alone and bare,
They expose me still to the grinning air,
I shall never gather my bones and my dust
Together (so changed and scattered, lost . . .)
So I can be decently burièd !
What is that whimpering like a child
That this mad ghost beats like a drum in the air ?
The heart of Sal
That once was a girl
And now is a calico thing to loll
Over the easy steps of the slum
Waiting for something dead to come.'

From Rotten Alley and Booble Street,
The beggars crawl to starve near the meat

Of the reeling appalling cannibal mart,
And Lady Bamburgher, smart Plague-cart.
Red rag face and a cough that tears
They creep through the mud of the docks from their
    lairs;
And when the dog-whining dawn light
Nosed for their hearts, whined in fright,
With a sly high animal
Whimpering, half-frightened call
To worlds outside our consciousness,
It finds no heart within their dress.
The Rat has eaten
That and beaten
Hope and love and memory,
At last, and even the will to die.
But what is the loss ?   For you cannot sell
The heart to those that have none for Hell
To fatten on . . . or that cheap machine,
And its beat would make springs for the dancing feet
Of Lady Bamburgher down in the street
Of her dogs that nose out each other's sin,
And grin, and whine, and roll therein.

Against the Sea-wall are painted signs
' Here for a shilling a sailor dines.'
Each Rag-and-Bone
Is propped up tall
(Lest in death it fall)
Against the Sea-wall.
Their empty mouths are sewed up whole
Lest from hunger they gape and cough up their soul.
The arms of one are stretched out wide. . . .
How long, since our Christ was crucified ?

Rich man Judas,
Brother Cain,
The rich men are your worms that gain
The air through seething from your brain ;

Judas, mouldering in your old
Coffin body, still undying
As the Worm, where you are lying
With no flesh for warmth, but gold
For flesh, for warmth, for sheet :
Now you are fleshless, too, as these
That starve and freeze,
Is your gold hard as Hell's huge polar street,
Is the universal blackness of Hell's day so cold ?

.   .   .   .   .

When, creeping over
The Sailor's Street
Where the houses like rat-skin
Masks flap, meet
Never across the murdered bone
Of the sailor, the whining overtone
Of dawn sounds, slaves
Rise from their graves,
Where in the corpse-sheet night they lay
Forgetting the mutilating day,
Like the unborn child in its innocent sleep.
Ah Christ, the murdered light must weep —
(Christ that takest away the sin
Of the world, and the rich man's bone-dead grin)
The light must weep
Seeing that sleep
And those slaves rise up in their death-chains, part
The light from the eyes,
The hands from the heart,
Since their hearts are flesh for the tall
And sprawling
Reeling appalling
Cannibal mart,
But their hands and head
Are machines to breed
Gold for the old and the greedy Dead.

I have seen the murdered God look through the eyes

Of the drunkard's smirched
Mask as he lurched
O'er the half of my heart that lies in the street
'Neath the dancing fleas and the foul news-sheet.

Where (a black gap flapping,
A white skin drum)
The cannibal houses
Watch this come —
Lady Bamburgher's party ; for the plan
Is a prize for those that on all fours ran
Through the rotting slum
Till those who come
Could never guess from the mud-covered shapes
Which are the rich or the mired dire apes,
As they run where the souls, dirty paper, are blown
In the hour before dawn, through this long hell of
    stone.

Perhaps if I too lie down in the mud,
Beneath tumbrils rolling
And mad skulls galloping
Far from their bunches of nerves that dance
And caper among these slums and prance,
Beneath the noise of that hell that rolls,
I shall forget the shrunken souls,
The eyeless mud squealing ' God is dead,'
Starved men (bags of wind) and the harlot's
    tread,
The heaven turned into monkey-hide
By Lady Bamburgher's dancing fleas,
Her rotting parties and death-slack ease,
And the dead men drunken
(The only tide)
Blown up and down
And tossed through the town
Over the half of my heart that lies
Deep down, in this meaner Death, with cries.

The leaves of black hippopotamus-hide
Black as the mud
Cover the blood
And the rotting world.   Do we smell and see

The sick thick smoke from London burning,
Gomorrah turning
Like worms in the grave,
The Bedlam daylight's murderous roar,
Those pillars of fire the drunkard and whore,
Dirty souls boiled in cannibal cookshops to paper
To make into newspapers, flags ? . . . They caper
Like gaping apes.   Foul fires we see,
For Bedlam awakes to reality.

The drunkard burning,
The skin drums galloping,
In their long march still parched for the sky,
The Rotten Alleys where beggars groan
And the beggar and his dog share a bone ;
The rich man Cain that hides within
His lumbering palaces where Sin
Through the eyeless holes of Day peers in,
The murdered heart that all night turns
From small machine to shapeless Worm
With hate, and like Gomorrah burns —
These put the eyes of Heaven out,
These raise all Hell's throats to a shout,
These break my heart's walls toppling in,
And like a universal sea
The nations of the Dead crowd in.

Bahunda, Banbangala, Barumbe, Bonge,
And London fall, . . . rolling human skin drums
Surrounded by long black hair, I hear
Their stones that fall,
Their voices that call,
Among the black and the bellowing bones.

But yet when the cannibal
Sun is high
The sightless mud
Weeps tears, a sigh,
To rhinoceros-hided leaves : ' Ah why
So sightless, earless, voiceless, I ? '

The mud has at least its skulls to roll ;
But here as I walk, no voices call,
Only the stones and the bones that fall ;
But yet if only one soul would whine,
Rat-like from the lowest mud, I should know
That somewhere in God's vast love it would shine :
But even the rat-whine has guttered low.

I saw the Blind like a winding-sheet
Tossed up and down through the blind man's street
Where the dead plague-spot
Of the spirit's rot
On the swollen thick houses
Cries to the quick,
Cries to the dark soul that lies there and dies
In hunger and murk, and answers not.

Gomorrah's fires have washed my blood —
But the fires of God shall wash the mud
Till the skin drums rolling
The slum cries sprawling
And crawling
Are calling
' Burn thou me ! '
Though Death has taken
And pig-like shaken,
Rooted, and tossed
The rags of me.
Yet the time will come
To the heart's dark slum

When the rich man's gold and the rich man's wheat
Will grow in the street, that the starved may eat, —
And the sea of the rich will give up its dead —
And the last blood and fire from my side will be shed.
For the fires of God go marching on.

LATER POEMS

(from 1940 onwards)

PART I

ဢ

1. Invocation

FOR ALEC AND MERULA GUINNESS

I WHO was once a golden woman like those who walk
In the dark heavens — but am now grown old
And sit by the fire, and see the fire grow cold,
Watch the dark fields for a rebirth of faith and of wonder.

The turning of Ixion's wheel the day
Ceased not, yet sounds no more the beat of the heart
But only the sound of ultimate Darkness falling
And of the Blind Samson at the Fair, shaking the pillars
    of the world and emptily calling.

For the gardeners cried for rain, but the high priests
    howled
For a darker rain to cool the delirium of gold
And wash the sore of the world, the heart of Dives,
Raise wheat for the hunger that lies in the soul of the
    poor —
Then came the thunderous darkness

And the fly-like whispering of small hopes, small fears,
The gossips of mean Death — gadflies and gnats, the
    summer world :
The small and gilded scholars of the Fly
That feed upon the crowds and their dead breath
And buzz and stink where the bright heroes die
Of the dust's rumours and the old world's fevers.
Then fell the world in winter.

But I, a golden woman like the corn goddess
Watch the dark fields, and know when spring begins
To the sound of the heart and the planetary rhythm,
Fires in the heavens and in the hearts of men,
Young people and young flowers come out in the
      darkness.
And where are they going ?   How should I know ?   I
      see only
The hierarchies love the young people — the Swan has
      given his snows
And Berenice her wild mane to make their fair hair,
And speaking of love are the voices that come from the
      darkness :

Of the nobler love of Man for his brother Man,
And of how the creeds of the world shall no more divide
      them
But every life be that of a country Fate
Whose wheel had a golden woof and warp, the Day —
Woven of threads of the common task ; and light
Tells to that little child the humble dust
Tales of the old world's holiness, finds veins of ore
In the unripe wheat-ear ; and the common fire
That drops with seed like the Sun's, is fallen from the
      long-leaved planets.

So when the winter of the world and Man's fresh Fall
When democratic Death feared no more the heart's
      coldness
Shall be forgotten,
O Love, return to the dying world, as the light
Of morning, shining in all regions, latitudes
And households of high heaven within the heart.

Be then our visible world, our world invisible !
Throughout our day like the laughing flames of the Sun
Lie on our leaves of life, your heat infusing
Deep in the amber blood of the smooth tree.

The panic splendour of the animal
Is yours — O primal Law
That rules the blood — (the solar ray in the veins,
The fire of the hearth, the household Deity
That shines not, nor does it burn, destroy like fire,
But nourishes with its endless wandering
Like that of the Golden Ones in the high heavens.)

Rule then the spirit working in dark earth
As the Sun and Planets rule the husbandman —
O pride that in each semitone
Of amber blood and bone
Proclaims the splendour that arose from the first Dark!

Be too the ear of wheat to the Lost Men
Who ask the city stones if they are bread
And the stones of the city weep. . . .
                       You, the lost days
When all might still be hoped for, and the light
Laid gold in the unhopeful path of the poor —
The shrunken darkness in the miser's heart.

Now falls the night of the world : — O Spirit moving upon
    the waters
Your peace instil
In the animal heat and splendour of the blood —
(The hot gold of the sun that flames in the night
And knows not down-going
But moves with the revolutions in the heavens.)

The thunders and the fires and acclamations
Of the leaves of spring are stilled, but in the night
The Holy Ghost speaks in the whispering leaves.
O wheat-ear shining like a fire and the bright gold,
O water brought from far to the dying gardens!

Bring peace to the famine of the heart and lips,
And to the Last Man's loneliness
Of those who dream they can bring back sight to the blind!

You are the Night
When the long hunt for Nothing is at rest
In the Blind Man's Street, and in the human breast
The hammer of Chaos is stilled.
                                        Be then the sleep
When Judas gives again the childish kiss
That once his mother knew — and wash the stain
From the darkened hands of the universal Cain.

2. *An Old Woman*

I

I, AN old woman in the light of the sun,
Wait for my Wanderer, and my upturned face
Has all the glory of the remembering Day,
The hallowed grandeur of the primeval clay
That knew the Flood, and suffered all the dryness
Of the uncaring heaven, the sun its lover.

For the sun is the first lover of the world,
Blessing all humble creatures, all life-giving,
Blessing the end of life and the work done,
The clean and the unclean, ores in earth, and splendours
Within the heart of man, that second sun.

For when the first founts and deep waterways
Of the young light flow down and lie like peace
Upon the upturned faces of the blind
From life, it comes to bless
Eternity in its poor mortal dress —
Shining upon young lovers and old lechers
Rising from their beds, and laying gold
Alike in the unhopeful path of beggars
And in the darkness of the miser's heart.
The crookèd has a shadow light made straight,
The shallow places gain their strength again —
And desert hearts, waste heavens, the barren height
Forget that they are cold.
The man-made chasms between man and man
Of creeds and tongues are fill'd, the guiltless light
Remakes all men and things in holiness.

And he who blessed the fox with a golden fleece,
And covered earth with ears of corn like the planets
Bearded with thick ripe gold,
For the holy bread of mankind, blessed my clay :
For the sun cares not that I am a simple woman,

To him, laughing, the veins in my arms and the wrinkles
From work on my nursing hands are sacred as branches
And furrows of harvest . . . to him, the heat of the earth
And beat of the heart are one, —
Born from the energy of the world, the love
That keeps the Golden Ones in their place above,
And hearts and blood of beasts ever in motion, —
Without which comets, sun, plants, and all living beings
And warmth in the inward parts of the earth would freeze.
And the sun does not care if I live in holiness,
To him, my mortal dress
Is sacred, part of the earth, a lump of the world
With my splendours, ores, impurities, and harvest,
Over which shines my heart, that ripening sun.

Though the dust, the shining racer, overtake me,
I too was a golden woman like those that walk
In the fields of the heavens : — but am now grown old
And must sit by the fire and watch the fire grow cold,
— A country Fate whose spool is the household task.
Yet still I am loved by the sun, and still am part
Of earth.   In the evenings bringing home the workers,
Bringing the wanderer home and the dead child,
The child unborn and never to be conceived,
Home to the mother's breast, I sit by the fire
Where the seed of gold drops dead and the kettle simmers
With a sweet sound like that of a hive of bees ;
And I wait for my Wanderer to come home to rest —
Covered with earth as if he had been working
Among the happy gardens, the holy fields
Where the bread of mankind ripens in the stillness.
Unchanged to me by death, I shall hold to my breast
My little child in his sleep, I shall seem the consoling
Earth, the mother of corn, nurse of the unreturning.

Wise is the earth, consoling grief and glory,
The golden heroes proud as pomp of waves, —
Great is the earth embracing them, their graves,

And great is the earth's story.
For though the soundless wrinkles fall like snow
On many a golden cheek, and creeds grow old
And change, — man's heart, that sun,
Outlives all terrors shaking the old night :
The world's huge fevers burn and shine, turn cold,
Yet the heavenly bodies and young lovers burn and shine,
The golden lovers walk in the holy fields
Where the Abraham-bearded sun, the father of all things,
Is shouting of ripeness, and the whole world of dews and
    splendours are singing
To the cradles of earth, of men, beasts, harvests, swinging
In the peace of God's heart.   And I, the primeval clay
That has known earth's grief and harvest's happiness,
Seeing mankind's dark seed-time, come to bless,
Forgive and bless all men like the holy light.

II. *Harvest*

TO STEPHEN SPENDER

I, AN old woman whose heart is like the Sun
That has seen too much, looked on too many sorrows,
Yet is not weary of shining, fulfilment and harvest,
Heard the priests that howled for rain and the universal
    darkness,
Saw the golden princes sacrificed to the Rain-god,
The cloud that came, and was small as the hand of Man.
And now in the time of the swallow, the bright one, the
    chatterer,
The young women wait like the mother of corn for the
    lost one —
Their golden eyelids are darkened like the great rain-clouds.
But in bud and branch the nature of Fate begins
— And love with the Lion's claws and the Lion's hunger
Hides in the brakes in the nihilistic Spring. —
Old men feel their scolding heart

Reproach the veins that for fire have only anger.
And Christ has forgiven all men — the thunder-browed
      Caesar,
That stone-veined Tantalus howling with thirst in the plain
Where for innocent water flows only the blood of the slain,
Falling for ever from veins that held in their noonday
The foolish companion of summer, the weeping rose.
We asked for a sign that we have not been forsaken —
And for answer the Abraham-bearded Sun, the father of
      all things,
Is shouting of ripeness over our harvest for ever.
And with the sound of growth, lion-strong, and the
      laughing Sun
Whose great flames stretch like branches in the heat
Across the firmament, we almost see
The great gold planets spangling the wide air
And earth —

                  O sons of men, the firmament's belovèd,
The Golden Ones of heaven have us in care —
With planetary wisdom, changeless laws,
Ripening our lives and ruling hearts and rhythms,
Immortal hungers in the veins and heart
Born from the primal Cause
That keeps the hearts and blood of men and beasts ever
      in motion,
The amber blood of the smooth-weeping tree
Rising toward the life-giving heat of the Sun. . . .
For is not the blood, — the divine, the animal heat
That is not fire, — derived from the solar ray ?
And does not the Beast surpass all elements
In power, through the heat and wisdom of the blood
Creating other Beasts — the Lion a Lion, the Bull a Bull,
The Bear a Bear — some like great stars in the rough
And uncreated dark — or unshaped universes
With manes of fire and a raging sun for heart.
Gestation, generation and duration —
The cycles of all lives upon the earth —
Plants, beasts and men, must follow those of heaven :

The rhythms of our lives
Are those of the ripening, dying of the seasons,
Our sowing and reaping in the holy fields,
Our love and giving birth — then growing old
And sinking into sleep in the maternal
Earth, mother of corn, the wrinkled darkness.
So we, ruled by those laws, see their fulfilment.
And I who stood in the grave-clothes of my flesh
Unutterably spotted with the world's woes
Cry, ' I am Fire.   See, I am the bright gold
That shines like a flaming fire in the night — the gold-
    trained planet,
The laughing heat of the Sun that was born from dark-
    ness —
Returning to darkness — I am fecundity, harvest.'
For on each country road
Grown from the needs of men as boughs from trees,
The reapers walk like the harvesters of heaven —
Jupiter and his great train, and the corn-goddess,
And Saturn marching in the Dorian mode.
We heard in the dawn the first ripe-bearded fire
Of wheat (so flames that are men's spirits break from
    their thick earth);
Then came the Pentecostal Rushing of Flames, God in the
    wind that comes to the wheat,
Returned from the Dead for the guilty hands of Caesar
Like the rose at morning shouting of red joys
And redder sorrows fallen from young veins and heart-
    springs,
Come back for the wrong and the right, the wise and
    the foolish
Who like the rose care not for our philosophies
Of life and death, knowing the earth's forgiveness
And the great dews that come to the sick rose:
For those who build great mornings for the world
From Edens of lost light seen in each other's eyes,
Yet soon must wear no more the light of the Sun,
But say farewell among the morning sorrows.

The universal language of the Bread —
(O Thou who art not broken, or divided —
Thou who art eaten, but like the Burning Bush
Art not consumed — Thou Bread of Men and Angels) —
The Seraphim rank on rank of the ripe wheat —
Gold-bearded thunders and hierarchies of heaven
Roar from the earth : ' Our Christ is arisen, He comes to
    give a sign from the Dead.'

3. Eurydice

TO JOHN LEHMANN

FIRES on the hearth ! Fires in the heavens ! Fires in the
     hearts of Men !
I who was welded into bright gold in the earth by Death
Salute you ! All the weight of Death in all the world
Yet does not equal Love — the great compassion
For the fallen dust and all fallen creatures, quickening
As is the Sun in the void firmament.
It shines like fire. O bright gold of the heat of the Sun
Of Love across dark fields — burning away rough husks
     of Death
Till all is fire, and bringing all to harvest !

See then ! I stand in the centre of my earth
That was my Death, under the zenith of my Sun
Bringing a word from Darkness
That Death too has compassion for all fallen Nature.
For as the Sun buries his hot days and rays
To ripen in earth, so the great rays of the heart
Are ripened to wisdom by Death, and great is our for-
     giveness.

When through the darkness Orpheus came with his Sun-
     like singing
Like the movements in the heavens that in our blindness
Could we but emulate, would set right our lives —
I came to the mouth of the Tomb, I did not know our
     meeting would be this :
— Only like the return at evening
Of the weary worker in the holy fields, —
The cry of welcome, the remembered kiss !

In the lateness of the season, I with the golden feet
That had walked in the fields of Death, now walk again
The dark fields where the sowers scatter grain
Like tears, or the constellations that weep for the late-
     ness of the season —

Where the women walk like mourners, like the Afternoon
    ripened, with their bent heads ;
Their golden eyelids like the drifts of the narcissus
In spring, are wet with their tears.   They mourn for a
    young wife who had walked these fields
— So young, not yet had Proserpina tied up her golden
    hair
In a knot like the branchèd corn. . . . So good was she, —
With a voice like the sweet swallow.   She lies in the
    silent Tomb

And they walk in the fields alone.   Then one of the Dead
    who lay
Beneath the earth, like the water-dark, the water-thin
Effigy of Osiris, with a face green as a moon,
— He who was lying in darkness with the wheat
Like a flame springing from his heart, or a gold sound,
Said to me, ' We have been blind and stripped God naked
    of things
To see the light which shines in the dark, and we have
    learned
That the gold flame of the wheat may spring from a
    barren heart.'

When I came down from the Metropolis of the Corn
Then said the ferine dust that reared about me,
' I have the famine of the lion, all things devour,
Or make them mine. . . . Venus was powerful as me —
Now is she but a handful of dry amber dust :
And my tooth cracked the husk, the dry amber wall
That held the fire of the wheat.   That fire is gone, —
And remember this, that Love, or I, have ground
Your heart between the stones of the years, like wheat.'

But as I left the mouth of the Tomb, far off, like the noise
    of the dark wild bees
I heard the sounds arise from the dwellings of Men, and I
    thought of their building,

Their wars, their honey-making, and of the gold roofs
    built against Darkness.

And I had learned beneath the earth that all gold nature
Changes to wheat or gold in the sweet darkness.
Why do they weep for those in the silent Tomb,
Dropping their tears like grain ?   Her heart, that honey-
    comb,
Thick Darkness like a bear devours. . . . See, all the gold
    is gone !
The cell of the honeycomb is six-sided. . . . But there,
    in the five cells of the senses,
Is stored all their gold. . . . Where is it now ?   Only
    the wind of the Tomb can know.
But I feared not that stilled and chilling breath
Among the dust. . . . Love is not changed by Death,
And nothing is lost and all in the end is harvest.

As the earth is heavy with the lion-strong Sun
When he has fallen, with his hot days and rays,
We are heavy with Death, as a woman is heavy with
    child,
As the corn-husk holds its ripeness, the gold comb
Its weight of summer. . . . But as if a lump of gold had
    changed to corn,
So did my Life rise from my Death.   I cast the grandeur
    of Death away
And homeward came to the small things of Love, the
    building of the hearth, the kneading of daily bread,
The cries of birth, and all the weight of light
Shaping our bodies and our souls.   Came home to youth,
And the noise of summer growing in the veins,
And to old age, a serene afternoon,
An element beyond time, or a new climate.

I with the other young who were born from darkness,
Returning to darkness, stood at the mouth of the Tomb
With one who had come glittering like the wind

To meet me — Orpheus with the golden mouth,
You — like Adonis born from the young myrrh-tree, you,
    the vine-branch
Broken by the wind of love. . . . I turned to greet you —
And when I touched your mouth, it was the Sun.

4. *Song for Two Voices*

' O Dionysus of the tree — you of the beard, you of the
    ripeness
Among the branches of my arms and hair
As the boughs of the vine hold the plane-tree —
You came like the wind in the branches.'

' And to the earth of my heart, O golden woman,
You are the corn-goddess.'

' O wind, come again to my branches.'

' O darkness of earth — O ripeness.'

PART II

ᕦ

1. *Still Falls the Rain*

The Raids, 1940.   *Night and Dawn*

STILL falls the Rain —
Dark as the world of man, black as our loss —
Blind as the nineteen hundred and forty nails
Upon the Cross.

Still falls the Rain
With a sound like the pulse of the heart that is changed to
    the hammer-beat
In the Potter's Field, and the sound of the impious feet

On the Tomb :
                  Still falls the Rain
In the Field of Blood where the small hopes breed and
    the human brain
Nurtures its greed, that worm with the brow of Cain.

Still falls the Rain
At the feet of the Starved Man hung upon the Cross.
Christ that each day, each night, nails there, have mercy
    on us —
On Dives and on Lazarus :
Under the Rain the sore and the gold are as one.

Still falls the Rain —
Still falls the Blood from the Starved Man's wounded Side :
He bears in His Heart all wounds, — those of the light
    that died,

The last faint spark
In the self-murdered heart, the wounds of the sad un-
    comprehending dark,
The wounds of the baited bear, —
The blind and weeping bear whom the keepers beat
On his helpless flesh . . . the tears of the hunted hare.

Still falls the Rain —
Then — O Ile leape up to my God : who pulles me
    doune —
See, see where Christ's blood streames in the firmament :
It flows from the Brow we nailed upon the tree
Deep to the dying, to the thirsting heart
That holds the fires of the world, — dark-smirched with
    pain
As Caesar's laurel crown.

Then sounds the voice of One who like the heart of man
Was once a child who among beasts has lain —
' Still do I love, still shed my innocent light, my Blood,
    for thee.'

2. *Lullaby*

THOUGH the world has slipped and gone,
Sounds my loud discordant cry
Like the steel birds' song on high :
' Still one thing is left — the Bone ! '
Then out danced the Babioun.

She sat in the hollow of the sea —
A socket whence the eye's put out —
She sang to the child a lullaby
(The steel birds' nest was thereabout).

' Do, do, do, do —
Thy mother's hied to the vaster race :
The Pterodactyl made its nest
And laid a steel egg in her breast —
Under the Judas-coloured sun.
She'll work no more, nor dance, nor moan,
And I am come to take her place.
Do, do.

There's nothing left but earth's low bed —
(The Pterodactyl fouls its nest) :
But steel wings fan thee to thy rest,
And wingless truth and larvae lie
And eyeless hope and handless fear —
All these for thee as toys are spread,
Do — do —

Red is the bed of Poland, Spain,
And thy mother's breast, who has grown wise
In that fouled nest.   If she could rise,
Give birth again,

In wolfish pelt she'd hide thy bones
To shield thee from the world's long cold,

And down on all fours shouldst thou crawl
For thus from no height canst thou fall —
Do, do.

She'd give no hands : there's naught to hold
And naught to make : there's dust to sift,
But no food for the hands to lift.
Do, do.

Heed my ragged lullaby,
Fear not living, fear not chance ;
All is equal — blindness, sight,
There is no depth, there is no height :
Do, do.

The Judas-coloured sun is gone,
And with the Ape thou art alone —
Do,
      Do.'

3. *Serenade: Any Man to Any Woman*

DARK angel who are clear and straight
As cannon shining in the air,
Your blackness doth invade my mind
And thunderous as the armoured wind
That rained on Europe is your hair;

And so I love you till I die —
(Unfaithful I, the cannon's mate):
Forgive my love of such brief span,
But fickle is the flesh of man,
And death's cold puts the passion out.

I'll woo you with a serenade —
The wolfish howls the starving made;
And lies shall be your canopy
To shield you from the freezing sky.

Yet when I clasp you in my arms —
Who are my sleep, the zero hour
That clothes, instead of flesh, my heart, —
You in my heaven have no part,
For you, my mirage broken in flower,

Can never see what dead men know!
Then die with me and be my love:
The grave shall be your shady grove
And in your pleasaunce rivers flow

(To ripen this new Paradise)
From a more universal Flood
Than Noah knew: but yours is blood.

Yet still you will imperfect be
That in my heart like death's chill grows,
— A rainbow shining in the night,
Born of my tears . . . your lips, the bright
Summer-old folly of the rose.

4. Street Song

' Love my heart for an hour, but my bone for a day —
At least the skeleton smiles, for it has a morrow :
But the hearts of the young are now the dark treasure of
    Death,
And summer is lonely.

Comfort the lonely light and the sun in its sorrow,
Come like the night, for terrible is the sun
As truth, and the dying light shows only the skeleton's
    hunger
For peace, under the flesh like the summer rose.

Come through the darkness of death, as once through the
    branches
Of youth you came, through the shade like the flowering
    door
That leads into Paradise, far from the street, — you, the
    unborn
City seen by the homeless, the night of the poor.

You walk in the city ways, where Man's threatening
    shadow
Red-edged by the sun like Cain, has a changing shape —
Elegant like the Skeleton, crouched like the Tiger,
With the age-old wisdom and aptness of the Ape.

The pulse that beats in the heart is changed to the hammer
That sounds in the Potter's Field where they build a new
    world
From our Bone, and the carrion-bird days' foul droppings
    and clamour —
But you are my night, and my peace, —

The holy night of conception, of rest, the consoling
Darkness when all men are equal, — the wrong and the
    right,

And the rich and the poor are no longer separate nations, —
They are brothers in night.'

This was the song I heard ; but the Bone is silent !
Who knows if the sound was that of the dead light call-
     ing, —
Of Caesar rolling onward his heart, that stone,
Or the burden of Atlas falling ?

5. *O yet forgive*

O YET forgive my heart in your long night!
I am too poor to be Death's self so I might lie
Upon your heart . . . for my mortality
Too sad and heavy is, would leave a stain
Upon young lips, young eyes. . . . You will not
    come again :
So the weight of Atlas' woe, changed to a stone,
And that stone is my heart, I laid above
Your eyes, till blind as love
You no more see the work of the old wise.

But you in your long night are not deceived :
And so, not heeding the world, you let it roll
Into the long abyss
And say, ' What is that sound ?   I am alone. . . .
Is it my great sunrise ? '

6. Poor Young Simpleton

I. *An Old Song Re-sung*

' ONCE my love seemed the Burning Bush,
The Pentecost Rushing of Flames :
Now the Speech has fallen to the chatter of alleys
Where fallen man and the rising ape
And the howling Dark play games.

For she leaned from the light like the Queen of Fairies
Out of the bush of the yellow broom . . .
" I'll take out that heart of yours," she said,
" And put in your breast a stone.
O, I'll leave an empty room," she said,
" A fouled, but an empty room." '

II

' I WALKED with my dead living love in the city —
The Potter's Field where the race of Man
Constructs a new world with hands thumbless from unuse
— (Pads like a tiger's) — a skeleton plan.

We walked in the city where even the lightning —
The Flag of Blood flying across the world,
The Flag of immeasurable Doom, of God's warning,
Is changed to a spider's universe, furled

For a banner of hunger . . . the world of the thunder
Is dulled till it seems but the idiot drum
Of a universe changed to a circus, — the clatter
Where the paralysed dance in the blind man's slum.

But the sun was huge as a mountain of diamonds
That starved men see on a plain far away :
It will never buy food, but its red fires glittered
On the Heart of Quietness, my Eden day.

For she was the cool of the evening, bringing
The dead child home to the mother's breast,
The wanderer homeward, far from the hammer
That beats in the Potter's Field : she was my rest,

And the Burning Bush, and the worker's Sunday,
The neighbour of Silence, speech to the still,
And her kiss was the Fiery Chariot, low swinging
To take me over the diamond hill.

Where the crowds sweep onward, mountaineers, nomads
From cities and continents man has not seen,
With beachcombers drifted from shores that no wave has
        known,
Pilgrims to shrines where no God-head has been,

We watched the somnambulists, rope-walkers, argonauts,
Avatars, tamers of steel-birds and fugitives
From dream and reality, emigrants, mourners,
And each with his Shadow, (to prove that Man lives !)

And with them come gaps into listening Darkness :
The gun-men, the molochs, the matadors, man-eaters,
Hiding in islands of loneliness, each one
Infections of hatred, and greed-plague, and fear.

For the season of red pyromaniacs, the dog-days
Are here, and now even the sun of a kiss
Sets a city on fire, and the innocent roses
Are the fever of foolish world-summers ; and this

Beloved of my skeleton laughed, and said, " Tell me —
Why give me your heart like an eagle that flies,
Or a sun ? — You should give me a crow for my dinner,
Or a flat dirty penny to lay on my eyes."

And how can I save the heart of my Eden
That is only the hammering heart of the town,

When the only world left is my skeleton's city
Where the sun of the desert will never go down ?

She has hearkened the Spider's prudence, the wisdom
That, spinning a foul architecture, unfurled
From his belly a city he made out of Hunger —
Constructed for Hunger's need : his is the world.

So what can I give to her ?   Civilisation's
Disease, a delirium flushed like the rose
And noisy as summer ?   Hands thumbless from unuse
— (From pads like a tiger's what bright claw grows ?)

Though faithless the rose and the flesh, yet the city,
That eternal landscape, the skeleton's plan,
Has hope for its worm. . . . I will give her the pity
For the fallen Ape, of the Tiger, Man.

For my Eden is withered.   I, damned by the Rainbow,
Near that fouled trodden alley, the bed where she lies,
Can wake no false dawn, — where, for want of a penny,
She lies with the sins of the world on her eyes.'

7. *Song*

ONCE my heart was a summer rose
That cares not for right or wrong,
And the sun was another rose, that year,
They shone, the sun and the rose, my dear —
Over the long and the light summer land
All the bright summer long.

As I walked in the long and the light summer land
All that I knew of shade
Was the cloud, my ombrelle of rustling grey
Sharp silk, it had spokes of grey steel rain —
Hiding my rose away, my dear,
Hiding my rose away.

And my laughter shone like a flight of birds
All in the summer gay, —
Tumbling pigeons and chattering starlings
And other pretty darlings, my dear,
And other pretty darlings.

To my heart like a rose, a rain of tears
(All the bright summer long)
Was only the sheen on a wood-dove's breast,
And sorrow only her song, my love —
And sorrow only my rest.

I passed a while in Feather Town —
(All the bright summer long) —
The idle wind puffed that town up
In air, then blew it down.

I walk alone now in Lead Town
(All in the summer gay . . .)
Where the steady people walk like the Dead —
And will not look my way.

For withering my heart, that summer rose,
Came another heart like a sun, —
And it drank all the dew from the rose, my love,
And the birds have forgotten their song
That sounded all summer long, my dear —
All the bright summer long.

8. *Green Flows the River of Lethe—O*

GREEN flows the river of Lethe — O
Long Lethe river
Where the fire was in the veins — and grass is growing
Over the fever —
The green grass growing. . . .

I stood near the Cities of the Plains
And the young girls were chasing their hearts like the gay
     butterflies
Over the fields of summer —
O evanescent velvets fluttering your wings
Like winds and butterflies on the Road from Nothing to
     Nowhere !

But in the summer drought
I fled, for I was a Pillar of Fire, I was Destruction
Unquenched, incarnate and incarnadine.

I was Annihilation
Yet white as the Dead Sea, white as the Cities of the Plains,
For I listened to the noontide and my veins
That threatened thunder and the heart of roses.

I went the way I would —
But long is the terrible Street of the Blood
That had once seemed only part of the summer redness :
It stretches for ever, and there is no turning
But only fire, annihilation, burning.

I thought the way of the Blood would never tire
But now only the red clover
Lies over the breath of the lion and the mouth of the
     lover —

And green flows Lethe river — O
Long Lethe river
Over Gomorrah's city and the fire. . . .

9. *A Mother to her Dead Child*

THE winter, the animal sleep of the earth, is over
And in the warmth of the affirming sun
All beings, beasts, men, planets, waters, move
Freed from the imprisoning frost, acclaim their love
That is the light of the sun.
                          So the first spring began
Within the heart before the Fall of Man.

The earth puts forth its sprays, the heart its warmth,
And your hands push back the dark that is your nurse,
Feel for my heart as in the days before your birth.
O Sun of my life, return to the waiting earth
Of your mother's breast, the heart, the empty arms.
Come soon, for the time is passing, and when I am old
The night of my body will be too thick and cold
For the sun of your growing heart.   Return from your
          new mother
The earth : she is too old for your little body,
Too old for the small tendernesses, the kissings
In the soft tendrils of your hair.   The earth is so old
She can only think of darkness and sleep, forgetting
That children are restless like the small spring shadows.
But the huge pangs of winter and the pain
Of the spring's birth, the endless centuries of rain
Will not lay bare your trusting smile, your tress,
Or lay your heart bare to my heart again
In your small earthly dress.
And when I wait for you upon the summer roads
They bear all things and men, business and pleasure,
          sorrow,
And lovers' meetings, mourning shades, the poor man's
          leisure,
And the foolish rose that cares not ever for the far
          tomorrow.
But the roads are too busy for the sound of your feet,
And the lost men, the rejected of life, who tend the wounds

That life has made as if they were a new sunrise, whose
    human speech is dying
From want, to the rusted voice of the tiger, turn not their
    heads lest I hear your child-voice crying
In that hoarse tiger-voice : ' I am hungry ! am cold ! '
Lest I see your smile upon lips that were made for the kiss
    that exists not,
The food that deserts them, — those lips never warm with
    love, but from the world's fever,
Whose smile is a gap into darkness, the breaking apart
Of the long-impending earthquake that waits in the heart.
That smile rends the soul with the sign of its destitution,
It drips from the last long pangs of the heart, self-devouring,
And tearing the seer.

                Yet one will return to the lost men,
Whose heart is the Sun of Reason, dispelling the shadow
That was born with no eyes to shed tears, — bringing peace
    to the lust
And pruriency of the Ape, from the human heart's sublimity
And tenderness teaching the dust that it is holy,
And to those who are hungry, are naked and cold as the
    worm, who are bare as the spirit
In that last night when the rich and the poor are alone,
Bringing love like the daily bread, like the light at morning.
And knowing this, I would give you again, my day's darling,
My little child who preferred the bright apple to gold,
And who lies with the shining world on his innocent eyes,
Though night-long I feel your tears, bright as the rose
In its sorrowful leaves, on my lips, and feel your hands
Touching my cheek, and wondering ' Are those your tears ? '
O grief, that your heart should know the tears that seem
    empty years
And the worlds that are falling !

10. Tattered Serenade: Beggar to Shadow

I

THESE are the nations of the Dead, their million-year-old
Rags about them, — these, the eternally cold,
Misery's worlds, with Hunger, their long sun
Shut in by polar worlds of ice, known to no other,
Without a name, without a brother,
Though their skin shows that they yet are men,

Airing their skeletons' well-planned cities whence
(Left by the rose, the flesh, with truth alone),
The fevers of the world and of the heart,
The light of the sun, are gone.

And to their only friend, the Shade
They cast, their muttering voices sing this Serenade :

' O Shade !   Gigantic and adaptable Ape,
With the elegance of the skeleton
In your black tattered cape —
How like, and yet how unlike, you are to our last state !

You, too, have giant hands, — but have no thumbs
In a world where nothing is to make or hold,
Nor have you that appalling gulf the heart, —
Or that red gulf the gullet where only Hunger comes.

For face, you have a hollow wolf-grey cowl
Like mine . . . no voice to howl —

(O plain of winter wolves beneath my heart !)
And no identity !   No face to weep !
No bed — unlike the rich men who can creep
Into the pocks made by that vast disease
That is our civilisation, once there, lie at ease !

No memory, — no years,
Nothing to feel or think,
No friend from whom to part with youthful tears.
But your unutterable tatters cannot stink !

My overcoat, like yours, is an Ideal,
With a gulf for pockets — nothing there to steal
But my empty hands, that long have lost their use,
With nothing now to make, or hold, or lose.

Yet when spring comes, a world is in my head,
And dreams, for those who never have a bed —

The thought of a day when all may be possible, — all
May come my way,' said small Rag-Castle to Rag-Castle
  tall, —
The young, that have no covering between
Their outer tatters and the worthless skin
That shows the air, the rain, they yet are men,

When remembering it is spring, falls the warm rain
Like lilies of the vale,
Buds golden-pale
Sprouting from pavements, or a universe of coins, endless
  gold

Pelting the homeless, those who have no dress
Against the winter cold,
But the skeleton, that burgh of idleness
Where only the worm works . . . those that are alone
Except for hunger, thirst, and lust ;
For the fevers of the world and of the heart,
The summer rose, are gone.

II

In the summer, when no one is cold,
And the country roads seem of hot gold,

While the air seems a draught of white wine
Where all day long golden stars shine, —

And the sun is a world of red meat
For those who have nothing to eat,

I walk the world, envying the roads
That have somewhere to go, that bear loads

Of happiness, business, and sorrow,
And the rose that cares not for tomorrow ;

But I've nothing to hold or to lose,
And my hands have long since lost their use ;

While my overcoat's but an Ideal, —
In my pockets there's nothing to steal.

But the roads have north, east, west, and south,
For their food, though I've none for my mouth

Or my empty red gulf of a heart —
I have no friend from whom I must part

But the shade that I cast, — my one friend
Till at last the world comes to an end.

His face is a wolfish grey cowl,
Like my own, but without the wolf's howl,

For like me, he's a face, but no tears
He can shed, neither memory nor years.

But the Shadow has never known cold,
And the Shadow will never grow old, —

The black tatters he wears cannot stink
And he neither can feel, fear, nor think,

While a universe grows in my head, —
I have dreams, though I have not a bed —

The thought of a world and a day
When all may be possible, still come my way

As I walk the long roads of hot gold
In the summer, when no one is cold.

11. *The Song of the Cold*

TO NATASHA LITVIN

HUGE is the sun of amethysts and rubies,
And in the purple perfumes of the polar sun
And homeless cold they wander.
But winter is the time for comfort, and for friendship,
For warmth and food —
And a talk beside a fire like the Midnight Sun, —
A glowing heart of amber and of musk.   Time to forget
The falling night of the world and heart, the polar
        chaos
That separates us each from each.   It is no time to roam
Along the pavements wide and cold as Hell's huge polar
        street,
Drifting along the city like the wind
Blowing aimlessly, and with no home
To rest in, only famine for a heart —
While Time means nothing to one, as to the wind
Who only cares for ending and beginning.

Here in the fashionable quarters of the city
Cold as the universal blackness of Hell's day
The two opposing brotherhoods are swept
Down the black marble pavements, Lethe's river.
First come the worlds of Misery, the small and tall Rag-
        Castles,
Shut off from every other.   These have no name,
Nor friend to utter it . . . these of the extinct faces
Are a lost civilisation, and have no possession
But the night and day, those centuries of cold.
Even their tears are changed now to the old
Eternal nights of ice round the loveless head
Of these who are lone and sexless as the Dead.
Dives of the Paleocrystic heart, behold
These who were once your brothers !   Hear their voices
Hoarsened by want to the rusty voice of the tiger, no
        more crying

The death of the soul, but lamenting their destitution.
What life, what solar system of the heart
Could bring a restitution
To these who die of the cold?
                              Some keep their youthful graces,
Yet in their winding-sheets of rags seem early
Made ready for the grave. . . . Worn to the bone by
      their famine
As if by the lusts that the poor Dead have known,
Who now are cold for ever. . . . Those who are old
Seem humbler, lean their mouths to the earth as if to
      crop
The kind earth's growth — for this is the Cainozoic period
When we must learn to walk with the gait of the Ape and
      Tiger:
The warmth of the heart is dead, or has changed to the
      world's fever —
And love is but masked murder, the lust for possession,
The hunger of the Ape, or the confession
Of the last fear, the wish to multiply
Their image, of a race on Oblivion's brink.

Lazarus, weep for those who have known the lesser
      deaths, O think
How we should pity the High Priests of the god of this
      world, the saints of Mammon,
The cult of gold! For see how these, too, ache with the
      cold
From the polar wastes of the heart. . . . See all they
      have given
Their god! Are not their veins grown ivy-old,
And have they not eaten their own hearts and lives in
      their famine?

Their huge Arithmetic is but the endless
Repetition of Zero — the unlimited,
Eternal. — Even the beat of the heart and the pulse is
      changed to this:

The counting of small deaths, the repetition
Of Nothing, endless positing and suppression of
                              Nothing. . . . So they live
And die of inanition. . . .
                      The miser Foscue
Weaving his own death and sinking like a spider
To vaults and depths that held his gold, that sun,
Was walled in that grave by the rotting hand of the dust,
    by a trap-door falling.
Do the enormous rays of that Sun now warm his blood,
    the appalling
Empty gulf of his veins — or fertilise
His flesh, that continent of dryness ? . . . Yellow, cold,
And crumbling as his gold,
Deserted by the god of this world, a Gold Man like a
    terrible Sun,
A Mummy with a Lion's mane
He sits in this desert where no sound of wave shall come,
And Time's sands are of gold, filling his ears and eyes ;
And he who has grown the talons of the Lion
Has devoured the flesh of his own hands and heart in his pain.

Pity these hopeless acolytes . . . the vain
Prudence that emulates the wisdom of the Spider
Who spins but for herself — a world of Hunger
Constructed for the needs of Hunger. . . . Soon
Their blankets will be thinner than her thread :
When comes the Night when they have only gold
For flesh, for warmth, for sheet —
O who would not pity these,
Grown fleshless too as those who starve and freeze !

Now falls the Night on Lazarus and Dives —
Those who were brothers, those who shared the pain
Of birth, and lusts, and the daily lesser deaths,
The beat of the dying heart, the careful breaths :
' You are so worn to the bone, I thought you were
    Death, my brother —

Death who will warm my heart.' ' Have you too known
        the cold ?
Give me your hand to warm me.   I am no more alone.
There was a sun that shone
On all alike, but the cold in the heart of Man
Has slain it.   Where is it gone ? '
So in the great Night that comes like love, so small they
        lie
As when they lay close to their mother's breast,
Naked and bare in their mortality.

Soon comes the Night when those who were never loved
Shall know the small immortal serpent's kiss
And turn to dust as lover turns to lover. . . .
Than all shall know the cold's equality. . . .
Young Beauty, bright as the tips of the budding vine,
You with the gold Appearances from Nothing rise
In the spring wind, and but for a moment shine.

Dust are the temples that were bright as heat . . .
And, perfumed nosegay brought for noseless Death,
Your brightest myrrh can not perfume his breath !

That old rag-picker blown along the street
Was once great Venus.   But now Age unkind
Has shrunken her so feeble and so small —
Weak as a babe.   And she who gave the Lion's kiss
Has now all Time's gap for her piteous mouth.
What lullaby will Death sing, seeing this
Small babe ?   And she of the golden feet,
To what love does she haste ?   After these centuries
The sun will be her only kiss — now she is blackened,
        shrunken, old
As the small worm — her kiss, like his, grown cold.

In the nights of spring, the inner leaf of the heart
Feels warm, and we will pray for the eternal cold
Of those who are only warmed by the sins of the world —

And those whose nights were violent like the buds
And roots of spring, but like the spring, grew old.
Their hearts are tombs on the heroic shore,
That were of iris, diamond, hyacinth,
And now are patterned only by Time's wave . . . the
    glittering plinth
Is crumbling. . . . But the great sins and fires break out
    of me
Like the terrible leaves from the bough in the violent
    spring . . .
I am a walking fire, I am all leaves —
I will cry to the Spring to give me the birds' and the
    serpents' speech
That I may weep for those who die of the cold —
The ultimate cold within the heart of Man.

12. *Tears*

My tears were Orion's splendour with sextuple suns and
the million
Flowers in the fields of the heaven, where solar systems
are setting —
The rocks of great diamonds in the midst of the clear
wave
By May dews and early light ripened, more diamonds
begetting.
I wept for the glories of air, for the millions of dawns
And the splendours within Man's heart with the darkness
warring,
I wept for the beautiful queens of the world, like a
flower-bed shining, —
Now gathered, some at six, some at seven, but all in
Eternity's morning.
But now my tears have shrunk and like hours are falling :
I weep for Venus whose body has changed to a meta-
physical city
Whose heart-beat is now the sound of the revolutions, —
for love changed
To the hospital mercy, the scientists' hope for the future,
And for darkened Man, that complex multiplicity
Of air and water, plant and animal,
Hard diamond, infinite sun.

PART III

∽

1. Heart and Mind

SAID the Lion to the Lioness — 'When you are amber
    dust, —
No more a raging fire like the heat of the Sun
(No liking but all lust) —
Remember still the flowering of the amber blood and bone,
The rippling of bright muscles like a sea,
Remember the rose-prickles of bright paws
Though we shall mate no more
Till the fire of that sun the heart and the moon-cold bone
    are one.'

Said the Skeleton lying upon the sands of Time —
' The great gold planet that is the mourning heat of the Sun
Is greater than all gold, more powerful
Than the tawny body of a Lion that fire consumes
Like all that grows or leaps . . . so is the heart
More powerful than all dust.   Once I was Hercules
Or Samson, strong as the pillars of the seas :
But the flames of the heart consumed me, and the mind
Is but a foolish wind.'

Said the Sun to the Moon — ' When you are but a lonely
    white crone,
And I, a dead King in my golden armour somewhere in a
    dark wood,
Remember only this of our hopeless love
That never till Time is done
Will the fire of the heart and the fire of the mind be one.'

2. *Green Song*

TO DAVID HORNER

AFTER the long and portentous eclipse of the patient sun
The sudden spring began
With the bird-sounds of Doom in the egg, and Fate in
    the bud that is flushed with the world's fever —
But those bird-songs have trivial voices and sound not
    like thunder,
And the sound when the bud bursts is no more the sound
    of the worlds that are breaking. —
But the youth of the world, the lovers, said, ' It is Spring!
And we who were black with the winter's shade, and old,
See the emeralds are awake upon the branches
And grasses, bird-blood leaps within our veins
And is changed to emeralds like the sap in the grasses.
The beast-philosopher hiding in the orchards,
Who had grown silent from the world's long cold,
Will tell us the secret of how Spring began
In the young world before the Fall of Man.
For you are the young spring earth
And I, O Love, your dark and lowering heaven.'

But an envious ghost in the spring world
Sang to them a shrunken song
Of the world's right and wrong —
Whispered to them through the leaves, ' I wear
The world's cold for a coat of mail
Over my body bare —
I have no heart to shield my bone
But with the world's cold am alone —
And soon your heart, too, will be gone —
My day's darling.'

The naked Knight in the coat of mail
Shrieked like a bird that flies through the leaves —
The dark bird proud as the Prince of the Air,
' I am the world's last love. . . . Beware —

Young girl, you press your lips to lips
That are already cold —
For even the bright earthly dress
Shall prove, at last, unfaithfulness.

His country's love will steal his heart —
To you it will turn cold
When foreign earth lies on the breast
Where your young heart was wont to rest
Like leaves upon young leaves, when warm was the green
    spray,
And warm was the heart of youth, my day's darling.

And if that ghost return to you —
(The dead disguised as a living man)
Then I will come like Poverty
And wear your face, and give your kiss,
And shrink the world, and that sun the heart
Down to a penny's span :

For there is a sound you heard in youth,
A flower whose light is lost —
There is a faith and a delight —
They lie at last beneath my frost
When I am come like Time that all men, faiths, loves,
    suns defeat,
My frost despoils the day's young darling.

For the young heart like the spring wind grows cold
And the dust, the shining racer, is overtaking
The laughing young people who are running like fillies,
The golden ladies and the ragpickers
And the foolish companions of spring, the wild wood
    lilies.'

But the youth of the world said, ' Give me your golden
    hand
That is but earth, yet it holds the lands of heaven

And you are the sound of the growth of spring in the
    heart's deep core,
The hawthorn-blossoming boughs of the stars and the
    young orchards' emerald lore.'

And hearing that, the poor ghost fled like the winter
    rain —
Sank into greenish dust like the fallen moon
Or the sweet green dust of the lime-flowers that will be
    blossoming soon —
And spring grew warm again —

No more the accusing light, revealing the rankness of
    Nature,
All motives and desires and lack of desire
In the human heart, but loving all life, it comes to bless
Immortal things in their poor earthly dress —
The blind of life beneath the frost of their great winter
And those for whom the winter breaks in flower
And summer grows from a long-shadowed kiss.
And Love is the vernal equinox in the veins
When the sun crosses the marrow and pith of the heart
Among the viridian smells, the green rejoicing.
All names, sounds, faiths, delights, and duties lost
Return to the hearts of men, those households of high
    heaven.
And voices speak in the woods as from a nest
Of leaves — they sing of rest,
And love, and toil, the rhythms of their lives,
Singing how winter's dark was overcome,
And making plans for tomorrow as though yesterday
Had never been, nor the lonely ghost's old sorrow,
And Time seemed but the beat of heart to heart,
And Death the pain of earth turning to spring again
When lovers meet after the winter rain.
And when we are gone, they will see in the great
    mornings
Born of our lives, some memory of us, the golden stalk

Of the young long-petalled flower of the sun in the pale
   air
Among the dew. . . . Are we not all of the same substance,
Men, planets and earth, born from the heart of darkness,
Returning to darkness, the consoling mother,
For the short winter sleep — O my calyx of the flower of
   the world, you the spirit
Moving upon the waters, the light on the breast of the
   dove.

3. *Anne Boleyn's Song*

FOR MINNIE ASTOR

'AFTER the terrible rain, the Annunciation' —
The bird-blood in the veins that has changed to emeralds
Answered the bird-call. . . .
In the neoteric Spring the winter coldness
Will be forgotten
As I forget the coldness of my last lover,

The great grey King
Who lies upon my breast
And rules the bird-blood in my veins that shrieked with
      laughter
— A sound like fear —
When my step light and high
Spurned my sun down from the sky
In my heedless headless dance —
O many a year ago, my dear,
My living lass !

In the nights of Spring, the bird, the Angel of the
      Annunciation
Broods over his heaven of wings and of green wild-fire
That each in its own world, each in its egg
Like Fate is lying.

He sang to my blood, as Henry, my first King,
My terrible sun
Came like the Ethos of Spring, the first green streak,
And to me cried,
' Your veins are the branches where the first blossom begins
After the winter rains —
Your eyes are black and deep
As the prenatal sleep
And your arms and your breasts are my Rivers of Life
While a new world grows in your side.'

Men said I was the primal Fall,
That I gave him the world of spring and of youth like an
    apple
And the orchards' emerald lore —
And sin lay at the core.

But Henry thought me winter-cold
When to keep his love I turned from him as the world
Turns from the sun . . . and then the world grew old —

But I who grew in the heart as the bird-song
Grows in the heart of Spring . . . I, terrible Angel
Of the emeralds in the blood of man and tree,
How could I know how cold the nights of Spring would
    be

When my grey glittering King —
Old amorous Death — grew acclimatised to my coldness?
His age sleeps on my breast,
My veins, like branches where the first peach-blossom
Trembles, bring the Spring's warmth to his greyness.

4. A Young Girl

Is it the light of the snow that soon will be overcoming
The spring of the world ?   Ah no, the light is the white-
    ness of all the wings of the angels
As pure as the lily born with the white sun.
And I would that each hair on my head was an angel,
    O my red Adam,
And my neck could stretch to you like a sunbeam or the
    young shoot of a lily
In the first spring of the world, till you, my grandeur of
    clay,
My Adam, red loam of the orchard, forgetting
The thunders of wrongs and of rights and of ruins
Would find the green shadow of spring beneath the hairs
    of my head, those bright angels,
And my face, the white sun that is born of the stalk of a
    lily
Come back from the underworld, bringing light to the
    lonely :
Till the people in islands of loneliness cry to the other
    islands
Forgetting the wars of men and of angels, the new Fall of
    Man.

5. *How Many Heavens . . .*

THE emeralds are singing on the grasses
And in the trees the bells of the long cold are ringing, —
My blood seems changed to emeralds like the spears
Of grass beneath the earth piercing and singing.

The flame of the first blade
Is an angel piercing through the earth to sing
' God is everything !
The grass within the grass, the angel in the angel, flame
Within the flame, and He is the green shade that came
To be the heart of shade.'

The grey-beard angel of the stone,
Who has grown wise with age, cried ' Not alone
Am I within my silence, — God is the stone in the still
    stone, the silence laid
In the heart of silence ' . . . then, above the glade

The yellow straws of light
Whereof the sun has built his nest, cry ' Bright
Is the world, the yellow straw
My brother, — God is the straw within the straw : —
    All things are Light.'

He is the sea of ripeness and the sweet apple's emerald
    lore.
So you, my flame of grass, my root of the world from
    which all Spring shall grow,
O you, my hawthorn bough of the stars, now leaning low
Through the day, for your flowers to kiss my lips, shall
    know
He is the core of the heart of love, and He, beyond
    labouring seas, our ultimate shore.

6. The Flowering Forest

THEY walked in the green wood, wild snows, soft,
    unchilling,
Falling upon their hair, touching their lips
In the undying ways, in the bright April land.
' See, Aldebaran, wild Cassiopeia
And Sirius are jealous of your white hand, —
Orion with sextuple suns and great nebulae,
Procyon and Vega and Altair, the parallax
Trail of the fixed stars are falling to greet you.
While the planetary systems and snows on the branches
Are shaking with laughter at seeing the old
World's follies that dream that the heart will grow cold.
And the drops of dew fall'n from the branches and white
    flowers,
Are young worlds that run to each other, their beings
Are one, in the green ways, the bright April land.'

7. *Holiday*

O YOU, all life, and you, the primal Cause —
The Sun and Planets to the husbandman,
The kernel and the sap, the life-blood, flower
Of all that lives, the Power
That holds the Golden Rainers in the heaven,

The wasteful Gardener Who to grow one flower —
Your life, like a long-petalled Sun, has strewn the infinite
Meadow of space with calyxes that die
Like dew, has sown the seed of this hour that comes no
     more —
Growing in Time, too thin as an abstraction
Yet holding in the end our bones like winter.

Come, we will leave the grey life, the half light
Where we are like the blind, live but in Time
When Toil, the arithmetician, rules the beat
Of blood and heart.
                    Beneath the flowering boughs of heaven
The country roads are made of thickest gold —
They stretch beyond the world, and light like snow
Falls where we go, the Intelligible Light
Turns all to gold, the apple, the dust, the unripe wheat-ear.
Young winds and people have winged feet like Mercury,
And distance is dead, the world ends in the heart.

On this great holiday
Dives and Lazarus are brothers again :
They seem of gold as they come up from the city
Casting aside the grave-clothes of their lives
Where the ragged dust is nobly born as the Sun.
Now Atlas lays aside his dying world,
The clerk, the papers in the dusty office ;
And lovers meet their bright Antipodes
To whom they are borne by the young siren seas
Of blood . . . he finds no more his dark night is her noon,

For they forget their minds' polarity,
The jarring atoms. . . . The least ore of gold
And quality of dust
Holds a vein of holiness . . . the laws that lie
In the irrefutable dust are Fate's decrees.
No more is Man
The noonday hope of the worm that is his brother —
He who begins with the shape of that eyeless one
Then changes to the world in the mother's side :
For the heart of Man is yet unwearied by Chaos,
And the hands grown thumbless from unuse, the work-
    less hands
Where the needs of famine have grown the claws of the
    lion
Bear now on their palms the wounds of the Crucified.

For now the unborn God in the human heart
Knows for a moment all sublimities. . . .
Old people at evening sitting in the doorways
See in a broken window of the slum
The Burning Bush reflected, and the crumb
For the starving bird is part of the broken Body
Of Christ Who forgives us — He with the bright Hair
— The Sun Whose Body was spilt on our fields to bring
    us harvest.

8. Song

WE are the darkness in the heat of the day,
The rootless flowers in the air, the coolness : we are the
    water
Lying upon the leaves before Death, our sun,
And its vast heat has drunken us . . . Beauty's daughter
The heart of the rose and we are one.

We are the summer's children, the breath of evening, the
    days
When all may be hoped for, — we are the unreturning
Smile of the lost one, seen through the summer leaves —
That sun and its false light scorning.

9. The Youth with the Red-Gold Hair

THE gold-armoured ghost from the Roman road
Sighed over the wheat
' Fear not the sound and the glamour
Of my gold armour —
(The sound of the wind and the wheat)
Fear not its clamour. . . .
Fear only the red-gold sun with the fleece of a fox
Who will steal the fluttering bird you hide in your breast.
Fear only the red-gold rain
That will dim your brightness, O my tall tower of the
    corn,
You, — my blonde girl. . . .'
But the wind sighed ' Rest.' . . .
The wind in his grey knight's armour —
The wind in his grey night armour —
Sighed over the fields of the wheat, ' He is gone. . . .
    Forlorn.'

10. Girl and Butterfly

I, AN old man,
Bent like Ixion on my broken wheel the world,
Stare at the dust and scan
What has been made of it . . . and my companion

Shadow, born with a wolfish pelt —
Grey dress to wear against the invincible cold
Sits at my feet. . . . We scan the old
And young, we stare at the old woman
Who bears a stone in her breast
That will not let her rest
Because it once was a world in the grey dawn
When sap and blood were one.

We stare at the young girl chasing a yellow butterfly
On the summer roads that lead from Nothing to Nowhere.

What golden racers, young winds, have gone ! For the
        dust like a great wave
Breaks over them — the shade of mortality lying
On the golden hand (the calyx outshining all flowers) —
The hand that drew the chart of the undiscovered,
And the smile for which great golden heroes marched
        with the pride
And pomp of waves — and like the waves they died.
The words that drew from the shade
A planetary system :
                        These are gone —

And the Grey Man that waits on the Road from Nothing
        to Nowhere
Does not care how the breezes and butterflies move their
        four wings —
And now the old woman who once was a world and my
        earth,
Lies like time upon my heart, or a drift of the grey dust.

But the young girl chases the yellow butterfly
Happiness . . . what is the dust that lies on its wings ?
Is it from far away
From the distance that lies between lover and lover, their
     minds never meeting —
Like the bright continents ? — are Asia, Africa, and
     Cathay
But golden flowers that shine in the fields of summer —
As quickly dying ?

II. Song

THE Queen Bee sighed, 'How heavy is my sweet gold!'
To the wind in the honey-hive.
And sighed the old King, 'The weight of my crown is
      cold —
And laden is life!'
'How heavy,' sighed the gold heart of the day, 'is the
      heat!'
Ah, not so laden sweet
As my heart with its infinite gold and its weight of love.

12. You, the Young Rainbow

TO ALICE HUNT

You, the young Rainbow of my tears, the gentle Halcyon
Over the troubled waters of my heart :
Lead now, as long ago, my grief, your flock, over the hollow
Hills to the far pastures of lost heaven.
But they are withered, the meadows and the horizon
Of the gentle Halcyon, hyacinthine sun ;
Cold are the boughs, the constellations falling
From the spring branches ; and your heart is far
And cold as Arcturus, the distance of all light-years
From the flowering earth and darkness of my heart.

13. The Poet Laments the Coming of Old Age

I SEE the children running out of school;
They are taught that Goodness means a blinding hood
Or is heaped by Time like the hump on an agèd back,
And that Evil can be cast like an old rag
And Wisdom caught like a hare and held in the golden
    sack
Of the heart. . . . But I am one who must bring back
    sight to the blind.

Yet there was a planet dancing in my mind
With a gold seed of Folly . . . long ago. . . .
And where is that grain of Folly ? . . . with the hare-
    wild wind
Of my spring it has gone from one who must bring back
    sight to the blind.

For I, the fool, was once like the philosopher
Sun who laughs at evil and at good :
I saw great things mirrored in littleness,
Who now see only that great Venus wears Time's filthy
    dress —
A toothless crone who once had the Lion's mouth.

The Gold Appearances from Nothing rise
In sleep, by day . . . two thousand years ago
There was a man who had the Lion's leap,
Like the Sun's, to take the worlds and loves he would,
But (laughed the philosopher Sun, and I, the fool)

Great golden Alexander and his thunder-store
Are now no more
Than the armoured knight who buzzed on the window-
    pane
And the first drops of rain.

He lies in sleep. . . . But still beneath a thatch
Of hair like sunburnt grass, the thieving sweet thoughts
    move
Toward the honey-hive. . . . And another sweet-tooth
    Alexander runs
Out of the giant shade that is his school,
To take the dark knight's world, the honeycomb.

The Sun's simulacrum, the gold-sinewed man
Lies under a hump of grass, as once I thought to wear
With patience, Goodness like a hump on my agèd back.
. . . But Goodness grew not with age, although my heart
    must bear
The weight of all Time's filth, and Wisdom is not a hare
    in the golden sack

Of the heart. . . . It can never be caught.   Though I
    bring back sight to the blind
My seed of Folly has gone, that could teach me to bear
That the gold-sinewed body that had the blood of all the
    earth in its veins
Has changed to an old rag of the outworn world
And the great heart that the first Morning made
Should wear all Time's destruction for a dress.

14. *O Bitter Love, O Death* . . .

I DREW a stalk of dry grass through my lips
And heard it sigh
' Once I was golden Helen . . . but am now a thin
Dry stalk of quaking grass. . . . What wind, what Paris
    now would win
My love ? — for I am drier than a crone.'

But the sap in those dry veins sang like a bird :
' I was the sea that knew the siren song
And my veins heard
A planet singing in the Dorian mode ! '

An old man weary with rolling wisdom like a stone
Up endless hills to lay on the innocent eyes
Said, ' Once I was Plato, wise
In the ripe and unripe weathers of the mind,
And I could draw

The maps of worlds beyond the countries of the blind
Sense ; I found the law
Uniting atoms of our Chaos like the love
Of boy and girl.'

                Another old man said,
' I was a great gold-sinewed King, I had a lion's mane
Like the raging Sun . . . but now I am alone —
And my love, that white lady, is but a thin white bone.

I live in my perpendicular grey house,
Then in my horizontal house — a foolish bed
For one whose blood like Alexander roamed
Conquering the countries of the heart.

                      All is the same :
The heroes marched like waves upon the shore :

Their great horizons, and the kiss
Of lovers, and of atoms, end in this.'

O bitter love, O Death that came
To steal all that I own !

15. A Sylph's Song

TO KATHERINE ANNE PORTER

THE cornucopia of Ceres
I seek not, fading not for this,

But fair Pomona, gardener's daughter,
Laughing like bird-feathered water.

Amid this hot green glowing gloom
A word falls with a rain-drop's boom;

And baskets of ripe fruit in air
The bird-songs seem, suspended where

Those goldfinches, the ripe warm lights,
Peck slyly at them, take quick flights.

I bring you branches green with dew
And fruits that you may crown anew

Your waspish-gilded hair until
That cornucopia doth spill

Dew, and your warm lips bear the stains,
And bird-blood leap within your veins.

Pomona, lovely gardener's daughter,
Fruits like ripples of the water

Soon will fade . . . then leave your fruits,
Smooth as your cheek or the birds' flutes,

And in this lovelier, smoother shade
Listen to my serenade.

16. Most Lovely Shade

FOR ALICE BOUVERIE

Most lovely Dark, my Æthiopia born
Of the shade's richest splendour, leave not me
Where in the pomp and splendour of the shade
The dark air's leafy plumes no more a lulling music
    made.

Dark is your fleece, and dark the airs that grew
Amid those weeping leaves.
Plantations of the East drop precious dew
That, ripened by the light, rich leaves perspire.
Such are the drops that from the dark airs' feathers
    flew.

Most lovely Shade . . . Syrinx and Dryope
And that smooth nymph that changed into a tree
Are dead . . . the shade, that Æthiopia, sees
Their beauty make more bright its treasuries —
Their amber blood in porphyry veins still grows
Deep in the dark secret of the rose
And the smooth stem of many a weeping tree,
And in your beauty grows.

Come then, my pomp and splendour of the shade,
Most lovely cloud that the hot sun made black
As dark-leaved airs, —
                Come then, O precious cloud,
Lean to my heart : no shade of a rich tree
Shall pour such splendour as your heart to me.

17. 'Lo, this is she that was the world's desire

In the green winter night
That is dark as the cypress bough, the pine,
The fig-tree and the vine
When our long sun into the dark had set
And made but winter branches of his rays,
The heart, a ghost,
Said to our life farewell — the shadow leaves
The body when our long dark sun has gone. . . .

And this is the winter's Æthiopian clime,
Darkening all beauty. . . .
                              Now in the winter night
The seed of the fire
Fallen from the long-leaved planets is of gold.
But she is old
And no more loved by the stars. . . . O now no more
The gold kiss of Orion burns her cheek.

Grey dust bent over the fire in the winter night,
Was this the crone that once Adonis loved,

Were those the veins that heard the sirens' song?
Age shrinks her heart to dust, black as the Ape's
And shrunk and cold
Is Venus now, grown blackened, noseless, old!

So changed is she by Time's appalling night
That even her bone can no more stand upright

But leans as if it thirsted — for what spring?
The Ape's bent skeleton foreshadowing

With head bent from the light, its only kiss.
Now she, too, knows the metamorphosis

When the appalling lion-claws of age
With talons tear the cheek and heart, yet rage

For life devours the bone, a tigerish fire :
The craters in the heart weep to that mire
The flesh . . . but the long wounds torn by Time in the
    golden cheek
Seem the horizons of the endless cold.
Lo, this is she that was the world's desire.

Crouched by the fire, blind from her earth's thick hood
Of dust, she, Atridae-like, devours her blood

With hopeless love, and knows the anguish of the bone
Deserted by all love, with Death alone.

And now the small immortal serpent cries,
' To my embrace the foolish and the wise

Will come,' and the first soundless wrinkles fall like snow
On many a golden cheek, and none may know

Seeing the ancient wrinkled shadow-shape
If this be long-dead Venus, or the Ape

Our great precursor. . . .
                      I felt pity for the dust,
And Time, the earth from which our beauty grows,
The old unchanging memory of the bone —
That porphyry whence grew the summer rose ;

For when spring comes, the dew with golden foot
Will touch the hidden leaf, the wrinkled root :

Then the grey dust that was the world's desire
Will sigh, ' Once I was wild and blind
In my desires as the snow.   I loved where I list

And was violent like spring roots. . . . O might I feel
    again
The violence, the uproar of bursting buds, the wild-beast
    fire

Of spring in my veins — and know again the kiss
That holds all the spring redness and the rose that weeps
    in the blood —
O might I know but this ! '

18. The Swans

In the green light of water, like the day
Under green boughs, the spray
And air-pale petals of the foam seem flowers, —
Dark-leaved arbutus blooms with wax-pale bells
And their faint honey-smells,
The velvety syringa with smooth leaves,
Gloxinia with a green shade in the snow,
Jasmine and moon-clear orange-blossoms and green
    blooms
Of the wild strawberries from the shade of woods.
Their showers
Pelt the white women under the green trees,
Venusia, Cosmopolita, Pistillarine —
White solar statues, white rose-trees in snow
Flowering for ever, child-women, half stars
Half flowers, waves of the sea, born of a dream.

Their laughter flying through the trees like doves,
These angels come to watch their whiter ghosts
In the air-pale water, archipelagos
Of stars and young thin moons from great wings falling
As ripples widen.
These are their ghosts, their own white angels these !
O great wings spreading —
Your bones are made of amber, smooth and thin
Grown from the amber dust that was a rose
Or nymph in swan-smooth waters.
                              But Time's winter falls
With snows as soft, as soundless. . . . Then, who knows
Rose-footed swan from snow, or girl from rose ?

PART IV

∽

1. One Day in Spring

GONE is the winter's cold
In the wild wood and the heart —
And warm are the young leaves and the budding spray.
' O heart, O eyes, O lips that will grow not old,
The waters love the moon, the sun the day,
As I love you, my day's darling ! '

Said the youth of the world.   But a living dead man walked
In the spring fire and talked
As if one heard him — though in all the spring
No heart was listening.
(' O heed him not, my dew with golden feet
Flying from me, my dew that is born of the spring heat.')

' On that last day she said, " I shall be cold
To the world's end, without your kiss . . . but when
Death is so old
He no more feels the pain
Of jealous love, I shall be yours again.

On that great holiday
There'll be no work, no fear for tomorrow's bread
Nor will the nations rage —
And only Death will feel the sorrow of old age."

Then, Sun of my life, she went to warm the Dead,
And I must now go sunless in their stead.

I felt not the cold wind blow, —
Nor the change of the sun :
For earth and sea
And my heart were one :
There nothing grew ; they nothing knew
Except the world was done !
They clothed a dead man in my dress
Who rose in the morning sorrow —
And all day walked the earth, waving at Nothingness
Now high, now low —
Changing with every wind like a scarecrow.

Sometimes my voice would sound from those dead lips :
For I who had seen
Each stain of age, fatigue, upon her cheek —
Dimming her beauty — I who had feared to see
That eternal truth the Bone
Laid bare by Death — cried now " Come home ! — whatever stain
Death laid upon you, in whatever guise
You are now, I should know your heart ! Come home,
out of the rain,

The cold ! How shall I bear my heart without its beat,
— My clay without its soul ? . . . I am alone —
More cold than you are in your grave's long night,
That has my heart for covering, warmth and light."

The cathedrals and their creeds were built above
Her heart. And all the Babels of the world,
Their bells and madness tolled — " Dead " — over her
love . . .
But the earth and all the roots of trees in the winter earth
Yet could not hold her down —
The tides of seas and seasons could not drown

Her heart. . . . So after twelve months in her grave
She came to me and gave

Her kiss . . . humbly and pleadingly she crept beside
My bed and looked at me with those hollow eyes
That seemed as if they had wept
For the stains Death left upon her beauty, fearing I might
Love her no more — so she came home from her endless
    night

— And the lips of my dead love were warm to me,
But the lips, the heart, should be dust-dun, death-cold
From that long night . . . and so I feared to hold
That heart that came warm from the grave . . . afraid
Of that eternity of love I laid
Death's earth upon her heart; for this
Dead man in my dress dared not kiss
Her who laid by Death's cold lest I
Should feel it when she came to lie
Upon my heart . . . my dead love gave
Lips warm with love though from her grave :
And I gave Death her love — the only light
And fire she had to warm her eternal night.'

So he went by.   The snowflake's star can see
Its ephemeral cold in the eternity

Of the rock-crystal's six rays . . . so light grief and
    waterfalls
See that eternal grief that melts not though the last spring
    calls

The heart. . . . But where the wild birds sing
We walked together
And pitied the poor Dead for whom the Spring
Is cold . . . for all the strange green fire
In eyes, on hair, — the world, the veins, changed into
    emeralds !

O Dead, your heart is gone ! you cannot weep ;
And like the unborn child's should be your sleep.

But on your lips, long worn away, a youthful smile
Remains, a thing of sorrow —

And wasted so thin by hopeless love you seem a
    shade —
An echo only —

You wait for one who comes not, for the hour
When your lips spoke, and winter broke in flower,

The Parthenon was built by your dead kiss . . .
But what should love seek now you are changed to
    this

Thin piteous wreck ! — yet strong as the Prophet's
    rock
No grief tears waters from that stone to mock

Death's immobility — and changed to stone
Those eyelids see one sight, and one alone.

What do they see ?   Some lost and childish kiss
In summer, in the dews of a dead morning —
The meeting, and clasp of hands, the last farewell
Among the morning sorrows ?   Now in spring

Beneath the young green-blooming strawberry
In the deep groves they sigh for the forgotten bliss
Grown dead and rotten, of their lover's kiss,
Forgetting the young heart grows old
And in the spring night they must sleep alone.

But in the spring warmth, creatures, faiths, and men
Awaken in the sun —
The coldness of the heart
Is with the winter done —

And the waters love the moon, the sun the day —
As I love my day's darling.

Though all the lovers of the world
Grow old, and fade, and die —
Yet how should you and I?
For the world was only made that we should love —
O hair, O eyes, O lips that will never grow old!

2. A Song at Morning

THE weeping rose in her dark night of leaves
Sighed ' Dark is my heart, and dark my secret love —
Show not the fire within your heart, its light —
For to behold a rainbow in the night
Shall be the presage of your overthrow.'

But morning came, and the great dews ; then her philo-
    sophies
Of the heart's darkness died.   And from the chrysalis of
    my thin sleep
That lay like light or dew upon my form
I rose and wrapped my wings about me, went
From that porphyrian darkness.   Like the rose

I too was careless in the morning dews
Seeing the dead and the dead hour return
To forgive the stain on our hands.   I too at morning
Am like the rose who shouts of the red joys and redder
    sorrows
Fallen from young veins and heartsprings that once held
The world's incendiarism and the redness of summer,
The hope of the rose.   For soon will come the morrow
When ancient Prudence and her wintery dream
Will be no more than the rose's idleness. . . .
The light of tears shall only seem the rose's light
— Nor sorrow darker than her night of leaves.

3. The Two Loves

TO PAVEL TCHELITCHEW AND HIS WORK IN PROGRESS

I

THE dead woman black as thunder, upright in the Spring's
    great shroud
Of flowers and lightnings, snows and sins and sorrows,
    cried like the loud
Noise of Spring that breaks in heart and bud . . .
' Oh should you pass —
Come not to this ground with your living lass :
For I have a light to see you by !
Is it the Burning Bush —
Is it Damnation's Fire . . .
Or the old aching heart with its desire ?
I only know I tried to bless
But felt that terrible fire burn to the bone —
Beneath Time's filthy dress.'

II

But where are the seeds of the Universal Fire
To burn the roots of Death in the world's cold 'heart ?
The earth of my heart was broken and gaped low
As the fires beneath the equator of my veins.
And I thought the seeds of Fire should be let loose
Like the solar rains —
The light that lies deep in the heart of the rose ;
And that the bloom from the fallen spring of the world
Would come again to the cheek grown famine-white
As winter frost —
Would come again to the heart whose courage is lost
From hunger.   When in this world
Will the cold heart take fire ?   In the hour when the
    sapphire of the bone —
That hard and precious fire wrung from the earth,
And the sapphire tears the heavens weep shall be made one.

But, in the summer, great should be the sun of the heart
And great is the heat of the fires from elementary and
      terrestrial nature —
Ripening the kernel of amethysts in the sun of the
      peach —
The dancing seas in the heart of the apricot.
The earth, the sun, the heart, have so many fires
It is a great wonder
That the whole world is not consumed.   In such a heat
      of the earth, under
The red bough, the Colossus of rubies the first husband-
      man and grave-digger, the red Adam,
Dug from the earth of his own nature, the corn effigy
Of a long-buried country god, encrusted with earth-
      virtues,
And brought to a new birth
The ancient wisdom hiding behind heat and laughter,
Deep-rooted in Death's earth.

Gone is that heat.   But this is the hour of brotherhood,
      the warmth that comes
To the rejected by Life — the shadow with no eyes —
Young Icarus with the broken alar bones
And the sapped and ageing Atlas of the slums
Devoured by the days until all days are done —
To the Croesus of the breadline, gold from the sun,
And the lover seeing in Woman the rankness of Nature, —
A monstrous Life-force, the need of procreation
Devouring all other life . . . or Gravity's force
Drawing him down to the centre of his earth.
These sprawl together in the sunlight — the negation
Of Life, fag-ends of Ambition, wrecks of the heart,
Lumps of the world, and bones left by the Lion.
Amid the assembly of young laughing roses
They wait for a re-birth
Under the democratic sun, enriching all, rejecting no
      one. . . .
But the smile of youth, the red mouth of the flower

Seem the open wounds of a hunger that is voiceless —
And on their lips lies the dust of Babel's city ;
And the sound of the heart is changed to the noise of
        revolutions —
The hammer of Chaos destroying and rebuilding
Small wingless hopes and fears in the light of the Sun.
Who dreamed when Nature should be heightened to a
        fever —
The ebullition of her juices and humours —
The war of creed and creed, of starved and starver —
The light would return to the cheek, and a new Word
Would take the place of the heart ?

                                    We might tell the blind
The hue of the flower, or the philosopher
What distance is, in the essence of its being —
But not the distance between the hearts of Men.

I see Christ's wounds weep in the Rose on the wall.
Then I who nursed in my earth the dark red seeds of
        Fire —
The pomegranate grandeur, the dark seeds of Death,
Felt them change to the light and fire in the heart of the
        rose. . . .
And I thought of the umbilical cords that bind us to
        strange suns
And causes . . . of Smart the madman who was born
To bless Christ with the Rose and his people, a nation
Of living sweetness . . . of Harvey who blessed Christ
        with the solar fire in the veins,
And Linnaeus praising Him with the wingèd seed ! —
Men born for the Sun's need —
Yet theirs are the hymns to God who walks in darkness.
And thinking of the age-long sleep, then brought to the
        light's birth
Of terrestrial nature generated far
From heaven . . . the argillaceous clays, the zircon and
        sapphire
Bright as the tears of heaven, but deep in earth —

And of the child of the four elements
The plant — organic water polarised to the earth's
    centre —
And to the light : — the stem and root, the water-plant
    and earth-plant,
The leaf, the child of air, the flower, the plant of fire —
And of One who contracted His Immensity
And shut Himself in the scope of a small flower
Whose root is clasped in darkness . . . God in the span
Of the root and light-seeking corolla . . . with the voice
    of Fire I cry —
Will He disdain that flower of the world, the heart of
    Man?

PART V

꙳

1. The Bee Oracles

I. *The Bee-Keeper*

TO DENYS AND ELIZABETH KILHAM ROBERTS

In the plain of the world's dust like a great Sea,
The golden thunders of the Lion and the Honey-Bee
In the Spirit, held with the Sun a Colloquy

Where an old woman stood — thick Earthiness —
Half Sun, half Clod,
A plant alive from the root, still blind with earth
And all the weight of Death and Birth.

She, in her primitive dress
Of clay, bent to her hives
And heard her sisters of the barren lives

Begin to stir . . . the Priestesses of the Gold Comb
Shaped by Darkness, and the Prophetesses
Who from a wingless pupa, spark of gold

In the Dark, rose with gold bodies bright as the Lion,
And the trace of the Hand of God on ephemeral wings
To sing the great Hymn of Being to the lost :

' This Earth is the honey of all Beings, and all Beings
Are the honey of this Earth . . . O bright immortal
     Lover
That is incarnate in the body's earth —
   bright immortal Lover Who is All ! '

'This Water is the honey of all Beings, and all Beings
Are the honey of this Water . . . O the bright immortal
    Lover
That is in water and that is the seed
Of Life . . . O bright immortal Lover Who is All!'

'This Fire is the honey of all Beings, and all Beings
Are the honey of this Fire . . . O bright immortal Lover
That is in fire and shines in mortal speech —
O bright immortal Lover Who is All!'

'This Air is the honey of all Beings, and all Beings
Are the honey of this Air . . . O bright immortal Lover
That is in air and is our Being's breath —
O bright immortal Lover Who is All!'

'This Sun is the honey of all Beings, and all Beings
Are the honey of this Sun . . . O bright immortal Lover
That is in the sun and is our Being's sight —
O bright immortal Lover Who is All!'

'This Thunder is the honey of all Beings, and all Beings
Are the honey of this Thunder . . . O the bright immortal
    Lover,
That is in thunder and all voices — the beasts' roar —
Thunder of rising saps — the voice of Man!
O bright immortal Lover Who is All!'

This was the song that came from the small span
Of thin gold bodies shaped by the holy Dark. . . .

And the old woman in her mortal dress of clay
(That plant alive from the root, still thick with earth)
Felt all the saps of Day.

And in the plain of dust like a great Sea
The Lion in the Spirit cried, 'Destroy — destroy
The old and wrinkled Darkness.' But the Sun
— That great gold simpleton — laughed like a boy,
And kissed the old woman's cheek and blessed her clay.

The great Sun laughed, and dancing over Chaos,
Shouts to the dust ' O mortal Lover !   Think what
        wonders
May be born of our love — what golden heroes ! '

The Bee in the Spirit said ' The gold combs lay
In the cold rock and the slain Lion, amid spent golden
        thunders.'

II. *A Sleepy Tune*

TO VIOLET GORDON WOODHOUSE

' I WAS a Gold Man. . . . Now I lie under the earth
And only the young wheat-ear
Grows from my hollow breast like a gold sound . . .
Amid the asp-aspersions of the dust,
The old assertions
Of that sleep-causing Asp with swelling head.
And only the bull-voiced thunders of the gold ripe wheat
Answer the Augur in this long and sleepy August.'

The Gold Man who was King raised up his sleepy head . . .
' Is this the time of our advance upon the Sun ?
Will he kiss the loveless
And stretch himself on our earth in love once more ?
Lions do not bury gold and seek again
Their treasure . . . but the Sun sees our gold nature
Sunken in earth, and comes again to the Ore,
The growing plant and the root with the nature of gold
(Whose generation is in earth) — the Ore, precursor
Of the Plant Kingdom, that with growth becomes alive.

In the time when the Sun of the heart is in the sign of
        the Lion
I lie far from the forgotten thunders. . . .'
But near the Tomb the Thriae, Priestesses of the Gold
        Comb,
Buzz and hum of the forgotten wonders,

And of the wind from the Tomb that is no more
Than the wind of the honey-hive that drifts to them over
　　their gold floor.
Their heads are white as if from barley-flour
— And thin are their gold bodies.

　　　　　　　　　　　　　　This is the hour
When they sing of the noon of the world : ' There was a
　　King
Who reigned in Babylon —
Grown sleepy now. . . . His hair was like the honey-red
　　foxes
Burned by fires like the Sun in the wheat-festival :
— He lies embalmed by bees . . . the sweetness lapping
　　over
Him, with only Darkness for a lover. . . .
And now is his town no more than our gold Comb.

　　　　　　　　　　　　And carrying a young lion,
A solar hero, King of Lydia,
Stood on his city walls. . . .
You would not know that King or lion now from the
　　dust ground from the wheat-ears.

Great Alexander lies in a mask of gold
White honey mummified . . . as if it were gold armour.
And now only the cold
Wind from the honey-hive can know
If still from strength comes sweetness — if from the
　　lion-heart
The winged swarms rise ! '

This was the song of the Bee-Priestesses. . . .
But the Gold Man lying in the dark like the wingless pupa
That lies in their cells, said ' I hear the solar jubilation
Come to the heart and saps of Being . . . the roar of
　　ripeness.

For the Sun is the Ardent Belief
That sees life in the aridities of the dust,
In the seed and the base excrement and the world's
      fevers. . . .

He loves alike, the common dust of the streets
And the lovers' lips like the gold fires burning Troy.
The Sun kisses the loveless,
The mouth of the condemned by Man, the dog-mouth
      and the lion-fang
Deep in the heart. . . . He comes to the criminal whose
      nature
Was crippled before his birth by a new gravitation
That changed the solar system of the heart
To a universe reigned over by deformation. . . .
None is condemned. . . . Then why should we lie
      loveless ?
He will clothe us again in gold and a little love.'

2. *Mary Stuart to James Bothwell*

(*Casket Letter No. II*)

O you who are my heavenly pain of Hell,
My element, my Paradise of the First Man
That knows not sin — the eternity wherein I dwell!
Before the Flood were you not my primeval clay?
Did you not shape me from that chaos to the form
Of that which *men* call Murder — I, the light of the
    First Day?

Leaving you, I was sundered like the Sea!
Departed from the place where I left my heart
I was as small as any body may be
Whose heart is gone — small as the shade of Spring
That has no heart.
                  My mate, the leper-King,
White as a man of diamonds, spotted over
With the ermines of God's wrath for a kingly robe
— My leper-stick of bone

Covered with melting snows, to which I am crucified —
— Saw not Death gape wide
Wearing my smile, and bade me come again as his lover.

I was the thunder of the seas within man's blood, and
    the world's wonder!
But he sold my kiss for that of the fair-skinned Sickness
Who melted him away like the spring snows:
The bite of the bright-spotted leopard from Hell's
    thickets — this he chose!
She devoured his bones like fire . . . the bite that tore
    him asunder
Hidden behind the mouth of the ultimate Rose.

I lodged him in a beggar's house, Death-low
And ragged as a leper's flesh. . . . Then, weeping like
    the Spring

341

From amid his melting snow
He begged me watch by him, night long. Did I not
 know
His heart is wax,
While mine is diamond that no blow can break —
But only the touch of your hand, I had pitied those lidless
 eyes that must wake
Until Death seal them, mimicking my kiss.

But how should Pity stand between you and me !
The Devil sunder us from our mates, and God
Knit us together
Until nor man nor devil could tell lover from lover
In our heaven of damnation ! Could these sunder our
 clay,
Or the seas of our blood ? As well might they part the
 fires
That would burn to the bottom of Hell. . . . But there
 is no Hell —
We have kissed it away.

3. *A Bird's Song*

THE fire high up in air,
The bird, cries, ' I am the seed of fire
From the Sun — although I wear
A bird-mask.   Now I swoop
Down to the archipelago of suns on the orange-tree in a
      dark sea of leaves.

O young Medea, fear
The sea in each fire that hangs upon your tree,
The cold in the heart of Man.
O guard that fleece of gold in your breast, your heart of fire ;
Too soon it stolen will be !

Between smooth leaves where still the drops of night
Lie, the gold cold water-drops, I take my flight,
Shaking down the water-drops like the dark drowsy bees.
Beneath the orange-tree, the sleeper lies —
A bone of fire in a body of thin amber ; the umbrageous
      tree
Has changed her to a bird of fire, feathered with shade,
      like me.

And I, the seed of the Sun in a bird-mask,
Fly where from the perfumed stem and wind-smooth fruits
      down-pour
Such amber tears as the rich Sun doth weep
In his deep noonday sleep.'

In this deep night of leaves
And seas in a fire of gold,
If Man, the marauding faithless Jason, came, how should
      he know
Which is the gilded fleece and which the long and legendary
      Sea —
Which is the Sleeper's long and tangled hair and which the
      water-cold gold orange-tree ?

4. Dido's Song

TO MARGARET DREW

My Sun of Death is to the deep, reversedly,
What the great Sun of heaven is to the height
In the violent heat
When Sirius comes to lie at the Sun's feet.
My Sun of Death is all depth, heaven's Sun
All height, and the air of the whole world lies between
Those Suns.
           Now only the Dog sits by my bier
Where I lie flaming from my heart. The five dogs of
    the senses
Are no more hunting now.
For after the conflagration of the summer
Of youth, and its violent Suns,
My veins of life that seemed so high, the pouring rivers
Of Africa and Asia were but brooks to them,
Were quenched, and Time like fire
Had changed the bone to knotted rubies like the horizons
    of the light ;
Beyond all summers lies the peony bud
In the veins, and the great paeons of the blood,
The empery of the rose !
Yet once I had thought my bed of love my bier the
    highest
Sun of heaven, the height where Sirius is flaming,
And then I thought it Death's Sun, and that there is no
    deep
Below. . . . But now I know
That even the hunters in the heart and in the heaven
At last must sleep.

5. *A Love Song*

IT was the time when the Day cried to me, ' Show me
    your heart, Medusa,
That I may be changed into stone,
And no more bear the grief of the all-seeing Sun !

Ah, stare with your eyes that are lidless as mine, are
    sleepless,
At the place where my heart was ! Change to immutable
    stone
The small equalities, reigned over now by the swift-
    wingèd

Scarlet Dust, brother of the three Furies — seeing all in its
    equilibrium :
The tides of the ocean, the temperature of the royal vein,
    the basilica, soon to be porphyry,
From whence grew the empery of the conquering rose.'

But I replied not. My eyes that are sleepless and lidless
As Day's see one sight alone.

For once it was Spring. And I with the other amaryllidi-
    ous girls of burning
Gold walked under the boughs and listened to the sweet
    chattering
Procne, and love began in the heart like the first wild
    spark in the almond-
Tree. But the heart of the Spring has been burned away.

Yet though the kingly vermilion Dust, the brother of the
    Erinyes,
Lies on my breast, and is my only lover, I yet am wingèd.
No more shall you escape me than the Sun
His heaven. I am blackened by my fires like the nights of
    the great Spring,

Yet am wingèd like the nightingale, like the Erinyes,
I, the spring night that lies on your breast like fire, the day
    that enfolds you,
The fire that springs up in your tears !

In the nights of spring I will clothe you with fire, like the
    nightingale.
In your veins I will run like the blood that is fire and is
    Fate, the blind impulse,
Predestination and Doom, crying to sins old as the Spring

Why, lovely swallow, weary me with thy sweet chattering ?
What dost thou hope to find in my heart ? The warmth
    of the Spring ?
In the great azure are flaming the almond bough and the
    almandine flower of the clear rose,
And my heart sheds its fire.

For once it was Spring. But now there is neither honey
    nor bee for me —
Neither the sting nor the sweetness.
Not mine the warm heart of Aprils and apricots, apricus,
Sunny, all gold within like the heart of the honeycomb,
Neither the honey-winged swarms of the gold thoughts of
    summer
Shall be mine again !

6. A Hymn to Venus

An old Woman speaks :

' LADY, beside the great green wall of Sea
I kneel to make my plea

To you, great Rose of the world. . . . Beyond the seeds
    of petrifaction, Gorgon of itself,
Behind the face bright as the Rose — I pray
To the seeds of fire in the veins that should
Hold diamonds, iris, beryls for their blood, —

Since you are grown old too, and should be cold,
Although the heat of the air
Has the motion of fire
And light bears in its heart
A cloud of colour . . . where

The great heat ripens in the mine
Of the body's earth, ruby, garnet, and almandine,

And in the dark cloud of the blood still grows
The rainbow, with the ruby and the rose.

Pity me then — a poor old woman who must wear a rag
Of Time's filth for a dress. . . .
O who would care to hold
That miserly rag now !

So I whose nights were violent as the buds
And roots of Spring, was taken by the Cold,

Have only the Cold for lover. Speak then to my dust !
Tell me that nothing dies
But only suffers change, —
And Folly may grow wise.

So we shall be transmuted — you who have grown chill,
    and I
Unto whose heart
My love preferred a heart like a winding-sheet of clay
— Fearing my fires would burn his body away !

Gone are your temples that were bright with heat.
But still I kneel at the feet
Of you who were built through aeons by a million lives,
Whispers and instincts, under the coralline light
That seems the great zone of sea-depths. . . .

                                    Though your grief
In my blood grows
Like chlorophyll in the veins of the deep rose,

Our beauty's earthly dress
(Shrunk now to dust) — shall move through all degrees
Of Life, from mineral to plant, and from still rock to the
    green laughing seas ;

From life's first trance, the mineral consciousness
That is deep blankness inside an invisible
And rigid box — defined, divisible

And separate from the sheath — (breathe not too deep
If you would know the mineral's trancèd sleep. . . .
So measure Time that you, too, are apart
And are not conscious of the living heart) —

To the plant that seeks the light that is its lover
And knows not separation between cover
And sentience. . . . The Sun's heat and the dew's chill
It knows in sleep with an undreaming thrill ;

And colour breathes that is reflected light.
The ray and perfume of the Sun is white :
But when these intermingle as in love
With earth-bound things, the dream begins to move,

And colour that sleeps as in a dreamless cloud
Deep in the mineral trance within that shroud
Then to a fluid changes, grows
Deep in the stem and leaves of the dark rose.

So could the ruby, almandine and garnet move
From this great trance into a dreaming sleep,
They might become the rose whose perfume deep
Grows in eternity, yet is
Still unawakened for its ephemeral hour
Beneath the great light's kiss ;

The rose might seek the untamed rainbow through
The remembering Eden of a drop of dew ;
Until at last in heavenly friendship grows
The ruby and the rainbow and the rose.
Nor will the one more precious than the other be —
Or make more rich the Shadow's treasury.

So, Lady, you and I,
And the other wrecks of the heart, left by the Lion
Of love, shall know all transmutations, each degree !
Our apeish skeletons, clothed with rubies by the light,
Are not less bright
In the Sun's eye than is the rose . . . and youth, and we,
Are but waves of Time's sea.

Folly and wisdom have dust equal-sweet,
And in the porphyry shade
Of this world's noon
The Poor seem Dives, burning in his robes bright as the
     rose
— Such transmutations even the brief moment made ! '

7. *Spring Morning*

TO KENNETH AND JANE CLARK

AFTER the thunders of night-wandering Zagreus,
The unseen suns were singing where, day-long, laughter
The Janus-face, turned black and terrible, as if lightning
Struck it among bright vine-tips.

The dancing seas of delight lie on young leaves,
Young heart upon young heart.   O night of ferment
    under earth !
The sapphire tears fallen from the heavens will reach
The fissures in the heart and rock, too deep
And narrow for the grandeur of the Sun.
But what has the Night ripened ?
What depths in that sapphiric mine, our bodies' earth ?

Then rose our Sun . . . He shouts through all Creation . . .
    His gold fires
Shake from each heaven to heaven . . . And at his kiss
From hemisphere to hemisphere the rising fires in all the
    hearts and homes of Men
Respond ; and I, still wrapped in darkness, cry
With the voice of all those rolling fires, ' Hail to the Sun,
    and the great Sun in the heart of Man '
Till the last fire fall in the last abyss.

In the violent Spring, amid the thunders of the sap and
    the blood in the heart,
The Sun answers the cries
From the frost that shines like fire or the dust of Venus in
    the time
That knows the first rites of the Croconides
Fertilising the saffron.

                        And the sound of Earth's desire
Reaches the bones of the Lion, the Horse, the Man,
For under their great Death

Like Spring, they feel the great saps rise —
The power of the Sun.

And in the House of Gold, the House of the Dead,
The bones of ancient lions shake like fire;
The dead men, the gold forms to whom all growth belongs,

Hear the shout of the god in the Gold Rain
And its marriage with the earth,
And the crocus, whose race has sprung from gold, is
    born again.

Then the King who is part of the saffronic dust —
He of the gold sinews, withered now —
Sighed ' Darkness clasps the root, the gold, the heart.

But the gold is brother to the root! Will it learn to grow
Through the long ages till it change to plant?
Will the Sun kiss its long hair? And will my heart
Be changed to gold? . . . Ah, when shall I know

Again the kiss outburning all the fires of the crocus?
When from gold lips that are dust shall I light my
    Sun?'

Then from the wide pale lips of the dust came the great
    sound
Of the Ritual Laughter
At the impiety of Death, the sacrilege.

' For,' said the great dust to the small serpent that
    devours
The saffronic dust of Venus, the spring hours, . . .
' See how the Sun comes with his gold love to kiss our
    baseness!

He pities the small worm and its lipless mouthing
At the earth's bosom like a babe at its mother's breast;

From the mouthing of the small worm, when the world
      began,
Arose the speech, arose the kiss of Man.

And the beast who shares with Man, Time and the
      beat of the heart,
And the great gold beasts who shake their fiery manes
Through all the pastures of high heaven, are as one.'

The Sun comes to the saps of Reason . . . sighs all sighs
And suffers all ambitions . . . cries
To the subterranean fires in Croesus' heart, the unborn
      wheat,
'Your gold must grow that the starved may eat!'

And from the Chaos of our Nature, the brute gold
In every seam and vein of earth roars to the Sun.

So day begins, the course of the fathering Sun
And the solar heroes, men of our common earth,
Of the common task,
With their gold sinews lift the world, reward the
      Morning
With the palms of all their martyrdoms and grandeurs,
The dews of Death. . . . And in the roads I see
The common dust change to an Archangel
Beneath the Sun's gold breath.

And I in answer raise
My arms and my long hands like the young vine-boughs
With the gold blood running and sunning
To the tips of the grape-shaped finger-ends,
Raise them in praise.

My blood is one with the young vines — part of the
      earth. I shout from my planet, quickening
As the great Sun in the void firmament:
My heart, that gives life to my earth, like water and the
      gold
Flames of the laughing Sun, grown strong as these.

8. *Out of School*

TO JOSÉ GARCIA VILLA

THE gold, the wild-beast fires begin again upon the fruit-
    boughs,
Running from branch to branch, and our gold veins
Catch fire.   In the caverns where our blood begins
Sound the ancestral voices

That are not fire but fate, blind impulse and predestination
Foretelling doom.
And the fleece of Marsyas, the last melting snow upon the
    branches,
Trembles no more at the flute-sound.
O heart, it is spring !

And the wild-beast fires (the furred-lynx fruit-buds) the
    young winds,
And the young tendrils of the vines, the gold spring rains,
Fall from the branches.

And from the hoarse voice of the stream freed from the ice
The animal laughters sound —
The neighings of the prophet horse arise
Who prophesied great evils once (and the spring thunders
    run
Along the ground
From his foretelling hoof) ; the bray
Of the world of asses following Darius —
The sound that scattered the great Scythian hordes,
The sound of the crowd's onolatry, and after
The Ritual Laughter at the escape from death :
For this is the age of the destroying Laughter.

In the forest there are great emerald mists from which the
    bird-songs
Fall, the Cassandra voices.   Through green lightnings and
    the emeralds
Fallen from the trees,

The young green sun of spring,
A laughing ghost, danced ; with a ghostly voice
Calls to the children, ' See ! New worlds and emeralds
and Fates begin.
Soon will my greenness fade and I shall wear my own gold
armour,
Fighting the mists.'

                        And the children run from school
To the sound of the planetary system in the veins,
The beat of the young rains,
And the thunder of the wild wood-lilies' growth beneath
the ground.

They flee the old man who all morning long
Sifted a little dust through his dry hands
And boomed at the children : ' Once this dust was
Socrates,

The first spring sage, the satyr under the furred-lynx fruit-
buds
Tearing the tendrils of the young spring rains
And — where the sap like peridots and beryls
Rises in the budding fig-branches, — foretelling perils
Upon his flute that seemed like the young mist
Of spring, to the caverns where our blood begins.

Now is he but the emerald dust of lilies :
He is alone
With but the small equalities of dust.
And the green mist of spring will soon be gone, the Sun
in his gold armour,
Shout through the budding branches. Ere it is too late
You must discriminate
Between true gold and false, between the Sun that is the
ghost
Of your own heart, and the Sun the world has lost.
When to your Sun

Gilding the cheeks of lemons on the trees and the young
        spring lemures,
The jonquils (rills of water born from rocks)
And veins of gold in rocks and hearts of men —

Arise the breath of the cultivated earth,
Gold mists from vines,
And all gold airs and prayers from cities, Man

Seeing his mirrored morning face, no more can find
The masks he wore (through centuries)
Of faith and hope.   The gold corrosive of the hyper-
        modern suns
Of unbelief have shone upon them, they are gone,
And only emptiness remains.   This is the only good.
O fear that laughing ghost in his gold armour high in air
Who calls to you ! '

                                But the children run from school
To learn their wisdom from the great gold fool
Who is to the world of sight
What truth is to the invisible — life-giver of all voices
In sap and bud, life-giver of mankind.

He sees through the rough Ape-dust the gold fires
Of the spirit spring like the wild-beast fires upon the
        branches ;
The little and the great,
The shadow of the crooked and the straight
Complete each other, and the cripple's hump,
The curve of the mountain hiding veins of gold
As equal in their grandeur.   Sees the common lump
Of the world hold the seed of the flower, the wisdom of
        the Dark
Formed with an angel's innocence ;   the old
And wrinkled mask of Pithecanthropus Erectus
Hide the great brow of Socrates ;   the ass's ears
And the almond husk of the beast as no wise less

In grandeur than the long rivers and the almond-husk
Of that great sleepy animal, the world.

He sees the gold blood in the veins of plants and men
Has the beat of the gold planetary system ; sees
The plant, a beast retarded by the dark
(Whose root had once been gold, but changed by growth),
The beast, a plant that blossoms, freed by light,
Devoid of root like the planets, (those bright bees
That move in heaven about their honeycomb of light,)
And are forms of Time that imitate the eternal — made
That from their unerring courses we might learn
From the intelligence in the wide heavens,
And the perturbed might learn from the unperturbed,
Set right the inharmonious errors of our lives,

And fear not change or Time and darkness, but behold
The elements are but as qualities
That change for ever, like all things that have known
        generation, like a gold
Image taking a new form for ever, — mutable
As the child who is innocence and oblivion, acceptance,
A new beginning, primal motion, a self-moving game that
        changes
Like the heart of forgetful spring.

9. *A Simpleton*

TO DAVID HORNER

IN the autumn, the season of ripeness, when final redness
Comes to the ore and the earth is with child by the Sun,
Like the bright gold spangles fall'n from the light of
    Nature
Flying over the happy fields, the Simpleton
Feeling the warm gold ripen, sat by the wayside
— His broad face having an animal nature (the beast of
    burden
Who has turned prophet, the beast in our earth
    unconscious),
A simple creature, happy as butterflies,
Or as the dancing star that has risen from Chaos.
And the world hangs like a ripe apple — the great gold
    planets
Lying with Evil and Good in the ripened core.
The old men, Abraham-bearded like the auburn
Sun of harvest, walk in the holy fields
Where the Sun forgives and remakes the shape of Evil
And, laughing, forgives lean Virtue. . . . Gravity yields
The gold that was hidden deep in the earth, in the map-like
Lines of a smile made holy by Light, and the Sun
With his gold mouth kisses the skin that shines like
    red fire,
And shouts to the lowly, the dust that is his lover:
' See how of my love and my shining I never tire,
But rule over thunders and Chaos : the lore of the bee
    and the great lion's raging
To me are equal in grandeur, the hump of the cripple
And the mountain that hides the veins of brute gold are
    as one —
And to me the jarring atoms are parted lovers ! '
And this is the lore the Simpleton learns from his
    nature —
Lifting his face in blindness and happiness up to the Sun.

10. *Street Acrobat*

TO CHARLES HENRI FORD

UPON the shore of noon, the wide azoic
Shore of diamonds where no wave comes, sprawled the
    nation
Of Life's rejected, with the vegetation
Of wounds that Life has made

Breaking from heart and veins. Why do they tend
With pride this flora of a new world ?   To what end ?

But wearing the slime of Lethe's river for a dress —
Peninsulas of Misery in the Sea of Nothingness

With waves of dead rags lapping islands of the Shade,
They seem.   With these for audience —
From whom you could not hope even for pence

To lay upon your eyes —
Street-corner Atlas, you support a world
Whose solar system dies in a slum room.
And what is the world you balance on your shoulder ?
What fag-ends of ambition, wrecks of the heart, miasmas
From all Time's leprosies, lie there ?   The diamonds of the
    heat

Clothe you, the being diseased by Civilisation —
(With a void within the soul that has attracted
The congestion or intoxication
Of Astral Light — a gulf of diamonds —
Gyrations, revolutions, vortices
Of blinding light timed by the new pulsation !)

You work false miracles of anarchies
And new moralities
Designed for Bird-Men, grown with the growth of wings
From needs of Fear —
And balance high above an immeasurable abyss
Of blinding emptiness and azure vast profundities.

To the sound of ragged Madness beating his drum
Of Death in the heart, you, the atavistic, the Ape-Man,
The World-Eater, call to Darkness your last Mate
To come from her world, the phantom of yours.   Then,
    a Strong Man, shake
The pillars of this known world, the Palace, and Slum.

Or bear this breaking world — turn acrobat
And execute dizzy somersaults from Real
To the Ideal — swing from desolate heavens
Of angels who seem Pharisees and Tartuffes,
Januses, gulls, and money-lenders, mediums,
In those false heavens of cloud — down to a comfortable
    hell —
And swing this easy world and watch it heel
Over before it fell,

To the admiration of the Lost Men nursing their wounds
And the children old in the dog's scale of years —
With only this sight for bread. . . . (Oh, seeing these,
I thought the eyes of Men
Held all the suns of the world for tears, and these were
    shed —
Are fallen and gone !
So dark are the inexpiable years.)

But I, whose heart broke down to its central earth
And spilled its fire, its rubies, garnets, like the heat
And light from the heart of the rose,
Still lie immortal in the arms of Fire
Amid the ruins.   The Acrobat on his tight-rope, stretched
    from beast
To God, over a vast abyss

Advances, then recedes.   Or, on his ladder of false light,
Swings from mock heaven to real hell.   And Galileo,
    blind,

Stares with his empty eyes on the crowds of planets and
     young roses
Beyond the arithmeticians'

Counting ! O, the grandeur of the instinct ! The young
     people and young flowers,
Who, careless, come out in green dark,
Are numberless as the true heavens ; still, in this world
We measure by means of the old mathematicians'
Rods, or by rays of light, by the beat of Time, or the
     sound of the heart,
And vibrating atoms that soon will be Man or Flower.

11. Song

TO JOHN AND ALEXANDRINE RUSSELL

Now that Fate is dead and gone
And that Madness reigns alone,
Still the Furies shake the fires
Of their torches in the street
Of my blood. . . . And still they stand
In the city's street that tires
Of the tread of Man.

Three old Rag-pickers are they
Clothed with grandeur by the light
As a Queen, but blind as Doom
Fumbling for the rag of Man
In an empty room.

Now they take the place of Fate
In whom the flames of Madness ran
Since her lidless eyes were cursed
With the world-expunging sight
Of the heart of Man.

How simple was the time of Cain
Before the latter Man-made Rain
Washed away all loss and gain
And the talk of right and wrong —
Murdered now and gone.

And the ghost of Man is red
With the sweep of the world's blood. . . .
In this late equality
Would you know the ghost of Man
From the ghost of a Flea ?

But still the fires of the great Spring
In the desolate fields proclaim

Eternity . . . those wild fires shout
Of Christ the new song.

Run those fires from field to field !
I walk alone and ghostlily
Burning with Eternity's
Fires, and quench the Furies' song
In flame that never tires.

12. The Stone-Breakers

A Prison Song

TO ZOSIA KOCHANSKA

(After the song of men condemned to 99 years on the Chain Gang:
'Ain no mo cane in de Brazis.')

Go down, red Sun, red Cain!
Or, if you rise again,
Bring us the last fires of the Judgment Day!

The red sea of the heat, the tide
Of all men's blood, divide
Us from our brother men: In all that Flood

There is no drop of mercy! Red dews lie on flower
and heart
In this red Morning of the World — no other rain!

The dead men rise with Cain the Sun;
They died on the chain, but rise to work again.

Dead men, rise, and help me break the stone!
Dead men, rise, and help me break the heart!
Lies not some drop of mercy there?

Among living men, in the Live Men's air,
Our emperor brothers, the Low-Man-Flea
And the tyrant's ghost, cast equal shades,
And the world yields them its heart and vein —
Bled white as innocence. But despair

And all the Furies in our hearts
Beat stripes that mark the prediluvian
Tiger. No flood washed away
That furious darkness striped upon
A heart light as Hell's day.

Now, naked as the worm, unarmed
As when in our first Hell, the womb,
That shaped us for damnation, we,
The outcast Tree of Bone

On which our Christ is crucified,
Are fleshless as the skeleton
Of Adam, and have known
All deaths, from Adam's first sin to the resurrection
Of the testifying, the accusing Dead.

The stone we beat upon, O brothers, seals Christ's Tomb
The red sea of the heat and heart will change. Oh, hear
    the rolling
Back of that sea ! Another sea rolls on
Across the world. And we from death on death shall rise
    again

To testify against the heart of Man
That dreamed our darkness could present a dam
To the Sea that comes — the infinite Blood of Christ.

13. The Coat of Fire

AMID the thunders of the falling Dark
In the Tartarean darkness of the fog
I walk, a Pillar of Fire
On pavements of black marble, hard
And wide as the long boulevard
Of Hell . . . I, in whose veins the Furies wave
Their long fires, move where purgatories, heavens, hells,
     and worlds
Wrought by illusion, hide in the human breast
And tear the enclosing heart. . . . And the snow fell
(Thin flakes of ash from Gomorrah) on blind faces
Turned to the heedless sky. . . . A dress has the sound
Of Reality, reverberates like thunder.
And ghosts of aeons and of equinoxes
(Of moments that seemed aeons, and long partings)
Take on the forms of fashionable women
With veils that hide a new Catastrophe, and under
Is the fall of a world that was a heart. Some doomed to
     descend
Through all the hells and change into the Dog
Without its faithfulness, the Crocodile
Without its watchfulness, and then to Pampean mud.
In the circles of the city's hells beneath the fog
These bear, to light them, in the human breast,
The yellow dull light from the raging human dust,
The dull blue light from the brutes, light red as rust
Of blood from eyeless weeping ghosts, light black as
     smoke
From hell. And those breasts bear
No other light. . . . They circle in the snow
Where in the dust the apterous
Fates turned insects whisper ' Now abandon
Man the annelida. Let all be wingless
That hangs between the abyss and Abaddon.'
The Catastrophes with veils and trains drift by,
And I to my heart, disastrous Comet, cry

'Red heart, my Lucifer, how fallen art thou,
And lightless, I!'
The dresses sweep the dust of mortality
And roll the burden of Atlas' woe, changed to a stone
Up to the benches where the beggars sway —
Their souls alone as on the Judgment Day —
In their Valley of the myriad Dry Bones under world-tall
  houses.
Then with a noise as if in the thunders of the Dark
All sins, griefs, aberrations of the world rolled to confess,
Those myriad Dry Bones rose to testify :
'See her, the Pillar of Fire !

      The aeons of Cold
And all the deaths that Adam has endured
Since the first death, can not outfreeze our night.
And where is the fire of love that will warm our hands ?
There is only this conflagration
Of all the sins of the world ! To the dust's busyness
She speaks of the annihilation
Of every form of dust, burned down to Nothingness !
To the small lovers, of a kiss that seems the red
Lightning of Comets firing worlds, — and of a Night
That shall outburn all nights that lovers know —
The last red Night before the Judgment Day !
O Pillar of Flame, that drifts across the world to Nowhere !
The eyes are seas of fire ! All forms, all sights,
And all sensations are on fire ! The storms
Of blood, a whirlpool of the flame ! the ears, all sounds
Of all the world, a universe of fire ! All smells, a ravening
Raging cyclone of wild fire ! The nose, burned quite away !
The tongue is on fire, all tastes on fire, the mind
Is red as noon upon the Judgment Day !
The tears are rolling, falling worlds of fire !
With what are these on fire ? With passion, hate,
Infatuation, and old age, and death,
With sorrow, longing, and with labouring breath,
And with despair and life are these on fire !
With the illusions of the world, the flames of lust,

And raging red desire !
A Pillar of Fire is she in the empty dust,
And will not change those fires into warmth for our hands,'
Said the beggars, lolling and rocking
The heedless world upon a heaving shoulder.

∽

PART VI

1. Dirge for the New Sunrise

*(Fifteen minutes past eight o'clock, on the morning
of Monday the 6th of August* 1945)

BOUND to my heart as Ixion to the wheel,
Nailed to my heart as the Thief upon the Cross,
I hang between our Christ and the gap where the world
    was lost

And watch the phantom Sun in Famine Street
— The ghost of the heart of Man . . . red Cain
And the more murderous brain
Of Man, still redder Nero that conceived the death
Of his mother Earth, and tore
Her womb, to know the place where he was conceived.

But no eyes grieved —
For none were left for tears :
They were blinded as the years
Since Christ was born. Mother or Murderer, you have
    given or taken life —
Now all is one !

There was a morning when the holy Light
Was young. The beautiful First Creature came
To our water-springs, and thought us without blame.

Our hearts seemed safe in our breasts and sang to the
        Light —
The marrow in the bone
We dreamed was safe . . . the blood in the veins, the sap
        in the tree
Were springs of Deity.

But I saw the little Ant-men as they ran
Carrying the world's weight of the world's filth
And the filth in the heart of Man —
Compressed till those lusts and greeds had a greater heat
        than that of the Sun.

And the ray from that heat came soundless, shook the sky
As if in search of food, and squeezed the stems
Of all that grows on the earth till they were dry
— And drank the marrow of the bone :
The eyes that saw, the lips that kissed, are gone
Or black as thunder lie and grin at the murdered Sun.

The living blind and seeing Dead together lie
As if in love. . . . There was no more hating then,
And no more love : Gone is the heart of Man.

2. *The Shadow of Cain*

TO C. M. BOWRA

UNDER great yellow flags and banners of the ancient Cold
Began the huge migrations
From some primeval disaster in the heart of Man.

There were great oscillations
Of temperature. . . . You knew there had once been
    warmth ;

But the Cold is the highest mathematical Idea . . . the
    Cold is Zero —
The Nothing from which arose
All Being and all variation. . . . It is the sound too high
    for our hearing, the Point that flows

Till it becomes the line of Time . . . an endless positing
Of Nothing, or the Ideal that tries to burgeon
Into Reality through multiplying. Then Time froze

To immobility and changed to Space.
Black flags among the ice, blue rays
And the purple perfumes of the polar Sun
Freezing the bone to sapphire and to zircon —
These were our days.

And now in memory of great oscillations
Of temperature in that epoch of the Cold,
We found a continent of turquoise, vast as Asia
In the yellowing airs of the Cold : the tooth of a
    mammoth ;
And there, in a gulf, a dark pine-sword

To show there had once been warmth and the gulf stream
    in our veins
Where only the Chaos of the Antarctic Pole
Or the peace of its atonic coldness reigns.

And sometimes we found the trace
Of a bird's claw in the immensity of the Cold:
The trace of the first letters we could not read:
Some message of Man's need,

And of the slow subsidence of a Race;
And of great heats in which the Pampean mud was
    formed,
In which the Megatherium Mylodon
Lies buried under Mastodon-trumpetings of leprous Suns.

The Earth had cloven in two in that primal disaster.
But when the glacial period began
There was still some method of communication
Between Man and his brother Man —
Although their speech
Was alien, each from each
As the Bird's from the Tiger's, born from the needs of
    our opposing famines.

Each said ' This is the Race of the Dead . . . their blood
    is cold. . . .
For the heat of those more recent on the Earth
Is higher . . . the blood-beat of the Bird more high
Than that of the ancient race of the primeval Tiger ':
The Earth had lived without the Bird

In that Spring when there were no flowers like thunders
    in the air.
And now the Earth lies flat beneath the shade of an iron
    wing.
And of what does the Pterodactyl sing —
Of what red buds in what tremendous Spring ? '

The thunders of the Spring began. . . . We came again
After that long migration
To the city built before the Flood by our brother Cain.

And when we reached an open door
The Fate said ' My feet ache.'
The Wanderers said ' Our hearts ache.'

There was great lightning
In flashes coming to us over the floor :
The Whiteness of the Bread —
The Whiteness of the Dead —
The Whiteness of the Claw —
All this coming to us in flashes through the open door.

There were great emerald thunders in the air
In the violent Spring, the thunders of the sap and the blood
    in the heart
— The Spiritual Light, the physical Revelation.

In the streets of the City of Cain there were great
    Rainbows
Of emeralds : the young people, crossing and meeting.

And everywhere
The great voice of the Sun in sap and bud
Fed from the heart of Being, the panic Power,
The sacred Fury, shouts of Eternity
To the blind eyes, the heat in the wingèd seed, the fire in
    the blood.

And through the works of Death,
The dust's aridity, is heard the sound
Of mounting saps like monstrous bull-voices of unseen
    fearful mimes :
And the great rolling world-wide thunders of that drum-
    ming underground

Proclaim our Christ, and roar ' Let there be harvest !
Let there be no more Poor —
For the Son of God is sowed in every furrow ! '

We did not heed the Cloud in the Heavens shaped like
     the hand
Of Man. . . . But there came a roar as if the Sun and
     Earth had come together —
The Sun descending and the Earth ascending
To take its place above . . . the Primal Matter
Was broken, the womb from which all life began.
Then to the murdered Sun a totem pole of dust arose in
     memory of Man.

The cataclysm of the Sun down-pouring
Seemed the roar
Of those vermilion Suns the drops of the blood
That bellowing like Mastodons at war
Rush down the length of the world — away — away —

The violence of torrents, cataracts, maelstroms, rains
That went before the Flood —
These covered the earth from the freshets of our brothers'
     veins ;

And with them, the forked lightnings of the gold
From the split mountains,
Blasting their rivals, the young foolish wheat-ears
Amid those terrible rains.

The gulf that was torn across the world seemed as if the
     beds of all the Oceans
Were emptied. . . . Naked, and gaping at what once had
     been the Sun,
Like the mouth of the Universal Famine
It stretched its jaws from one end of the Earth to the other.

And in that hollow lay the body of our brother
Lazarus, upheaved from the world's tomb.
He lay in that great Death like the gold in the husk
Of the world . . . and round him, like spent lightnings,
     lay the Ore —
The balm for the world's sore.

And the gold lay in its husk of rough earth like the core
In the furred almond, the chestnut in its prickly
Bark, the walnut in a husk green and bitter.

And to that hollow sea
The civilisation of the Maimed, and, too, Life's lepers,
    came
As once to Christ near the Sea of Galilee.

They brought the Aeons of Blindness and the Night
Of the World, crying to him, ' Lazarus, give us sight !
O you whose sores are of gold, who are the new Light
Of the World ! '
                They brought to the Tomb
The Condemned of Man, who wear as stigmata from the
    womb
The depression of the skull as in the lesser
Beasts of Prey, the marks of Ape and Dog,
The canine and lemurine muscle . . . the pitiable, the
    terrible,
The loveless, whose deformities arose
Before their birth, or from a betrayal by the gold wheat-
    ear.
' Lazarus, for all love we knew the great Sun's kiss

On the loveless cheek. He came to the dog-fang and the
    lion-claw
That Famine gave the empty mouth, the workless hands.
He came to the inner leaf of the forsaken heart —
He spoke of our Christ, and of a golden love. . . .
But our Sun is gone . . . will your gold bring warmth to
    the loveless lips, and harvest to barren lands ? '

Then Dives was brought. . . . He lay like a leprous Sun
That is covered with the sores of the world . . . the
    leprosy
Of gold encrusts the world that was his heart.

Like a great ear of wheat that is swoln with grain,
Then ruined by white rain,
He lay. . . . His hollow face, dust white, was cowled
     with a hood of gold :
But you saw there was no beat or pulse of blood —
You would not know him now from Lazarus !

He did not look at us.
He said ' What was spilt still surges like the Flood.
But Gold shall be the Blood
Of the world. . . . Brute gold condensed to the primal
     essence
Has the texture, smell, warmth, colour of Blood. We
     must take

A quintessence of the disease for remedy. Once hold
The primal matter of all gold —
From which it grows
(That Rose of the World) as the sharp clear tree from
     the seed of the great rose,

Then give of this, condensed to the transparency
Of the beryl, the weight of twenty barley grains :
And the leper's face will be full as the rose's face
After great rains.

It will shape again the Shadow of Man. Or at least will
     take
From all roots of life the symptoms of the leper —
And make the body sharp as the honeycomb,
The roots of life that are left like the red roots of the rose-
     branches.'

But near him a gold sound —
The voice of an unborn wheat-ear accusing Dives —
Said ' Soon I shall be more rare, more precious than
     gold.'

There are no thunders, there are no fires, no suns, no
    earthquakes
Left in our blood. . . . But yet like the rolling thunders
    of all the fires in the world, we cry
To Dives : ' You are the shadow of Cain. Your shade is
    the primal Hunger.'
' I lie under what condemnation ? '
' The same as Adam, the same as Cain, the same as Sodom,
    the same as Judas.

And the fires of your Hell shall not be quenched by the
    rain
From those torn and parti-coloured garments of Christ,
    those rags
That once were Men. Each wound, each stripe,
Cries out more loudly than the voice of Cain —
Saying " Am I my brother's keeper ? " ' Think ! When
    the last clamour of the Bought and Sold
The agony of Gold
Is hushed. . . . When the last Judas-kiss
Has died upon the cheek of the Starved Man Christ,
    those ashes that were men
Will rise again
To be our Fires upon the Judgment Day !
And yet — who dreamed that Christ has died in vain ?
He walks again on the Seas of Blood, He comes in the
    terrible Rain.

3. The Canticle of the Rose

TO GEOFFREY GORER

THE Rose upon the wall
Cries — ' I am the voice of Fire :
And in me grows
The pomegranate splendour of Death, the ruby, garnet,
  almandine
Dews : Christ's Wounds in me shine.

I rise upon my stem,
The Flower, the whole Plant-being, produced by Light
With all Plant-systems and formations. . . . As in Fire
All elements dissolve, so in one bright
Ineffable essence all Plant-being dissolves to make the
  Flower.

My stem rises bright :
Organic water polarised to the dark
Earth-centre, and to Light.'

Below that wall, in Famine Street
There is nothing left but the heart to eat

And the Shade of Man. . . . Buyers and sellers cry
' Speak not the name of Light —
Her name is Madness now. . . . Though we are black
  beneath her kiss
As if she were the Sun, her name is Night :
She has condemned us, and decreed that Man must die.'

There was a woman combing her long hair
To the rhythm of the river flowing. . . .
She sang ' All things will end —
Like the sound of Time in my veins growing :
The hump on the dwarf, the mountain on the plain,
The fixed red of the rose and the rainbow's red,
The fires of the heart, the wandering planet's pain —

All loss, all gain —
Yet will the world remain ! '

The song died in the Ray. . . . Where is she now ?
Dissolved, and gone —
And only her red shadow stains the unremembering stone.

And in Famine Street the sellers cry
' What will you buy ?

A dress for the Bride ? '
(But all the moulds of generation died
Beneath that Ray.)
                        ' Or a winding-sheet ? '
(Outworn. . . . The Dead have nothing left to hide.)

' Then buy ' said the Fate arisen from Hell —
That thing of rags and patches —
' A box of matches !
For the machine that generated warmth
Beneath your breast is dead. . . . You need a fire
To warm what lies upon your bone. . . .
Not all the ashes of your brother Men
Will kindle that again —
Nor all the world's incendiaries !
Who buys — Who buys — ?
Come, give me pence to lay upon my staring lidless eyes !

But high upon the wall
The Rose where the Wounds of Christ are red
Cries to the Light
' See how I rise upon my stem, ineffable bright
Effluence of bright essence. . . . From my little span
I cry of Christ, Who is the ultimate Fire
Who will burn away the cold in the heart of Man. . . .
Springs come, springs go. . . .
' I was reddere on Rode than the Rose in the rayne.'
' This smel is Crist, clepid the plantynge of the Rose
     in Jerico.'

PART VII

THE ROAD TO THEBES

(Three Poems on a Theme)

TO HUMPHREY AND GILLEN SEARLE

Is the road from Thebes to Athens and the
road from Athens to Thebes the same?
ARISTOTLE: *Physica*

∽

1. Beside the Yellow Foam that Sings of Lydian Airs

BESIDE the yellow foam that sings of Lydian airs and of
    the lyre —
And vines taut as the lyre, the earth seems of sardonyx
Where the hot juices fall like yellow planets — earth
    striped like the lynx.

Along the road to Thebes
All polished speeds,
Men, horses, seeds,
Are blown by the bright wind, the young flute-player,
Who kindles every vine-bough, sharp
As shrill spring lightnings.
                 But what golden speed
Now lies beneath the earth, like the soul maimed
By the rough centaur-husk? For in the Pliocene
Strata lies the Horse,
The Pliohippus and Hipparion
Whose skin shone like the Pleiades — once fleet as the
    spring rain,

Or young desire, were they — as quickly gone.
Yet still the sound of waves and the long-dying
Airs and the great veils and veins and voices
Of vines are theirs,

The thunders of the bull-voiced mimes, unseen, unknown,
The thunders of saps rising, and of all things sown

In far-off gardens.
                              Ghosts rise from gold seeds
In the mist from vine-branches. ' And were you
      Agamemnon
Or the shrill ghost of a vine-tendril ? ' ' Should I know ? '

I only know my form
Is the great logic of the winter, the geometry
Of Death : the world began with these :
The numbers of Pythagoras,
The seeds of Anaxagoras ;
And the winter at my heart, whose Zero is
An infinite intensity, yet holds
The seeds and beginning of the fires of spring.

Now for the sound of wars, I hear bees among vine-
      blooms
Singing of growth — they, yellow as the planets,
Like Capricornus, Lynx, and Taurus swarming.

The Dead Man, thin as water,
Or as a vine-tendril, and shod with gold
As for a journey — (but upon what road ?) —

Answered the thunders of the saps rising
Under the dust that shines like the glittering skin
Of centaurs in horse-bearing Thessaly :

' Is your gold-sinewed body still a vine-branch
In the vineyards of great Venus ? ' ' Shrunk to this

Poor span, I have returned to the likeness of the first and
      final Worm that is my brother :
For were we not born of the same holy mother —

Alike in holiness ? . . . Now black as earth.
Yet great queens found my mouth
As a dark leaf of nardus brought from Syria —
Of the gold door of the South.
                                Ah, who
Would kiss it now ?
                        And those queens' dust is but as
      frost that shines like fire
Or the gilded dust of Venus in the spring,
Fertilising the crocus.

                    As I went on my long road
From Birth to Death, I learned that Birth and Death,
The road to Thebes from Athens, and the road
From Thebes to Athens, coming and going, praise and
      blame,
Are like the angry kings, the ghosts of gold
That hide from Man his sun : they are the same.

Upon my road from Birth to Death, to Thebes from
      Athens,
I heaped gold dust in hills.
                      With the blind mole,
On my returning way, I heaped another mound
Of dust. And as I came

On my Night-Road, the four gigantic thunders sounded :
And the four worlds were gone : Earth, Water, Fire, and
      Air.
With Death, in nakedness, I was alone :
But then heard the great thunders of saps rising and of all
      things sown.

The four worlds came : Love, Hate, Belief, and Unbelief :
(The raging human dust, dull dust of brutes,
The groping dust of plants, the earth's blind dust).

On my Day Road, the four gigantic thunders sounded :
Those worlds fell from the living heart, were gone,
And I was alone with Life — the Naked Man.

The worlds went : I was a clod of earth
Blown by the wind along the road from Death to Birth.
The worlds came : I was clothed with a little dust,
And blown along the road from Birth to Death.

I cried at the light, as I had cried at the dark.
I found a little rest upon my way, a small child growing
Deep in the tomb, or in my mother's womb —
But still unknowing.

In my canicular days, I, the companion
Of the high Sun, could never dream of setting,
Or that I should not find the answer to the Question.'

   . . . . .

There was no sign of the lion-bodied one
Between the vineyards and the heroic sea,
There was no glitter of her mane, strong as the wave,
Bright as the treasure on the ocean-floor,
And the glittering orange-tree.   There was no sound

Where the lion-coloured dusts are numerous as Time's
  sands,
Under the heavens masked with gold like Agamemnon,

And bordered with great vines whose solar system of the
  grapes
Shines like the centaur's skin, hard as cornelian grains,
The hue of honey sarcophagising or of sard —
Holding small stars for seeds
And planets of noon-dew, and the long rains
And the cool sea-winds from the far horizons.

As I went my way from the cities of the living
Dead to cities of the dead Living, airs and prayers
Arose from the fertility of vines,

From cornucopias and corruptions, continents
Of growth, from where those seeds, the Dead, are sown
To be reborn, and germs of evil that exist in Matter
Are changed by holy earth, to the common good,

To usefulness, fertility. The breath
Of the Ardent Belief, of the cultivated earth
Drifts through the city streets, to kings turned dust-
    worms,
To beggars and bugbears, dusty thunders, Cerberus
Changed to a dog, and Niobe to a stone lest she should
    weep —

To palaces of Commerce, the machine, the revolutions
Rushing toward the vortices (gyrations
Of empty Light), and Man, like Ixion, bound
Upon that wheel, all in the conquering dust ;
To palaces of Justice — a projection of the Darkness :
(Domitian, the mad Emperor, catching flies, and
    Harcateus,
The King of Parthia, a blind mole-catcher) —

To Afternoon-Men, Giddy-heads, the chrysalides,
The Golden Outsides, drones, flies, and philosophers,
A world of busy sleep
Where the horse drives the man, the palace builds
The slave, the judge the criminal, and the sun gilds

Laughing and weeping, hatred, fear, and love, and lust
With royal robes, soon to be changed to dust.

Then comes the hour of consolation, and the evening,
Sighing all sighs and knowing all ambitions, walks like
    the wave
To cities whose names are like the sound of waves,
    Aomono,
Quezaltenango, Wawasee, Tandora,
London, and Paris.

A sound drifts through the streets to
the homeward-going —
A golden dust — from the evening ? From the hives of
Midas ? From the Lion-gate ?
Or the sands of Time whence the Lion-bodied asks the
Question
On roads sacred to Man, who is great as a planet moving
On its gold tendril, — small as a grain of dust.

2. *Interlude*

AFTER the intolerable weight of tyrant suns
(Caesars with masks of gold), wave after wave the early
    evening
Comes with the sound of sea and siren cave
To continents and cities after the long heat,

And echoes in buried cities — the azoic azure
Calls to the sphinxes of the silence and the unburied
    sapphires
Staring across the lion-breasted sands in the great deserts,

And to the azoic heart (where Time, that Medusa, reigns,
    turns all to stone) —
To the orange-flower, the oragious hair of youth that cool
    airs lift, the orb ;
And the golden nodding nurse that we call Eve

And evening, sighed, ' The first and final Adam — he who
    is one with the immense Ceres
And all day broke the gold body of the giantess as in love

And he who forsook her for that other giantess
The city, the vast continent of stone

Are homeward-going.'
           Soon night falls like fire, yet vine-dark.
        In the cities
The girls with breasts like points of sun in the vine-dark
    night
And gowns the colour of the thunder's reverberations
Among the forests, seek a love in which to sink like the sea.

What do the seraphs and sapphires of air among the
    branches
Hear as the voices pass ?   ' Your hair is ringed as the
    tendrils
Of the first plantations of the Vine after the Flood.'

' The vines of the Sun ?   Or the vines of Darkness and of
     all damnations —
The vines of Medusa's serpents ? '   ' Ah, your kiss is the
     light of the planets, burning among the leaves ! '
                                   ' No.   It was Lucifer,

Son of the Morning — then it changed to the Prince of
     the Air, the brightness
That rules in Hell !   Grown cold !   I am Medusa — and
     my other
Name is Time !

                         Come to my lips — the long horizon —
Cold with the serpents' buried wisdom, that has known
     the azoic
Continents, the secrets and night-haunted jewels of the
     catafalques !

Come !   I will seal your eyes that they no more shall
     weep,
No more behold another.   Once, at your grief,
The unfraught sea would swell, and the unsought
     diamonds

Rise with your tears.
                         Now you shall faithless be
To the flesh of orange-blossom and arbutus honey-
     hearted,
Seeing my lips cold as the unburied sapphires in the
     desert air
Approach your own —
The one horizon — the azoic continent of night and
     stone.'

3. The Night Wind

O HEART, great equinox of the Sun of Night
Where life and death are equal — Lion — or Sphinx !
What can you tell of Darkness
To the great continent of hungry stone ?

Heart, (Lion or Sphinx) what can you tell the city
Of breasts like Egypt where no lightning shines,
Because of their great heat ? This is the hour the night-
      wind
Asks those born in Hell concerning their foredoom.

Now in the streets great airs the colour of the vines
Drift to the noctuas, veiled women, to the faceless ones,
      the nameless ones —
To Lot's wife staring across the desert of her life.

Those airs of sapphire drift from violet vines —
Elixirs and saps of sapphire beloved of Saturn,
And planets of violet dew from vine-branches

Fall on the lips of fashionable women —
The abominable Koretto and Metro (cities buried
Under the sands of the Dead Sea : Adama and Gomorrah,
      Segor) ;
And cool the cheeks where the long fires of all Hell are
      dyed ;

Drifting to women like great vines : (what was the first
      plantation since the Flood ?
The vines of Grief ?
The first sin of the new world, and the last
Of the ancient civilisation ? You, the night-wind,
What was the first plantation since the Flood ?)

And to old Maenads of the city, where the far-off music,
Dying in public gardens, wraps their flesh —

That vast immundity from which the Flood receded,
Their hearts, those rocks from which no Moses could
    strike tears,

With a little comfort ; they, awhile forgetting
The mobilisation of the world's filth, the garrets, garners
Of Nothingness, and the sparse fire's infrequent garnets,
The ragpicker's great reign, their empty mouths like
    Chaos ruined,
Speak for a moment with their other lives :

' What is it knocks at that tomb my heart ? Is it the
    grave-digger,
The final Adam ? There was one knocked so :
He would not know me now. For all Time's filth, the
    dress
I stole from the habitations of the Dead,
Hides me — a body cold as the wind-blown vines,
And the sad sapphire bone shrunk by Time's fires

To this small apeish thing.'
                   ' Ah, what was I inferior to Death,
That you should be untrue ? Now, kindly Age,
My one companion, holds me close, so I
Forget your kiss. The fires in my heart are gone.
And yet, as if they had melted into rain,

The heart itself, my tears
Are faithful yet.'
              ' Is there another language of the
    Dead ?
Is that why those for whom we long return
No more ? For the small words of love they say —

How should we hear them through the Babel-clamour ?
They make no sound :
All the great movements of the world pass with no noise :
The golden boys,

The great Spring, turn to dust as to a lover —
The heart breaks with no sound.'

' And in the day, the empire of hatred and of hunger,
Even the Dog pities us ! " I would be destitute as Man,
So cast from me my faithfulness, my one possession.
All day, my throat must multiply its thunder
To the triple violence of Cerberus
To proclaim your misery and mine ! Why should the
        Beast and Reptile
Be imprisoned in their small empire of aggression —
The claw, fang, sting, the twining, the embrace ? "
Has Man no more than this ? Does not the lover say to
        lover :
" Is that your kiss ?

It is more cold than the python, the shining one, the
        viper ;
Its venom is perfidy, outshining all the stars." '

Then where the suns of Night seek in the rock for unborn
        sapphires
And cornflowers like blue flames or water-drops from
        wells of blue fire
Deep as the heart of Man, from which to build the Day,

I went upon my road to Thebes from Athens, Death
        from Birth,
And to my heart, that last dark Night in which the long
        Styx weeps its woe,
Held close the world, my wound.

PART VIII

1. *Bagatelle*

FOR JOHN GIELGUD

Upon the soil — (crushed rubies ? Or the pomegranate's
    garnet seeds ?)
And ridged with mounds like graves
Of giants and earth-worms, two Noachian survivors
    contemplate
Their glories of the past, their future state.

The small red Worm, rubied with dews of Death,
    declared :
' My redness is from Adam. I, the coral-plant,
Built by a million lives, endeavours, toils, loves, glories,
Am the first and last Democracy. The sun
Is not more universal in its love. And I have brothers
Who live in the flesh of Negroes, and are thick
As lute-strings, and as powerful. I have others
Who sing the praise of Death with a sweet tongue —

Great venomous serpents in the unknown Africa ; they
    carry
A gold bell on their tails, which ever ringeth
As they proceed, and like an angel singeth.'

Then said her enemy the Hen — the musty, dusty density,
The entity of primal, flightless, winged Stupidity :
' See how the Eagle falls like thunder from his height
And tears that continent of raging fire,
The heart, from the Tiger roaring like the sea,

And bears it to his nest
Wherein the huge eggs rest
From whence will break the young, the unfledged
        Murders :

(So, young ambitions lie in the heart of Man).
O you into whose maw
The heart of Man will fall
As you will fall to mine :
I am more powerful than the father of those Murders.

It was no Eagle, but a fusty Hen
That pecked the fire-seeds from Prometheus' heart, a
        crazy chilling
Hen-coop Laughter, the first Criticism, killing
The fire he brought to men,
As Age kills young Desire.'

The Worm said, ' I am small, my redness is from Adam.
But conquerors tall
Come to my embrace as I were Venus. I
Am the paramour in the last bed of love, and mine, the
        kiss
That gives Eternity.
I am Princess of Darkness. Yet the huge gold world,
With all plantations, powers of gold growth that shall be
        the bread of men,
Arise from the toil of the small, the mighty Worm beneath
        the earth —
The blind, all-seeing Power at her great work of death
        and of rebirth.'

2. *Gardeners and Astronomers*

TO J. M. AND AUDREY COHEN

WHERE the green airs seem fanning palms and the green
    psalms
Of greater waters, where the orange hangs huge as Orion,
    and day-long great gauds and lauds of light

Pierce their gold through the seeds, behold their secrets,
And the weight of the warm air
Shapes the exquisite corolla to a world of gold rain
Closed in thick gold armour like a King's,

Old men, dark-gold with earth and toil,
Praise their green heavens. ' Who would look dangerously
    high in air
At planets, who may safely watch the earth
For the lesser solar system of the plants,
And for the spring's rebirth ?

Then why are we less than the astronomers ?
Than Hipparchus, who saw a comet that foretold
The birth of Mithridates and began
To form his catalogue of stars that are no more
Than the long-leaved planets in our garden-shed.

And men of emeralds walking through the night
Of early Chinese annals, Emperor Hwan-Té
Whose pleasure-dome was an observatory, Chien-Ké
Who shook a branch and all the stars together glittered
    bright :
Now are they but the dust of lilies on our garden-bed.

And why are we less than these ?
Does not each dark root hold a world of gold ?
And was not Aristophanes,
Who gave the world green laughter, son of the garden-
    goddess ? '

So said the old men, gold with toil and ripeness,
As their great fathering Sun.
                                    But in the cities,
New criminals and sages, pariah Suns in heavens of evil
Ripen new forms of life from primeval mud.

And Man, the planet-bacillus, acts new virtues,
(The eunuch's chastity, the gentleness of the untoothed
        tiger,
More insolent than youth, more cruel than spring),

And longs for the night when each has his own world.
                                    Some dream that all are equal,
As in the gardener's world of growth, the plant and
        planet, King and beggar ;
And Fallen Man dreams he is falling upward.   And the
        eyeless
Horizontal Man, the Black Man, who in the Day's blazing
        diamond-mine, follows the footsteps
Of Vertical Man, is ever cast by him
Across all growth, all stone — he, great as Man's
        ambition,
And like to Man's ambition, with no body
To act ambition — he, the sole horizon,
Epitome of our age, now rules the world.

Their faces stained by the cool night like wine
Under the violet planets of night-dew, Night-roamers,
        Magians,
And the Bacchantes of the suburbs with their hair like the
        torn vines
That are lifted by the night-wind, know all things are equal
Hades and Dionysus, Being, Not-Being.

And those who see the virtues hidden in the compass
Of the green mantles, see the lamentable planets of those
        lives
As no more than the planets in green heavens of the
        gardens.

And in the gardens the airs sing of growth :
The orange-tree still sighs,
' I am the Dark that changed to water and to air,
The water and the air that changed to gold —
The gold that turned into a plant.   From the cool wave
    of the air grows a smooth
Stem, and from this the gold, cold orange-tree.'

And happy as the Sun, the gardeners
See all miasmas from the human filth but as the dung
In which to sow great flowers,
Tall moons and mornings, seeds, and sires, and suns.

3. Two Songs

FOR ROY AND MARY CAMPBELL

I

You said, ' This is the time of the wild spring and the
    mating of the tigers,
This is the first vintage of the heat like the budding of
    wild vines —
The budding of emeralds and the emerald climate,

When flowers change into rainbows and young insects
Are happy, the people have heart-strings like the music
Of the great suns, oh never to be quenched by darkness.'

But I am the water-carrier to the Damned, and dark as
    water.
Only those nights, my eyes, have no more rain,
And dead are the merciful fountains
Since the world changed into a stone again.

I am the grave of the unpitied Sisyphus,
My heart, that rolled the universe, a stone
Changed to me, like your heart, up endless mountains.

II. *The Song of the Beggar Maid to King Cophetua*

I saw the Gold Man with the lion's head
Reflected deep
In the waters of the well when in the great heat
I went to draw their cold : he gave to me a flower
Petalled with gold and glittering beams and said,
' You must not tell
What you have seen reflected.'

(The King to whom my sister flower, the marigold,
Turns her bright head . . .)
But mine is another Sun.   Come from the night,
    Cophetua !
I will unclose my corolla to my Sun —
Still wet with the tears of night, each golden beam
About my head !   But with your rising they are gone.

I am your Marigold, O royal star !

My birth was Darkness.   But your light
Gave me the corolla of my bright flower
Like to your crown !

The Kings bow their bright shining heads adown —
Like flowers of the Sun, those marigolds !
But the Sun of Fate has beat on them till they grew faint
And flaccid, no more fit
To bear the corolla of a bright crown.

' Kings and bright lovers all must come to this.'
So sighed the dews of night that from the leaf
Fade and are gone.

Yet when in a thick and cloudy air none may espy
Your beauty, so obscurèd, I
Still turn to you the bright beams of my head, my golden
    skin,
And close in your golden beams for my long night,
O royal star, for whom the poor Marigold must live and
    die !

4. *Butterfly-Weather*

FOR BETSEY AND JOCK WHITNEY

WHAT were the sounds I heard through the begonia-
    yellow music
(Spangled with gold as if by Sirius and his bright train)
In public gardens, in hot afternoons when old crones,
Featureless as the shores of Lethe, and the fashionable
    women
(Aeons of emptiness and the long equinoxes
Where all is equal) lean together, talking?

' I think but rarely of the past : it is a ghost.'
' What is a ghost ? ' ' One who has gone away —
Or a belief that faded.'
                 ' And do you remember
Semiramis, who was bright as all September ? Gone is her
    kiss,
And the golden racers, young winds from the shores of
    our lost youth.'
' But look at the children chasing the butterflies ! '

     .   .   .   .   .

I think we live now in the age of the terrible Furies
Changed into Butterflies, and of the Butterfly-weather,
    gilding the hopeless heart

With the hues of false victories, of the fallen suns, fallen
    Caesars and cities —
The brightness of air — the Nothing-country that has no
    chart

Like our world that is drifting to Nowhere. Once the
    astronomer
Kepler, in plague-time, foretold a pestilence ending Man,

Having seen on his hands and his feet the Stigmata. But
    what were those signs of the Crucifixion ?
Only a little bright dust from a butterfly's wing !

Those moments of summer happiness, the sweet innocent
 butterflies
Are bright as the apricot cheeks of the young girls chas-
 ing them,
And as their water-soft long yellow hair soft as bird-
 bosoms, soft as all Aprils —

Flashing among the dark woods, and their laughter.   The
 butterflies'
Auburn air-thin glittering velvets and gauzes are flying —
Holy with happiness, shining with Heaven's light.   But
 of the Furies changed into butterflies —
What of that terrible lightness, ephemeral brightness —
The Butterfly-pestilence ending the race of Man ?

5. The Madwoman in the Park

TO HORACE GREGORY

THERE were no lines of violent diamonds, blinding light.
There were no sharp guitar-notes of the rain
Amid the tiger-purring greenery. All through the night
I dreamed the King of Diamonds was sick and like to die.

Only small dusty deaths remain. For this is the time of the
    dryness.
The Dead have stolen the rain that they may weep
For us. . . .

              One sat beside me in a gown
That seemed as if long since it had been stolen
From one the waters of long Lethe drown.

Such was her dress.
And she was veiled like the long Niobean November when
    old Nothingness
Waits like the Minotaur in the long Cretan maze of the
    rain.

The rubies of the heat high up among the leaves
Burn in Egyptian darkness ; Reigns and Dynasties of
    light
War in the leaves. . . . There is no mask now of Erigone
Or Helen, Dionysus, swinging from the branches,
Moved by the young wind whose long dark hair
Seems like the rain, the dying spirit of the air.

There is only now the mask of our despair.
She talked with her one companion, the Fly,
The brother of the imperial Dust and the three Furies,
The avenging black-winged ones. ' Ah, why do they
    pursue us ?
I, the aurelia from which the great purple butterfly of the
    Night arises !

Am I not like to thee, with all-embracing sight ?
I am not like the race of Man, grown blind
Between the Scylla and Charybdis of the new and murder-
ous Light.

Why, then, do men despise us ? ' Then said Musca, the
Fly,
' Men say I am the ghost of Civilisation,
The epitome of the great conquering nation
Of the all-seeing Dead. But they lie. I am Life. And
would God prefer
The dream of a possible Angel to that of my plight,
Whose wings, though sprung from the uttermost filth of
the world,
Have all the grandeurs and jewels of the Dust about them,
And are made holy by Light ? '

Said the lady whose veils were like the black wings of the
Furies :
' Now there is no horizon but the lips of Medusa,
The all-embracing. Beyond that horizon, where is the day
Of Man's lost innocence — where is the clime
Of his forgiveness ? ' The Fly

Said, ' See how the works of Generation, the insect's egg
and the larvae,
Are warm on the garden wall and soon will be changed
To the great butterfly with the wings that are purple like
roses,
Where the great pattern dozes
Of Sirius and Aldebaran. The child
Who chases it into green darkness has the mane
Of the planets. To what realm do they fly and run ?
To what Antipodes of the heart ? With your all-seeing
sight
Can you tell ? — O you, the aurelia from which that great
butterfly the Night arises ! '

6. *The Blinded Song-Bird near the Battle-Field*

TO C. W. MCCANN

HERE, in the terrible Butterfly-climate of this world
Where the Stigmata are changed to the sign of the
    Feather —

I sit within my cage, am blind as the world.
Once I was Daedalus
And flew too near the sun.   But in my fall

Brought back a feather from those thunderous wings for
    song —
To comfort my world's darkness, the world's wrong.
And now one goldfinch light
Sings ' Happy are you that you have no sight ! '

For as I flew, I saw upon the earth
One limbless, eyeless, as before his birth, —
And torn by all the nails upon Christ's Cross :
He bore the Stigmata of the sins of the whole world.

And from the little span
Of his heart fell the blood — the sea of Galilee
Whereon Christ walked . . . that ghost of Abel whispers
    o'er the world :
' Brother, I come.
I have no eyes
But my all-seeing wounds ; and I am dumb,
But yet from all the open mouths of the world's wounds
    I rise :
I come to testify.'

7. *The Wind of Early Spring*

TO EVELYN SHRIFTE

THE ass-voiced wind of early spring brays over the wide
    plain —

The lynx-furred and lynx-purring plain of snow where
    branches of red coral
Hum of the spring to come. Not yet is there a fire
Of jacynth or of pyrope — first buds bursting through
    the apple-branch.
Only the lynx-furred and lynx-purring snow is over
    all.

What does the wind say ? ' In the plain, far away,
The fleece of Marsyas hangs upon a fruit-bough
(The fading snow) and trembles at the flute-sound.'

Was Marsyas a satyr or silenus ?
Was his the bray
That could foretell the spring, the wild-beast fire,
And imitate the cold wind of the spring ?

Apollonane the ass-god had a bray
Was thought to be an oracle . . . the crowd's onolatries
Echo that laughter. Yet was he burned to dust
As if by a sudden red spark on the apple-twigs,
And asses now are sacrificed to Apollo.

And Midas, the King who had an ass's ears,
Was grey as earth, or moss on the apple-trees —
Was half ass and half god. The spring by which
He caught Silenus, forced him to reveal
His secret that lies hidden in the thunders
Of spring beneath the earth, had for a name,
Mule : Ninna — Ninnus.

                    Blown by the cold wind of spring
From the very fact of the long years
Of the sage we see the long ears of the ass growing.

Where in the fruit-trees shrill sap rises bright
And clear as jacynth, pyrope, chrysolite,

An old man plays a flute —
A sound of two dimensions, like the beast-world's
Consciousness, or the cold wind of spring.

But the cold, like Time, has only one dimension —
A line, extending from the infinite past
Into a future that is infinite. . . . To this,
Only one point is known, the rest is Zero.

And all that is seen and touched will only seem
A budding out of Time, and then the flight
Of those buds to the Nothing that is all the world : (all
        forms and beings
Are only buddings from that line to the Infinite) :

But the gardener as he plays the flute has changed
The line and Zero of the Cold to curve and number,
Like the first budding of the small red satyr-hairy leaves
        upon the fruit-boughs ;
He shakes down from the branches a few tears
Brought by the wind from lost Persephone.

And what does the wind of spring, what does the flute
Tell of the beast-philosopher in the orchard —
Long silent from the cold ?
                    Does the flute fire the spark

Upon the branch ? Does it speak to the Chthonian
        dwellings, bring reply ?
' O think how your thin girl must feel the cold
Beneath the earth, who, in the nights of spring,
Once lay, a fire in your arms ?

Ah, long ago! When I was your living lass
My lips seemed the red fire upon the apple-branch,
The brand of rubies in the fire of spring —

Now quenched by the long cold
At the root of the sweet apple-tree. The Dust, grey
    glittering King,
Forced your bright-burning girl and made me one with him.
Yet am I not untrue!

For when green lightnings fall among the trees,
And I shall hear the strange bird-augur who is King
Picus, the guardian of the trees and Kings, the bird-
    magician,
In the green mists, my lips would burn again
With all the fires of spring, to hear you pass!'

This is the sound the cold wind blew from the Chthonian
    dwellings
In the early spring that makes the dead and living one —
The beast-fire and the soul-fire.

                  And the flute said:
' There is much to be learned in early spring from the
    wild-beast fires,
The centaur-red furred fruit-buds, — beast-fur shielding
    the clear sap
As the body shields the soul.

           And from the philosopher Ammonias
Who took an almond-furrèd ass,
Grey as the fruit-trees, for his pupil. Why? Mayhap

From his two see-saw syllables
All language rose. The human race began
With but a single word.'
               This is the sound
The gardener plays upon his sap-clear flute,
To bring red satyr-hairy fruit-buds to perfection.

Then came the words the cold wind brought our springs
And sprigs of blood : ' The past and present are as one —
Accordant and discordant, youth and age,
And death and birth.   For out of one came all —
From all comes one.'

8. *Sailor, What of the Isles?*

TO MILLICENT HUDDLESTON ROGERS

' SAILOR, what of the isles —
The green worlds grown
From a little seed ?   What of the islands known and those
    unknown ? '

' I have returned over the long and lonely sea ;
And only human need
For the world of men is mine ; I have forgot Immensity.

The rustling sea was a green world of leaves ;
The isle of Hispaniola in its form
Was like the leaf of a chestnut-tree in June.
And there is the gold region — the gold falls like rain
    with a long and leafy tune.

An old man bore us lumps of gold . . . the small,
Like walnuts husked with earth ; the great,
As large as oranges, and leafy earth
Still clung to them.   And when you thought that fireflies
    lit the night,
These were but nuggets, lying on the dark earth, burning
    bright.'

' Sailor, what of the maps of the known world ? ' ' The
    old Chinese,
Whose talk was like the sound of June leaves drinking
    rain,
Constructed maps of the known world — the few
Islands and two countries that they knew.

They thought the heavens were round,
The earth square, and their empire at the earth's
    centre . . .
                just as you
And I believe we are the world's centre and the stars

Are grown from us as the bright seas in a rind of gold
Are grown from the smooth stem of the orange-tree.

Those maps of the Yellow Empire then were drawn,
As we think, upside down :
Tongking was placed
Where usually the North stands, and Mongolia graced
The South.   The names, too, were writ upside down.
For how is it possible, in this flat world, to know
Why South should be below, the North above —
Why man should hold creeds high one moment, the next
    moment low ? '

' Sailor, what of the maps of skies ?   Is that Orion ? '
                                ' No, the sight
Is of a far island.   What you see
Is where they are gathering carbuncles, garnets, diamonds
    bright
As fireflies with a gardener's rake under the spice-trees
    and the orange-trees.'

' Sailor, what do you know of this world, my Self . . . a
    child
Standing before you ? — Or an isle
To which no sail has crossed over the long and lonely
    sea ?
What do you know of this island, of the soil
In which all sainthood or insanity, murder or mockery
    grows — a leafy tree ? '

' No more than the gardeners and astronomers who
    make
Their catalogues of stars for heavens and seeds for garden
    beds
Know of their green worlds ; or the soil, of the great
    beasts
Whose skin shines like gold fire or fireflies, and whose
    nostrils snort great stars —

The beasts — huge flowers grown from the stem of the
    green darkness ; each beast holds
The entire world of plants,
All elements and all the planetary system in
Itself (while the flower holds only the plant-world)
And freed from its stem by light, like the flowers in air —

No more than the father knows of the child, or the sailor
    of chartless isles.'

9. *The April Rain*

TO CONNIE GUION

Boy to Girl :
' FROM the sly mocking innocence of the azure
Where the amaryllid stars are not yet breaking
Out of their sapphire soil the air, a few raindrops are
        falling —

Shining and falling.
                    Such is our world, my love —
A bright swift raindrop falling.

The sapphire dews sing like a star ; bird-breasted dew
Lies like a bird and flies

In the singing wood and is blown by the bright air
Upon your wood-wild April-soft long hair
That seems the rising of spring constellations —
Aldebaran, Procyon, Sirius
And Cygnus who gave you all his bright swan-plumage.
                                            You —

The young Rainbow, risen from the spring, the sap, and
        singing
Of this old world — see the bright raindrops falling

On the blue flames of honey, water-drops of sapphire,
The bluebells (the blue fires of deepest air).

Such are the wisdoms of the world — Heraclitus
Who fell a-weeping, and Democritus
Who fell a-laughing, Pyrrho who arose
From Nothing, and ended in believing Nothing — fools,
And falling soon :
Only the April rain, my dear,
Only the April rain !

That fool-begotten wise despair
Dies like the raindrop on the leaf
Fading like young joy, old grief,
And soon is gone —

Forgot by the brightness of the air ;
But still are your lips the warm heart of all springs,
And all the lost Aprils of the world shine in your hair.'

10. *Two Songs*

FOR GORDON WATSON

(Written after hearing his Liszt recital, 8 May 1952)

I. *Prometheus' Song*

I⊤ was the time when the vulture left my heart
In cold December,
And I did not know which was my heart and which the
    rock.
But I remember

The echo of my breath in the streets' winter weather
When Kings' and Beggars', Lovers', Haters' breath is
    blown together
As by the wind of Death :

                          ' See that poor stick of bone
To which my body and my soul are nailed
As the Thief upon the Cross,
As I upon the rock !
Once she was the whole world's gain and loss !

She, the foul path I trod
From Chaos unto God !
What now is left ? That cross-road stake thrust through
    my heart —
And those poor rags of Heaven or of Hell
Blown here, blown there, upon that stick of bone.

Her tongue, a clacking bell
That speaks of Paradise —
But the grey ice
In which the world must end — such are her eyes.

Once I thought she would burn
My body and soul away
Like the fire that seals the heart from all other fires —

The red noon of the lovers' Judgment Day.
But then, a stick upon Time's shore
And broken by its wave —
Not even a spark to warm my hands
That dead stick gave.'

II. *The Queen of Scotland's Reply to a Reproof from John Knox*

SAID the bitter Man of Thorns to me, the White
        Rose-Tree :
' That wonted love of yours is but an ass's bray —
The beast who called to beast
And kicked the world away ! '
(All the wisdom of great Solomon
Held in an ass's bray.)

When body to body, soul to soul
Were bare in the fire of night
As body to grave, as spirit to Heaven or Hell,
What did we say ?
' Ah, too soon we shall be air —
No pleasure, anguish, will be possible.
Hold back the day ! '
For in this moment of the ass-furred night
You called the hour of the Beast, was born
All the wisdom of great Solomon
From the despisèd clay !
All the wisdom of Solomon
Held in an ass's bray.

11. *Two Songs of Queen Anne Boleyn*

TO NATALIE PALEY

I

THE King of Nowhere said to me,
Nodding his wintry crown
That seemed an ass's crown of ears
Or a broken town,

' Young girl, your love begs, " Give to me
Your body, for your soul
Is only an illusion." But,'
Said the winter air
(The aged King of Nowhere),

' You must lay your body by,
As other women may lay bare
Their bodies to the foolish air
That they call " Love " ; Nowhere, alone,
Shall then be Lovers' Town ;

Though you have little shelter there
From Truth that is the winter air,
Yet you will share my crown.'
That old King grey as olive-trees
Sighed in the withering winter wind.

' If,' said the nodding King of Nothing,
' Your body be the stepping-stone
For your love's path to Heaven from Hell,
Young girl, you must beware.

For stone when fretted upon stone
In the body's death-ghosted despair
May breed the all-devouring fire —
The lovers' Judgment-noon.

Then the heart that was the Burning-Bush
May change to a Nessus-robe of flame
That wraps not only its true love
But all the gibbering ghosts that came.
That flame then dies to a winter candle,
Lightless, guttering down.
And the soul that was the root of Being
Changes to Nothing-town.'

II. *At Cockcrow*

As I lay in my love's low bed
That is the primal clay
From which the night and day arise,
My love said, ' It is day.

That red glare on the window-panes
Is from the rising sun. . . .
Fear not it is the Judgment Day
Or Blood from the Crucified's Veins.

Shall I not feel your kiss again —
Its red light on my brow ? '
' I only know that kiss will change
Into the brand of Cain.'

I sleepy sighed, ' What is that sound ? '
' The world turns in its sleep
From good to ill, from ill to good
On what was once God's ground.'

You'll hear my bone clack on your heart —
Your heart clack on my bone.
That sound once seemed the first sunrise :
Now I must sleep alone.

The cock crowed thrice and men arise
To earn two pence or thirty pence
That on the last day nothing buys
Excepting dark for the Dead,

Weighing their eyelids down. . . . But I
Must have a dark more deep —
Lest when I hear the cock crow thrice
I turn like the world in my sleep

And know that red blare (three cock-cries)
Heralds the lovers' dawn —
The first kiss and last sound we hear
When we (alone) lie on the bier
With the two pence and the thirty pence
And the sins of the world on our eyes.

12. *Of the Wise and the Foolish*

A FOOL sat by the roadside
Upon a lonely stone.
His hair was grey as ass-fur.
He sang ' Alone — alone — '
To the ass-grey dust singing,
' Brother, to thee I come.
The ass that prophesied to Augustus
The victory of Actium.'

13. Song

TO ALBERTO DE LACERDA

WHERE is all the bright company gone —
The Trojan Elaine and the Knight Sir Gawaine ?
Why have they glided out of the rain ?
The Queens were bright as the waters' sheen,
Beautiful, bountiful as the grain ;
The Knights were brighter than stars in the sky
(The moons thick as roses in hot July) —
As bright as the raindrops and roses in June,
And many and merry as notes in a tune.
Alas, they are gone and I am alone,
For all they glided out of the rain.
And now I sit under the bright apple-tree
And weep that ever the speech was spoken
That the false angel said unto me.
For had I never the apple-branch broken,
Death had not fallen on mankind and me.

14. *A Song of the Dust*

TO JACK AND ANN LINDSAY

THE raging Dust said : ' See ! I come from the tomb of
    the three Furies,
Only to climate, or to ghost, your heart —
In the great guise of Love.' No Iris comes
With saffron wings from any clime of hope.

Only her sisters, harpy winds, black-winged like flies,
    Aello,
Ocypete, Celaeno, from the Harpies' tomb in Zanthus, far
    in Libya,
Proclaim their divinations from the Dust :
Which shall be king, which beggar, planet, plant,

Or the Arachnoian in the city office
Who spins gold webs to lead us from the Labyrinth
But taught the Minotaur Dark, born of the seed of the
    Sun,
New ways to kill.

' All things,' they said, ' are equal in this night —
The gilded dust of Jezebel, gilded dust
Of Dives, these that shone like fire by night
Are now at one
With the yellow jasmine, and the boughs of the trembling
    yellow stars.'

Who knows which dust is Dives, which black dust
Is Lazarus, changed into garden loam
To await the fertile universal will ?

For does not the dust of the common world hold the
    dark seed
Of a humble plant that grows
Beyond its morning wisdom — changed, one side, to
    gold,

And, on one side, to beast —
From which grows Pithecanthropus Erectus. What is
    Man
But a hybrid between beast and plant and God ?

Who knows which dust is Silence, and which Thunder ?
    All the dynasties
Of darkness rolling onward . . . phantoms, Pharaohs
Of dust whose crowns are comets of an awe-inspiring
    blackness
Foretelling doom . . .

                        Or the silence that foretells the
    spring . . .
The change in the spark upon the almond bough
Like the change in the word from smaragdum to
    smeraldo,
From émeraude to emerald. . . . So the first spark in the
    great silence of the earliest spring begins.

Who knows the history of Silence, or of Thunder ? Did
    the wave
Tell its long secret to Pythagoras who all night lay
Face downward to the sea, wreathed in black wool,
That he might learn from those depths like the violet
    heart of forests
Before the spring, the thunder's nature ? What did the
    wave say —

The black wave rearing like a horse, tall as the Manes,
And with a horse's mane, in the subsiding thunder,
A Delphic deluge presaging disaster ?

                        Only the night-wind sighs
Like the Oracle of Delphos : ' From the wave of the Night
    grows
A smooth stem ; from the orageous
Stem of darkness grows the orange-tree, the aurantium,
The hidden gold.'

And on the great roads of Night
The unseen suns are singing of their triumph.

All things lie in the clime of Man's forgiveness.
O tell me not we are face to face with our own dust —
That Judas creeps, night-long, from each crevice like the
      spring,
Only to meet Judas, and again Judas!
There is Another Who has shed all but the thunder's
      glory,
All but the heart of dust.

And I, whose heart is formed of the dust of the three
      Furies
Where still the fires are! I, who was once the nightin-
      gale —
I who burned my heart that was the blind nightingale
Whose song was a fire in the darkness . . . I who ate my
      heart, the flesh of the wakeful nightingale —
And now am awake for ever! —

                         This was the song I heard
When eastern light ripens the precious dew
In the bare rock and barren heart, and men pluck and bring
      home in stillness the great sapphire grape-clusters:

Beyond the ripening stillness
I heard the thunder of the growth of vines
And the great thunders in the veins of youth.

And now the amethyst stars of the night dew
That fall upon our hair lifted like vines
By the wind of night, hold all tomorrow's heat
And the violet heart of oceans in each sun,

And morning comes to the heart and the heart's warmth,
      its fevers,
Rapacity and grandeur — comes to the dress

Of flesh inconstant as the splendours and the rubies
Of the day's heat, the pity and glory of the rainbow.

And still the uncombatable song rose to the light
From all the heights of Being, and from the depth of the
　　　last abyss :

　If every grain of my dust should be a Satan —
If every atom of my heart were Lucifer —
If every drop of my blood were an Abaddon,
— Yet should I love.'

15. Elegy for Dylan Thomas

BLACK Venus of the Dead, what Sun of Night
Lies twined in your embrace, cold as the vine?
O heart, great Sun of Darkness, do you shine

For her, to whom alone
All men are faithful — faithless as the wave
To all but her to whom they come after long wander-
ing. . . .

Black giantess who is calm as palm-trees, vast
As Africa! In the shade of the giantess
He lies in that eternal faithfulness.

He, made of the pith and sap of the singing world —
Green kernel of a forgotten paradise
Where grass-hued, grass-soft suns brought the first spring
(Green fervours, singing, saps, fertilities)
And heat and moist lay on unseeing eyes
Till shapeless lumps of clay grew into men, now lies
Far from the Babel clamour. In his rest
He holds the rays of the universe to his stilled breast.

Before our Death in Birth, our Birth in Death,
Teaching us holy living, holy dying, we who cry
At the first light and the first dark, must learn

The oneness of the world, and know all change
Through the plant, the kingly worm (within whose shape
    all Kings begin,
To whom all Kings must come) through beast, to Man.

The fraternal world of beast and plant lies on his eyes:
The beast that holds all elements in itself —
The earth, the plant, the solar system: for each beast
Is an infinity of plants, a planet, or a moon,
A flower in the green dark, freed from its stem in earth,

Shrouded with black veils like the mourning Spring,
Under the vines of Grief (the first plantation since the
     Flood)
The mourners weep for the solary iris that God showed to
     Noah —

Our hope in this universe of tears. But he is gone —
He sleeps, a buried sun
That sank into the underworld to spread
A gold mask on the faces of the Dead —

Young country god, red as the laughing grapes
When Sirius parches country skins to gold and fire.

And he, who compressed the honey-red fire into holy
     shapes,
Stole frozen fire from gilded Parnassian hives,

Was Abraham-haired as fleeces of wild stars
That all night rage like foxes in the festival
Of wheat, with fire-brands tied to their tails under the
     wheat-ears
To avert the wrath of the Sun, gold as the fleeces
Of honey-red foxes. Now he is one with Adam, the first
     gardener. He sang

Of the beginning of created things, the secret
Rays of the universe, and sang green hymns
Of the great waters to the tearless deserts. Under
The fertilisation of his singing breath
Even the greyness and the dust of Death
Seemed the grey pollen of the long September heat

On earth where Kings lie wearing the whole world as
     their crown,
Where all are equal in the innocent sleep
That lulls the lion like a child, and is the clime
Of our forgiveness. Death, like the holy Night
Makes all men brothers. There, in the maternal

Earth, the wise and humbling Dark, he lies —
The emigrant from a forgotten paradise —
The somnambulist
Who held rough ape-dust and a planet in his fist —

Far from the empires of the human filth
Where the Gorgons suckle us with maternal milk
Black as the Furies', and the human breast
Can yield not even the waters of the Styx.   But rest

For these he brought ; to the Minotaur in the city office
Crying to the dunghill in the soul ' See, it is morning ! '

And seeing all glory hidden in small forms,
The planetary system in the atom, the great suns
Hid in a speck of dust.
                              So, for his sake,
More proudly will that Sisyphus, the heart of Man,
Roll the Sun up the steep of heaven, and in the street
Two old blind men seem Homer and Galileo, blind
Old men that tap their way through worlds of dust
To find Man's path near the Sun.

NOTES

JODELLING SONG

Page 142

THIS is founded on Gertrude Stein's ' Accents in Alsace' (The Watch on the Rhine) contained in her book, *Geography and Plays* :

' Sweeter than water or cream or ice. Sweeter than bells of roses. Sweeter than winter or summer or spring. Sweeter than pretty posies. Sweeter than anything is my queen and loving is her nature.

' Loving and good and delighted and best is her little King and Sire whose devotion is entire, who has but one desire to express the love which is hers to inspire.

' In the photograph the Rhine hardly showed.

' In what way do chimes remind you of singing ? In what ways do birds sing ? In what way are forests black or white ?

' We saw them blue.

' With forget-me-nots.

' In the midst of our happiness we were very pleased.'

METAMORPHOSIS

Page 225, *lines* 1 and 2

Dryden, ' Annus Mirabilis.'

Page 225, *line* 26

' The Word was from the beginning, and therefore was and is the divine beginning of all things, but now that He has taken the name, which of old was sanctified, the Christ, He is called by me a New Song.' — St. Clement, ' Address to the Greeks.'

Page 226, *lines* 3 and 4

' The Lord, having taken upon Him all the infirmities of our body, is then covered with the scarlet-coloured blood of all the martyrs.' — St. Hilary, quoted by St. Thomas Aquinas, *Catena Aurea*.

GOLD COAST CUSTOMS

Page 237

' The Negroes indulge that perfect contempt for humanity which in its bearing on Justice and Morality is the fundamental characteristic of the race. They have, moreover, no knowledge of the immortality of the soul, although spectres are supposed to appear. The under-valuing of humanity among them reaches an incredible degree of intensity. Tyranny is regarded as no wrong, and cannibalism is looked upon as quite customary and proper. Among us instinct deters from it, if we can speak of instinct at all as appertaining to man. But with the Negro this is not the case, and the devouring of human flesh is altogether consonant with the general principles of the African race ; to the sensual Negro, human flesh is but an object of sense — mere flesh. At the death of a king hundreds are killed and eaten ; prisoners are butchered and their flesh sold in the market-place ; the victor is accustomed to eat the flesh of his fallen foe.' — Hegel, *Philosophy of History*.

It is needless to add that this refers only to a past age, and that, in quoting this passage, I intend no reflection whatever upon the African races of our time. This passage no more casts a reflection upon them than a passage referring to the cruelties of the Tudor age casts a reflection upon the English of our present age. — E. S.

Page 237, *line* 5

' Munza rattles his bones in the dust.' King Munza reigned, in 1874, over the Monbuttoo, a race of cannibals in Central Africa. These notes are taken from Dr. Georg Schweinfurth's *The Heart of Africa* (translated by Ellen Frewer, published by Messrs. Sampson Low). Of the Monbuttoo and their neighbours the Niam-Niam, we read : ' Human fat is universally sold. . . . Should any lone and solitary individual die, uncared for . . . he would be sure to be devoured in the very district in which he lived. During our residence at the Court of Munza the general rumour was quite current that nearly every day some little child was sacrificed to supply his meal. There are cases in which bearers who died from fatigue had been dug out of the graves in which they had been buried . . . in order that they might be devoured. The cannibalism of the Monbuttoo is the most pronounced of all the known nations of Africa. Surrounded as they are by a number of people who, being inferior to them in culture, are consequently held in great contempt, they have just the opportunity which they want for carrying on expeditions of war and plunder, which result in the acquisition of a booty which is especially coveted by them, consisting of human flesh. But with it all, the Monbuttoos are a noble race of men, men who display a certain national pride . . . men to whom one may put a reasonable question and receive a reasonable answer. The Nubians can never say enough in praise of their faithfulness in friendly intercourse and of the order and stability of their national life. According to the Nubians, too, the Monbuttoos were their superiors in the arts of war.'

Page 241, *lines* 31 and 32

' And her soul, the cannibal Amazon's mart.'
' Tradition alleges that in former times a state composed of women

426

made itself famous by its conquests : it was a state at whose head was a woman. She is said to have pounded her son in a mortar, and to have had the blood of pounded children constantly at hand. She is said to have driven away or put to death all the males, and commanded the death of all male children. These furies destroyed everything in the neighbourhood, and were driven to constant plunderings because they did not cultivate the land. . . . This infamous state, the report goes on to say, subsequently disappeared.' — Hegel, *Philosophy of History*, chapter on Africa.

INVOCATION

Page 259, lines 3 to 7

' The blood, when present in the veins as part of a body, a generative part, too, and endowed with soul, being the soul's immediate instrument, and primary seat . . . the blood, seeming also to have a share of another divine body and being suffused with divine animal heat, suddenly acquires remarkable and most excellent powers, and is analogous to the essence of the stars. In so far as it is spirit, it is the hearth, the Vesta, the household divinity, the innate heat, the sun of the microcosm, the fire of Plato ; not because like common fire it lightens, burns, and destroys, but because, by a vague and incessant motion, it preserves, nourishes, and aggrandizes itself. It further deserves the name of spirit, inasmuch as it is radical moisture, at once the ultimate and the proximate and the primary aliment.' — William Harvey (*The Works of William Harvey, M.D.*, translated from the Latin by R. Willis, Sydenham Society, 1847).

HARVEST

Page 264, lines 24 to 28

' It is obvious that the heat contained in animals is not fire, neither does it derive its origin from fire ' : Aristotle, quoted by William Harvey (*The Works of William Harvey, M.D.*, translated from the Latin by R. Willis, Sydenham Society, 1847). Harvey continues : ' I maintain the same thing of the innate heat and the blood : I say that they are not fire and neither do they derive their origin from fire. They rather share the nature of some other, and that a more divine body and substance. They act by no faculty or property of the elements . . . as, in producing an animal, it ' (the generative factor) ' surpasses the power of the elements — as it is a spirit, namely, and the inherent nature of that spirit corresponds to the essence of the stars, so is there a spirit, or certain force, inherent in the blood, acting superiorly to the power of the elements.'

Page 264, lines 32 and 33

' The inferior world, according to Aristotle, is so continuous and connected with the superior orbits, that all its motions and changes appear to take their rise and to receive directions from thence. . . .

Inferior and corruptible things wait upon superior and incorruptible things ; but all are subservient to the will of the supreme, omnipotent, and eternal creator.' — *Ibid.*

Page 265, *lines* 10 and 11

' Best is water of all, and gold, as a flaming sun in the night shineth eminent.' — Pindar.

Page 266, *lines* 2 to 4

' He gives us men for our refreshment the bread of angels. . . . On the breaking of the Bread Thou art not broken, nor art Thou divided, Thou art eaten, but like the Burning Bush, Thou art not consumed.' — St. Thomas Aquinas, *Sermon of the Body of Our Lord.*

EURYDICE

Page 268, *line* 4

'. . . A most sweet wife, a young wife, *Nondum sustulerat flavum Proserpina crinem* (not yet had Proserpina tied up her golden hair) — such a wife as no man ever had, so good a wife, but she is now dead and gone, *Lethaeoque jacet condita sarcophago* (she lies buried in the silent tomb).' — Robert Burton, *The Anatomy of Melancholy.*

Page 268, *lines* 12 and 13

' The light which God is shines in darkness, God is the true light : to see it one has to be blind and strip God naked of things.' — Meister Eckhart, *Sermons and Collations*, XIX.

Page 269, *lines* 14 and 15

' And her deadness
Was filling her with fullness
Full as a fruit with sweetness and darkness
Was she with her great death.'
— R. M. Rilke (translated J. B. Leishman).

LULLABY

Page 274, *line* 5

The phrase ' out-dance the Babioun ' occurs in an Epigram by Ben Jonson.

POOR YOUNG SIMPLETON : II

Page 282, *line* 15

' *Damné par l'arc-en-ciel.*' — Arthur Rimbaud, *Une Saison en enfer.*

THE SONG OF THE COLD

Page 292, *line* 2

' There was the morning when, with Her, you struggled amongst those banks of snow, those green-lipped crevasses, that ice, those

black flags and blue rays, and purple perfumes of the polar sun. . . .'
— Arthur Rimbaud, *Metropolitan* (translated by Helen Rootham).

Page 292, lines 6 and 7

' This evening, Devotion to Circeto of the tall mirrors, fat as a fish and glowing like the ten months of the red night (her heart is of amber and musk) — for me a prayer, mute as those regions of night. . . .'
— Arthur Rimbaud, *Devotion*.

Page 294, line 4

The miser Foscue, a farmer general of France, existing in Langue-doc about 1760. These lines tell his actual story.

TEARS

Page 297, lines 7 and 8

'. . . Methusalem, with all his hundreds of years, was but a mush-room of a night's growth, to this day ; and all the four monarchies, with all their thousands of years, and all the powerful Kings and the beautiful Queens of this world, were but as a bed of flowers, some gathered at six, some at seven, some at eight, all in one morning, in respect of this day.' — John Donne, Sermon LXXIII.

GREEN SONG

Page 301, line 17

' I wept for names, sounds, faiths, delights and duties lost, taken from a poem, on Cowley's wish to retire to the Plantations.' — Dorothy Wordsworth, *Grasmere Journal*, May 8, 1802.

A YOUNG GIRL

Page 305, line 5

An adaptation from a line in Rilke's ' Venus.'

HOW MANY HEAVENS . . .

Page 306

'. . . The Stancarest will needs have God not only to be in every-thing, but to be everything, that God is an angel in an angel, and a stone in a stone, and a straw in a straw.' — John Donne, Sermon VII.

HOLIDAY

Page 308, line 19

' God is Intelligible Light.' — St. Thomas Aquinas, *Summa Theo-logica.*

THE YOUTH WITH THE RED-GOLD HAIR

Page 311

' Did ghosts from those thickets walk about your land
So the tent of the shepherdess was cumbered with gold armour
Till the hero left your mother and turned back into the glade,
Bright as his armour ? '

— Sacheverell Sitwell, ' Black Shepherdess.'

GIRL AND BUTTERFLY

Page 312, line 25

' How Butterflies and breezes move their four wings.' — Sir Thomas
Browne, *The Garden of Cyrus.*

THE POET LAMENTS THE COMING OF OLD AGE

Page 316, line 16

This is a reference to a passage in Plato's *The Sophist.*

' LO, THIS IS SHE THAT WAS THE WORLD'S DESIRE '

Page 322, line 22

' Venus.' . . . I used the name merely as a symbol. The poem is
not about a far-off myth. . . . It is equally, let us say, about the girl
who once walked under the flowering trees in the garden next door,
and who is now old and bent, waiting for death in a shuttered house.
. . It is about all beauty gone.

THE SWANS

Page 325, lines 12 to 15

A rough adaptation into English of a prose passage by Paul
Éluard.

ONE DAY IN SPRING

Page 329, line 21

' And in the spring night they must sleep alone.' — An adaptation
of a line by Sappho.

THE TWO LOVES

Page 334, lines 11 to 13

'. . . tell the blind
The hue of the flower, or the philosopher
What distance is, in the essence of its being.'

— A paraphrase of a passage by William James.

' umbilical cords that bind us to strange suns.'
— A paraphrase of a sentence by a French author — I do not
know his name.

' Bless Jesus Christ with the Rose and his people, which is a nation
of living sweetness.' — Christopher Smart, ' Rejoice with the Lamb.'

came into my head after reading a passage in Lorenz Oken's *Element
of Physiophilosophy*; the lines are in part a transcript.

THE BEE-KEEPER

These verses are founded on the great Second Adhyāya of the
Brihadāranyaka Upanishad : ' This earth is the honey (madhu, the
effect) of all beings, and all beings are the honey, or madhu, the effect,
of this earth. Likewise this bright immortal fusion incorporated in
the body (both are madhu). He indeed is the same as that Self, that
Immortal, that Brahman, that All,' etc.

I have founded the lines on this great Hymn with all reverence.

A SLEEPY TUNE

' When shall you see a lion hide gold in the ground ? ' — Robert
Burton, *The Anatomy of Melancholy.*

Reference to Lorenz Oken, *Elements of Physiophilosophy.*

Homeric Hymn to Mercury. Passage about the Bee-Priestesses.

An ancient Persian manuscript speaks of drowning and embalming
a red-haired man in honey.

The solar hero, King of Lydia, appears in *The Golden Bough.*

The tale of Alexander the Great's being embalmed in white honey
occurs more than once in Sir Ernest Wallis Budge's *Life and Exploits
of Alexander the Great.*

MARY STUART TO JAMES BOTHWELL
Casket Letter No. II
Page 341

This is the actual story of the Second Casket Letter, used as proof that Mary was guilty of complicity in the murder of Darnley.

Page 341, *lines* 8 and 9

A transcript of words ascribed to Mary.

Page 341, *line* 12

Darnley was known as 'the leper-King.' Towards the end of his life, he suffered from a disease which necessitated the hiding of his face behind a taffeta mask. This disease was ascribed by Mary's enemies to the result of poison, by her friends to the result of Darnley's excesses.

Page 341, *line* 25

It was a complaint against Mary that she lodged Darnley, at Kirk o' Field, the place of his death, in 'a beggarly house.'

Page 342, *lines* 2 to 4

A transcript of the Letter.

Page 342, *lines* 8 and 9

A transcript of the Letter.

A LOVE SONG

Page 346, *line* 7 and *second sentence line* 11

Sappho.

HYMN TO VENUS

Page 347, *line* 3

' seeds of petrifaction, Gorgon of itself.'
— Sir Thomas Browne, 'Of Vulgar Errors.'

SPRING MORNING

Page 350, *line* 1

' Having accomplished the thunders of night-wandering Zagreus.'
This beautiful and mysterious fragment was preserved by Porphyry, and the translation is given by Dr. Jane Ellen Harrison in 'Themis.' She inquires, ' What are the thunders, and how can they be accomplished ?'

As I have used the phrase, the thunders refer to the rising of the sap and blood in the heart, the ferment in the spring night.

' The rites of the Croconides.'

These were Greek minor rites, supposed to make the flowers of the saffron fertile.

The House of Gold was the name given to the ante-chamber to the Tombs of the Kings of Egypt.

OUT OF SCHOOL

Founded on a passage in *Chance and Symbol* (Richard Hertz).

Founded on a passage in Plato.

THE COAT OF FIRE

contain references to the Tibetan Book of the Dead.

refer to the Buddha's Fire Sermon.

THE SHADOW OF CAIN

'. . . the Point that flows
Till it becomes the line of Time . . . an endless positing
Of Nothing, or the Ideal that tries to burgeon
Into Reality through multiplying.'
— A reference to Oken, *op. cit.*

Arthur Rimbaud's *Metropolitan*.

'. . . monstrous bull-voices of unseen fearful mimes.' — A fragment of the lost play by Aeschylus, *The Edonians*.

' Irenaeus expressed it so elegantly as it is almost pity if it be not true. " *Inseminatus est ubique in Scripturis, Filius Dei*," says he. The Son of God is sowed in every furrow.' — John Donne, Sermon XI.

Transcript of an actual report by an eye-witness of the bomb falling on Hiroshima. — *The Times*, September 10, 1945.

Page 373, lines 19, 20 and 22

Founded on a passage in Burnet's *Theory of the Earth.*

Page 374, lines 12 to 14

These are references to descriptions given by Lombroso and Havelock Ellis of the marks and appearance borne by prenatally disposed criminals.

Page 374, lines 24 and 25

' Also we must say that this or that is a disease of Gold, and not that it is leprosy.' — *Paracelsus*, Appendix I, Chapter VI.

Page 375

' Gold is the most noble of all, the most precious and primary metal. . . . And we are not prepared to deny that leprosy, in all its forms, can be thereby removed from the human frame.' — *Paracelsus.*

Page 375, lines 9 to 14 and 15, 16

These verses also contain references to Hermetic Writings.

Page 376, lines 4 and 5

John Donne, Sermon CXXXVI.

THE CANTICLE OF THE ROSE

Page 377, lines 7 to 13

These verses contain references to Oken.

Page 378, lines 3 to 5

Transcript of an eye-witness' description of Nagasaki after the falling of the atomic bomb.

Page 378, line 31

Anturs of Arthur, 1394.

Page 378, line 32

Wyclif, *Selected Writings*, vol. I.

THE ROAD TO THEBES

1. — *Page 382, lines* 1 and 2

bear reference to the Tibetan Book of the Dead.

Page 383, lines 17 and 18

The Anatomy of Melancholy.

2. — *Page 385, lines* 19 and 20

are founded on lines in André Breton's *Un Homme et une femme tout blancs.*

Page 386, line 12

Milton.

434

3. — *Page* 389

Final line inspired by a line from 'Altarwise by Owl-light,' by Dylan Thomas :

'The world's my wound, God's Mary in her grief.'

GARDENERS AND ASTRONOMERS
Page 393, *line* 13

Fritz Werfel, quoted by Richard Hertz in *Chance and Symbol*.

THE MADWOMAN IN THE PARK
Page 400, *lines* 7 and 8

'And would God prefer
The dream of a possible angel'
is from a sermon by John Donne.

THE WIND OF EARLY SPRING
Page 405, *lines* 2 to 5

Heraclitus.

SONG
Page 417, *lines* 13 to 15

Founded on Eva's Lament in the Coventry Plays.

A SONG OF THE DUST
Page 418, *lines* 14 and 15

A transcript of a passage in a Sermon by John Donne.

Page 419, *line* 3

An adaptation of a phrase by Nietzsche.

Page 420, *lines* 5 and 6

An adaptation of a phrase by Maeterlinck.

Page 420, *line* 14

'Eastern light ripens the precious dew' : John Dryden.

ELEGY FOR DYLAN THOMAS
Page 423, *line* 10

A transcript of a phrase from Porphyry, quoted in Jack Lindsay's *Byzantium into Europe*.

INDEX TO TITLES

INDEX TO FIRST LINES

From gold-mosaic'd wave, 235
'From the sly mocking innocence of the azure, 409

Go down, red Sun, red Cain, 363
'God Pluto is a kindly man ; the children ran, 141
Gone is the winter's cold, 326
Great Snoring and Norwich, 132
Green flows the river of Lethe — O, 285
Green wooden leaves clap light away, 27
Grey as a guinea-fowl is the rain, 19

Heat of the sun that maketh all men black, 232
Here, in the terrible Butterfly-climate of this world, 401
'Here in this great house in the barrack square, 181
His kind velvet bonnet, 150
Huge is the sun of amethysts and rubies, 292

I, an old man, 312
I, an old woman in the light of the sun, 261
I, an old woman whose heart is like the Sun, 263
I drew a stalk of dry grass through my lips, 318
'I had a mother-in-law, 167
I saw the Gold Man with the lion's head, 395
I see the children running out of school, 316
'I walked with my dead living love in the city, 280
'I was a Gold Man. . . . Now I lie under the earth, 338
I who was once a golden woman like those who walk, 257
In a room of the palace, 125
In his tall senatorial, 110
In Summer when the rose-bushes, 40
In the autumn, the season of ripeness, when final redness, 357
In the cold wind, towers grind round, 44
In the early springtime, after their tea, 128
In the great gardens, after bright spring rain, 69
In the great nursery where the poppet maids, 68
In the great room above the orangery, 99
In the green light of water, like the day, 325
In the green winter night, 322
In the hot noon — like glowing muscadine, 97
In the huge and glassy room, 9
In the plain of the world's dust like a great Sea, 336
In the summer, when no one is cold, 289
Is it the light of the snow that soon will be overcoming, 305
It was the time when the Day cried to me, 'Show me your heart, Medusa, 345
It was the time when the vulture left my heart, 411

Jane, Jane, 16
Jumbo asleep, 119

THE END